Reflections on a Disruptive Decade

Reflections
on a
Disruptive
Decade

Essays from the Sixties

Eugene Davidson

University of Missouri Press
Columbia and London

148916

University of Missouri Press, Columbia, Missouri 65201
Printed and bound in the United States of America
5 4 3 2 1   04 03 02 01 00

Library of Congress Cataloging-in-Publication Data

Davidson, Eugene, 1902–
    Reflections on a disruptive decade : essays from the sixties /
Eugene Davidson.
        p.   cm.
    The introductory essays to each quarterly issue of Modern
age during the 1960s.
    Includes index.
    ISBN 0-8262-1297-2 (alk. paper)
    1. Civilization, Modern—20th century.   2. Ninteen sixties.
3. World politics—1955–1965.   4. World politics–1965–
1975.   I. Modern age (Chicago, Ill.)   II. Title.
CB427 .D34 2000
909.82' 6—dc21   00-032556

    This paper meets the requirements of the
American National Standard for Permanence of Paper
for Printed Library Materials, Z39.48, 1984.

Text Design: Elizabeth Young
Jacket Design: Kristie Lee
Typesetter: Bookcomp, Inc.
Printer and binder: Thomson-Shore, Inc.
Typefaces: Goudy, Gill Sans

Contents

A Note to Readers

Eugene Davidson was born in New York City in 1902, graduated from Yale College in 1927, and became head of the Yale University Press in 1929, which post he occupied for thirty years. At Yale he possessed many scholarly friends, and both from within the faculty and without published an extraordinary series of volumes. Thereafter he removed to Chicago, where for ten years he edited the periodical *Modern Age*. The horrendous winter of 1978–1979 took the edge off the attractions of Chicago, and with his wife Suzette he sought out California, where he lives in Santa Barbara.

As head of one of the major university presses Davidson had many tasks. During his press work he took interest in poetry. After moving to Chicago and then to Santa Barbara he published five books on what befell Germany in the twentieth century, the tragic era of Adolf Hitler with its aftermath including the Allied occupation and the Nuremberg trials. His recently completed two-volume account of Hitler's rise and fall, or to use his words Hitler's making and unmaking, is classic.

The pages that follow are a truly remarkable addition to his hitherto published work. They are introductory essays to each quarterly issue of *Modern Age* during the 1960s. They appear together here for the first time.

Reflections on a Disruptive Decade

1960

Mr. Dallin among the Scholars

David J. Dallin, whose article "The New Class in Russia" appears in this issue,[1] is a historian of remarkable gifts and the reception his books have received in academic circles in this country seems worth considering. Three of them appeared during the war—*Soviet Russia's Foreign Policy, 1939–1942, Russia and Post-War Europe,* and *The Big Three.* In them Mr. Dallin told some new things to American readers—for example, the terms of the secret treaty of August 1939 between the Soviet Union and Nazi Germany, although the documents which he accurately described came to light only in 1946 during the first Nuremberg trial. Mr. Dallin had not seen them but he knew they had to exist to account for the frictionless division of the newly occupied territories and the respective spheres of interest of Russia and Germany after the conquest of Poland. Mr. Dallin also wrote that Russia, when the war was over, would bring into its orbit a portion of Germany, which would then become a claim—as the true People's Republic—on the non-Communist part of the country. Mr. Dallin had discerned the pattern when Russia had recognized the so-called Finnish Karelian Republic, which had promptly called upon Soviet troops to liberate the rest of Finland from its imperialist exploiters.

These extraordinary insights accumulated in Dallin's books as he clearly saw the direction and purposes of the Soviet policies that were so baffling to so many in high places. And not only were they mysterious at the time; some of their former supporters were determined to keep them enigmatic. When, for example, postwar writers pointed out the patent misconceptions of Russia on the part of Mr. Roosevelt and many of his advisers, what was said was likely to be dismissed by tried and true reviewers among the academic critics as "Monday morning quarterbacking." The circumstance that people like Mr. Dallin had diagnosed the plays on Saturday afternoon was studiously ignored.

Dallin, although he had never been a Communist, knew from a lifelong concentration on Russian policies how the men in the Kremlin thought and acted. A theorist in the search for a new social order, he had been in exile in England before the Russian revolution (when Litvinov, too,

1. *Modern Age* 5, no. 1 (winter 1960–1961).

was there) and had returned to the Soviet Union, as a member of the Moscow Soviet, for the brief period when the Bolsheviks had permitted an opposition to function. He managed to leave before the early quasi-tolerance faded and the GPU looked after any opposition.

Despite the evidence with which he supported his analyses, the reception of his books in academic circles was always less than enthusiastic. Although he had scattered admirers among the professoriat he had far more opponents, who ranged from the violently hostile to those who merely called him anti-Soviet and who said in effect that even if he was right he made the future look too grim, that we must try to see a better face on our Russian allies or they would never have one. Even in 1947, when *Forced Labor in Soviet Russia* (which he had written with B. I. Nicolaevsky) was published, the academic furors did not subside. On the contrary, when Vishinsky denounced the book in the United Nations, professors in some of our foremost institutions of higher learning joined with him or shook their heads over the carefully arrived at findings that ten to fifteen million slaves were working in the Soviet economy. Subsequent investigations and the testimony of survivors of the system so strongly corroborated the book, forced labor became such a liability in the propaganda wars for a regime representing the workers of the world, that for once the men in the Kremlin were affected by public opinion and the institution of the forced labor camps was whittled down. It is not too much to say that thousands of people owe their freedom to the events set in motion by this book. But it had made its way against the academic procession.

What are the causes of this *trahison des clercs*? Why did these scholarly books arouse the wrath or passive resistance of scholars? And not only scholars. A conservative businessman once told me Dallin could not be right because—unlike so many accredited travelers—he had not been in the Soviet Union since 1921. What image of respectability for himself and for the Soviet Union had come into the head of this solid citizen, and how had it got there?

Enthusiasm for the wartime ally is not enough to explain this benevolence, which existed with fluctuating intensity before the war and has continued after it despite Korea, the East German rising, the Hungarian revolt, the unremitting attacks on the United States. Churchill, long the symbol of resistance to tyranny, himself became a dubious figure for many intellectuals when he made his Fulton, Missouri, speech about the Iron Curtain and two worlds. The myth of the Chinese agrarians that was cherished in academic circles as it was in American high policy was part of this image making, and the cadres of the Communist conspiracy could never have achieved their successes without the eagerness to believe they encountered among the intellectuals. Hitler-Stalin pacts were waved aside or explained as part of a wily long-range plan of the Kremlin to come to grips in due course with the arch enemy (an explanation that, incidentally, is the same as the one Hitler used to justify his attack on Russia); the shooting down of unarmed civilians in East Germany and Hungary was followed by mass meetings of protest and then by demands for America to sit down and talk over our right to stay in Berlin as with a partner seeking a reasonable solution. Any sign of joviality is seized upon as evidence of latent friendship and the two standards of judgment emerge: one for what Khrushchev says and does, the other for the men of the West. The bonhomie of Macmillan or Eisenhower or even de Gaulle would be no cause for flights of optimism.

For reasons which we shall pursue in future issues of *Modern Age*, too many intellectuals have consciously or unconsciously placed their hopes for the good society in a totalitarian system that has betrayed these docile admirers over and over again. They discover new phrases to find the Soviet Union better than before—it is reaching a new stage in its development, it has been won over to the idea of two worlds and peaceful coexistence, Khrushchev is not Stalin. . . . It is no wonder that the explanations of the Communist *Apparat*, of the full-time purveyors of opinion in the Kremlin, find these people ready to see their enemy, not in the perverters of truth, but in the Dallins—without whom the security and assurance with which they themselves write would be more endangered than they will ever know.

1961

Conservatism, Reaction, and Fascism

From time to time the question of the curious as well as of the ill-intentioned is raised—"How would you define the difference between the conservative, the reactionary, and the fascist?" Since the historians, political scientists, philosophers, and metaphysicians who write for *Modern Age* will continue to search out the roots and forms of conservatism, I shall try here only to make some distinctions that seem to have clearly separated these positions.

The historical meaning of "conservative" as it supplanted Tory in the early nineteenth century has changed as must every word that has to do with political contexts. The conservative in post–World War II England is above all the one who rejects the welfare state of the Labour party; the one who saw in it, and caused the uncommitted electorate to see in it, the party of economic stagnation and of diminishing returns, while nevertheless accepting some of its popular—if theoretically reprehensible—devices such as that of the National Health Service Program.

In West Germany, too, a conservative party has been in power since a federal government was established in 1949, despite the fact that all the rehabilitated parties licensed under the Four Power Occupation in 1945 or 1946 were originally addicted to some form of socialism. The conservatives in the Bundesrepublik are democrats by way of the bitter history they have experienced. That is why Germany has legislation outlawing any party of the Right or Left that threatens the democratic order. They have unleashed the energies of the free market and thus have enabled the country to bear its heavy burdens of restitution, war pensions, rebuilding, the upkeep of West Berlin, and to absorb the thirteen million or more people who have found refuge inside its borders. In addition, in the political forms and purposes they have helped to create, they have restored to the refugees as well as to the native population virtues that had been wholly lost of a free community accepting its responsibilities to a malign past and to a new European and Western order.

In Spain, as Mr. Wilson's article shows,[1] the conservative is of another

---

1. Francis G. Wilson, "The New Conservatives in Spain," *Modern Age* 5, no. 2 (spring 1961).

9

kind, a monarchist very likely, but here again pulling his weight against the pretensions of a state to impose its naked power—whether for the public welfare or what it takes to be the glory of God. Thus the postwar conservative in Western Europe has been *l'homme révolté*, the rebel against statist prescription, and it is mainly this reaction, in the case of the Germans to a criminal state that called itself socialist, in the case of the English to the bureaucratic benevolence and fatuity of a genuinely socialist government, that has been the source of the coalitions behind the conservative rise to power and public approval. Of course, conservatives everywhere oppose the kind of régime Mrs. Conant so well describes in her article on East Germany; there are no "yes, buts" in their opposition to a so-called revolutionary government that is reactionary as Hitler and Mussolini were reactionary, where any conservatives who survive have had to deal for thirty years with the same masters in different uniforms reciting contradictory slogans. The conservative Germans and Italians and Czechs who made common cause with the authoritarian state in its beginnings, whether reluctantly, or naively, because they thought they could bring it to reason, have long since discovered their powerlessness once the force of reaction, of the revolutions of both the Left and Right, is in motion. Konrad Adenauer, who has led the conservative party of postwar Germany, languished in a Nazi prison. So did men like Schacht, who once thought they could tame Hitler, and the revolt of July 20, 1944, sent to their deaths soldiers and civilians who believed they had the right and duty to judge the head of state and find him guilty. Nor had this been the first resistance of German conservatives in high and low places in the army and government who, before Munich and in the early stages of Hitler's Germany, tried first to curb and then depose him. They failed and they paid full measure, as they had known they would, for their failure.

In the United States, conservatism until recently has been swamped, among intellectuals, writers, teachers, politicians, and in the press, by the shallow tides of a pseudo-liberalism bringing in our own kind of welfare state. A conservative like Robert Taft was spoken of admiringly only after he died, for doing battle against Harry Truman's intention of putting striking railroad workers into the Army, for speaking up against the newly invented law of Nuremberg where men were tried for real crimes but also for others, like the alleged crime of aggression, contrived for the occasion and for which no one in history had ever been tried before. Now Khrushchev, Mao Tse-tung, and Castro, too, are able to identify an aggressor long before they see one, and there is small doubt of the uses they would make, if they could, of the Nuremberg precedent.

It is true that a coalition of expediency may unite conservatives with temporary allies who have no genuine belief in their principles. Anti-communism, like any embattled movement, brings people of widely disparate views together for what seems to be a moment of truth. But the conservative may be readily distinguished from those who are merely anti-Communist. He believes that the state exists for the individual, not the other way around, in the need to extend as far as possible the choice and consent of the individual in a time of technology and vast enterprises both private and public with their enormous power to submerge him. He rejects an affluent society where a government determines how he may best buy something or whether he will be allowed to buy it. He may, like Ludwig von Mises, give mankind the heady vision of a promised land far removed from Mr. Roosevelt's airy vistas of one world under four policemen. In Mises' free economy, goods, raw materials, and people of the entire earth could travel without let or hindrance where they were needed, and thus deprive even the most underdeveloped nation of any serious cause of war. This, like Voegelin's transcendental view of the political process, takes men further from reaction, further from the measures of coercion for a better life for which there is so much nostalgia among people who call themselves liberals.

Conservatism, it should be added, is compatible with radical forms in the arts. Eliot, who helped turn academic notions about the nature of poetry upside down in the 1920s, is a conservative in philosophy and politics. Kafka dredging among nightmares that came true of the twentieth century, Joyce recasting the ancient myths and journeying of mankind, St. John Perse, Claudel, Rilke—all write about the human condition *sub specie aeternitatis*. No struggle of the artist to make plain something never seen before or, out of the stresses and turbulence of his time, to restate a truth about people in their societies can be limited by inherited techniques. Here, too, it is the reactionary literature of the Soviet Union, of East Germany, of Yugoslavia that returns to rituals in praise of the Ruler, of the status quo kept inviolate in the local Koran, to borrow Voegelin's word. The conservative in his belief in criticism, in his individual quality of a judging, evaluating man, sifts experience in an attempt to enhance it, to turn the ruin and triumph of the past to a somehow wiser account.

Eichmann in Israel

As these words are being written, Adolf Eichmann, son of Karl Adolf Eichmann, as the trial record faithfully records every day, has been in the hands of the Israelis for a year. His long deposition—more than thirty-five hundred pages—tape-recorded and then typed for his corrections, the statements of people who knew him before and during the period of his lethal activities, the testimony of his jailers, leave him as open to observation as does the glass enclosure wherein he sits pale and shrunken in his sober blue suit. He makes many notes, leafs busily through the pile of documents on his table, looks toward his lawyer, the witnesses, and the judges, never at the audience in the courtroom, his eyes blinking, his face twitching now and then, but otherwise tense and expressionless behind his glasses. Even when a man in the gallery rose and shouted incoherent words, among them "Bloodhound!" before the police could lead him from the courtroom, Eichmann did not turn as did everyone else toward the sudden bustle of the disturbance. His persona, as is evident from his statement as well as from his stiff carriage in the courtroom, is that of the "treue Husar," a grotesquerie of the military virtue of obedience unto death, of "Traveller, go tell the Laodiceans that here, obedient to their words, we lie." All his life, he has said, he was brought up to obey orders, to that ideal of *Kadaver Gehorsam* under which any command whatever is mechanically carried out. He would without hesitation have shot his own father had he known him to be a traitor and had he been ordered to do so, he has said, and it is easy to believe him. But he is also in this persona a man of taste, of sensibility, he cannot bear the sight of a wound, he could not have been a doctor, and when reluctantly, but under orders, he visited in 1941 the first extermination camp where gas was to be used, he was revolted not only by its purpose but also by the man who had it in charge. This person, although a police officer, appeared without his coat, his sleeves rolled up, and he gave Eichmann the distasteful impression of having built the camp with his own hands. In addition he used coarse language, spoke a south German dialect and, who can tell? may even have been drinking—another possibility distressing to Eichmann. Finding himself in 1942 as the chief expert on the Jewish problem, at the Wannsee conference among ministers of state, Eichmann remembers gratefully the gentility of the gathering where cognac was served and the ministers spoke with few words and to the point. That is what he recalls about the meeting convened to arrange for the destruction of all the Jews in Europe. At the scenes of the killings Eichmann, although the most ardent of hunters in his pursuit of Jews for delivery to the extermination camps, has to look away, as he does during the forced marches of exhausted prisoners—men and women—where thousands died or were shot on the roadsides. On the occasion of another visit to check on the killings at Minsk and Lwów, Eichmann while invited to do so cannot bring himself to watch more than a small part of the executions, and he takes his mind off the horror of the scene by admiring the charming railroad station built to celebrate the sixtieth year of the reign of Franz Josef.

His habits of obedience have remained with him. Soon after being brought to Israel, Eichmann asked for something to eat, and one after the other as they were handed to him he solemnly chewed up seven slices of bread. He then thanked his jailer and said he had a request, would it be possible next time to give him only six slices? He is elaborately polite to his questioner from the Israeli police as he undoubtedly was to Himmler and to Heydrich. "Yes indeed, Herr Hauptmann," he says to his interrogator, "Please do not disturb yourself, Herr Hauptmann, on my account," when the officer suggests he may want to rest. "I am here to tell you everything," he says, "even things that are damaging." And he recounts how he once forced a man out of the SS because he beat two or three Jews for no reason. It is a story, obviously, in which he plays an uncommonly humane role although he wishes to point out, since he's concealing nothing, that he is responsible; the man had served under him. He himself, he says with shame, in a moment of anger once boxed the ears of a Jew who stood before him. But he was never an anti-Semite, through his stepmother he was even related to Jews, and helped one of them escape to Switzerland. In short Eichmann, like Himmler, like Hoess the commandant of Auschwitz and thousands of other murderous operators was able to take his part in organizing the killings and then live more or less in a normal fashion by a fantastic legerdemain of self-idealization. These men who stood in no danger, in well-pressed uniforms, while defenseless people were slaughtered, became for themselves heroes performing difficult tasks more abhorrent to their inner natures than to others less sensitive, but nevertheless stoically doing their duty to their Leader, to the State and its higher order. One of the witnesses in the trial described this scene: as Jews were gathered in a town for transport to the place of execution, a young baby held in the arms of its mother began to cry. An SS man went to her and said: "May I take the child, please?"

The mother hesitated for a moment before handing over the baby and the SS man took the child and dashed its head against the ground. Men like this told one another they had an assignment beyond the ordinary call of duty but like the soldiers at the front they had to carry it out if the enemies of the race and its future were to be made harmless.

The Eichmann trial will contribute to history in its side effects, as Nuremberg did, by being the occasion for the accumulation of documents, of eyewitness accounts out of which we may one day be able to explain how in the twentieth century such events, on such a vast, efficient, and continuous scale could be organized. But just as Nuremberg was the trial of the vanquished by the victors, so is this the trial of the persecutors, of the hangmen by their victims. Eichmann fades into the background as the witnesses tell their stories of murder and heroism, of the manner of dying of millions of people. For the trial is a point of concentration, like a medieval theater where the audience knows the play, knows the characters and the tragic end and nonetheless relives each scene as though seeing it for the first time.

For the government, the prosecution, the trial is another proof of the need for this state of Israel to exist, of the Jews to rely on themselves for justice, or for mere survival—were not the doors of escape, even those in the hands of their friends, closed to them? And who else in the course of fifteen years ferreted out Eichmann and brought him before a court of law? That the law under which he is being tried is retroactive is conceded, but it is argued that necessity makes law, that the chaos, the nihilism, of the Hitler period have forced the courts at Nuremberg and those of subsequent trials, including this one, to deal with the perpetrators of a new crime, genocide, as nations dealt with pirates who could be captured and punished by any power. That this court is prejudiced may be admitted says the attorney general, what human being would not be? But the judges will be fair, which is all any judge, Israeli or not, could be. Even in Nazi Germany, he points out, the Communist Dimitrov was freed by a court that could not be convinced of his guilt for the Reichstag fire.

The behavior of the court substantiates his view. The three judges are learned, courteous, patient, although one in the early part of the trial nodded and awakened with a perceptible start when a question was asked. While they hand down the expected decisions confirming their own competence, they check the attorney general from over-elaborating his case but in the interest of the historical record and of the world television audience, they permit wide latitude to the prosecution in producing witnesses who testify to atrocities they saw but which have no direct connection with the defendant. They listen carefully to Dr. Servatius, Eichmann's lawyer, and in its procedures, its externals this is a true court, weighing objections, the evidence, seeking the truth. And that Eichmann since his kidnapping has been well treated is evident from the tone of his rambling deposition; the conduct and interrogations of his jailers seem to have been impeccable however roughly handled he may have been in the Argentine. While Servatius, here as in Nuremberg, is working under considerable handicaps, he will be able to make his case. He has obstacles not shared by the prosecution: insufficient funds (the twenty thousand dollars he was paid was furnished by Israel and he says he has already spent it), witnesses who cannot be brought from Germany or wherever they are, either because they are unwilling to come, or would be in danger of arrest if they did. Their testimony, however, may be taken in a German court and will be admitted as evidence. And on the whole Servatius can probably present as good a defense as can be made for his client; no money and no witnesses are likely to affect the record, which is so damaging and which has been so thoroughly preserved.

The flaw of the trial is not in its forms but in its structure. It is like Nuremberg a trial with political overtones. No one questions Eichmann's guilt; he himself admits it in the context of the post-Nazi world and has even offered, because of his complicity in the mass murders, to hang himself in public. Chancellor Adenauer denies that Eichmann is a German citizen, and Austria, the only other country that might claim his allegiance, has made no request for his deportation. For the representatives of East Germany the trial is solely an opportunity for propaganda. They are present to show that Nazism survives in the Bundesrepublik, in its army and government, and Eichmann as such has no interest whatever for them. The representatives of the Bundesrepublik who are here as observers have kept an ostentatious distance from the accused and his counsel; they comport themselves as the representatives of a neutral power whose interest at some point may conceivably be involved. The Russian concern with the trial is limited to the line of the anti-West German press of the Iron Curtain countries. A request on the part of the Israeli government for the delivery of copies of documents kept by the Soviet government in Vilna was not even answered. Such matters come under the jurisdiction of the desk of Middle Eastern Affairs, not under the department of historical research, certainly not of justice.

Despite the outward correctness of the proceedings it is evident that Israel has missed an opportunity to forward the cause of law as well as justice and international comity in a time when all three are inconspicuous in international relations. "We shall neither forgive nor forget," says the attorney general, and this remote thunder of the prophets is heard too in the Israeli press. What then becomes of a distressed humanity, no part of which is wholly without guilt in history? Does it live forever in the massacres, the St. Bartholomew nights, the endless injustices of the past? And of course, in fact, the Israelis like people everywhere do forgive. The mark of Cain is not on all Germans. Ben-Gurion and Adenauer, simple Israelis and Germans have pleasant, even friendly, relations—but the rhetoric, for political purposes no doubt, is unrelenting. Yet Israel herself is surrounded by enemies who can and do point to the thousands of Arab refugees, whose property is held by the Israelis, to the punitive killing of defenseless Arab civilians. For this latter offense it is true, the responsible Israelis were given heavy sentences, but it is also true that the sentences were later commuted and the perpetrators only lightly punished. And if Israel has jurisdiction over crimes committed before its laws were written and can act on behalf of Jews in any country, what is to prevent, as Servatius among others has asked, one of the new African states from claiming the right to kidnap and to try the persecutors of the Negro in South Africa or Tennessee? But conceding the primary need to try Eichmann, and the fact that no other country took the pains to find him and bring him to trial, what aside from chauvinism kept Israel from asking that an international court be convoked to try the accused who had participated in crimes against the nationals of many countries? If the representatives of these two and a quarter million people had been ready to share their hard-won sovereignty to this extent, the verdict of any court could not conceivably be different from what this one will be. But the cause of manifest justice would have been better served and Israel would have taken a historic step toward a new order of the West, plainly dissociating herself from doctrines that have made so many victims of her people.

The Divided Cities

It is possible to travel from Chicago to West Berlin in half a day but on the way you must cross territory in East Germany where you may not enter nor may its inhabitants leave although for the time being the lines of communication from the West to Berlin are open. And in Berlin itself where people until mid-August had been able to cross back and forth between the east and west sectors with relative freedom, the Iron Curtain, although not then visible in the form of the barbed wire that marks the frontier between the Federal Republic and East Germany, was nevertheless always there, and the moment the Brandenburger gate was crossed, the West German conducted himself with the same caution as did the East German. They were both in dangerous territory where the wrong word overheard by the man at the next table could send anyone to jail for calumniating the People's State, sowing treason, or sabotaging the progressive, peace-loving activities of the progressive, peace-loving, and democratic republic.

It is possible, too, to make the journey to Jerusalem in less than a day. And Jerusalem is also a divided city where the barbed wire that cuts through it is visible enough and no Jew may cross it to the Jordanian part of the city nor any Jordanian to the Israeli sector. Children play in front of the barriers, people on both sides of the boundary go peacefully about their daily business but they are further apart than Jerusalem and New York; than Beirut and San Francisco. The barbed wire goes through other towns in Israel and Jordan; it is a boundary marking another cold war although here as in Berlin, the people living on both sides of it may be of the same race and language, for many of these frontier towns are inhabited by Arabs. The warning signs, however, speak of the peril lying ahead at the frontier where the enemy waits, since not peace but an armistice is in force, leaving both sides with their hands on their guns.

After so much confident talk of "one world" it is worth looking again at the divided cities. For they are, both Berlin and Jerusalem, evidences of a world more deeply divided than it has been by merely national, or religious, or geographical separation. Jerusalem as a whole is a city of many faiths, Moslem, Jewish, Protestant, and Catholic, and in sacred places on the Jordanian side of the line, even in one of the holiest, in the Church of the Nativity in Bethlehem, Moslem guards keep the peace in the birthplace of Christ, between the sects who struggle for position in the shrine that is common to them all. But it is no longer religion that divides the city: the mosques and the Christian and Jewish shrines could share the amenities of Jerusalem as they have before. What divides it is a neo-nationalism, an Arab nationalism tapering off to the pro-Russian "neutralism" of a segment of the Arab states (all of which are belligerently anti-Communist in their domestic policies) confronting the pro-Western Israelis, many of whose political leaders have markedly leftist leanings. In the search for a Big Brother in the postwar years, only two possibilities exist—either Russia or America, although both Arabs and Israelis may seek to build up their position in the camp of the other. No Communist party is permitted to exist in the lands of the Arabs who get their military support from Soviet Russia, while Israel not only has a legal Communist party but much of the program of the non-Communist parties, as well as the idealistic thinking of the Kibbutzim, which is more communal than anything Soviet Russia has been able to make work.

In Berlin, too, there are divisions within the great schism. Before the barriers were put up in August five thousand people fled across the boundary from the East to the West sectors in one weekend, keeping up the flow of the exodus that has, it is calculated, drained East Germany of more than four million people since the end of the war.[1] The counterflow from West Germany has been negligible by comparison—the population of West Germany wants and is getting a steadily improving standard of living in a climate of freedom. Nevertheless, the strains of Communist propaganda from East Berlin and East Germany, making adroit use of isolated cases, are repeated in the West, where many political observers agree that men like Hans Globcke, Staatssekretär in the office of the Chancellor, who for whatever reason served the Nazi state in its years of power, have too much place and influence. In Jerusalem, during the Eichmann trial, it was hard to find a West German newspaperman who disagreed with the East Germans on Globcke, although he could be warmly defended by Americans who had screened him in the early postwar years and who agreed with Adenauer that he had worked with the anti-Nazi underground, had kept his post and carried out his lugubrious assignments even unto writing a commentary on the Nuremberg laws, not to serve Hitler but to help destroy him. After the Globcke accusations there must be others, for Communist propaganda in the West and in Israel woodenly repeats that the present German government is a projection

1. Willi Kinnigkeit, Die Angst im Nacken, *Süddeutsche Zeitung*, July 25, 1961.

of Hitler's regime of Nazi militarism (a point of view that in a slightly different form was shared by almost the entire Roosevelt administration with its belief in the historic evils of Junkers, German big business, and the German General Staff, as an alliance that made and unmade governments at its will).

The Communist attack on the West in the Arab countries moves on another flank, against Western imperialism and colonialism and its pro-Israeli policies, and makes common cause, as it has before, with military rulers like Nasser who proscribe the party. On both sides of the line in Jerusalem are evidences of the struggle reaching into every conflict and corner of the globe. The anti-Americanism of people opposing King Hussein's government may echo the Moscow propaganda about American imperialism, but it also attacks American aid to Jordan, accusing the United States of helping to keep a corrupt and incompetent administration in power and funds—a charge that is difficult to refute because it appears to be true. The Jordanian government with "neutralist," anti-Western leanings claps its local Communist leaders in jail, while in the Israeli sector of Jerusalem, American money is gratefully put to work and a Communist party plies its trade in a modern, underdeveloped, welfare state.

Communism has kept the initiative against the West almost uninterruptedly since 1943. The documents of the Potsdam conference show Churchill, after the experiences of Yalta and Teheran, urging on Harry Truman that the Big Three meeting be held in territory where the Western powers would not again be guests of the Red Army. But the conference was nevertheless held in Berlin, where the United States even then had to ask for Russian permission to supply the tiny force responsible for the security of the president through Russian-held territory. It was a fathomless incomprehension of the nature of communism together with the terrible simplification of the one-world concept that determined Roosevelt's foreign policy. It was this policy inherited by Harry Truman complete with advisers like Harry Hopkins and Joe Davies who wanted nothing better than to please Mr. Stalin and thus to win their imaginary postwar world that gave Russia the opportunity to strangle Berlin. Their formula was so grandiose, so without content, that it could be confuted in the very city where the last seal of approval was being placed on the delivery of Eastern Europe to communism.

In Jerusalem and along the Arab-Israeli borders a cease-fire exists. What in other days would have been another major territorial change in a land that has experienced invasions and conquests from all points of the compass now narrows itself to one more outpost in the struggle between East and West. Here at least the intentions of American policy have been clear; to keep the lines of communication between the Arab states and the West open; to keep an independent Israel in the Western camp. But the failures in the Middle East, like those in Berlin, are tied to grandiose sentiments; formulae that work against the goals they set. In what it does and does not do the United States can be too easily identified with the party of the status quo, with the inheritors of power, while Russia, a new and virulent form of ancient despotism, flies the flag of native independence. Here again as once in Berlin the United States has helped to maneuver itself into a defensive position it will be long maintaining. Its policies lack flexibility and drive; instead of working within the contradictions of the Communist strategies, exploiting their weaknesses, it is caught in the rhetoric of Point 4, substituting money for intelligence, do-goodism for morality.

At the Sign of No Dollars

Certain Marxist dogmas, it has often been observed, are more deeply rooted in the thinking of American intellectuals than they are in the Kremlin. No country has manifested more faith, spent more money, or taxed itself more heavily in the conviction that economic factors determine political, and indeed, existential decisions than has the United States. In the dominant social science gospel of decision makers, a low standard of living is the chief cause of any people's adopting principles pleasing to Moscow and the latter day missionaries of the Foreign Aid Program are sent forth to raise the resistance levels of native populations by way of the checkbook if not of the substance of the democracy whose largesse they bestow. But the nudging, affluent approach is by no means confined to the aid of foreign countries. Here is a quotation from a recruiting bulletin addressed to the faculty of an American university on behalf of the State Department:

> Sign up for our mission to Yekrut. You get an increase in salary, overseas incentive pay, hardship differentials, free housing, post exchange privileges, and all the other perquisites of Foreign Service officers . . . Your wife will have servants; you will be invited to diplomatic receptions; you will rub shoulders with the local elite; you can entertain all sorts of VIPs, and Scotch sells at $1.75 a fifth. There are plenty of opportunities for travel and adventure. Yekrut is a charming little country and so are its neighbors. Besides, on your way out there and back you can take your family on a little tour of Europe. Above all, keep in mind that this is your chance to be somebody and accumulate a bankroll at the same time.[1]

It is difficult to imagine blandishments better designed to get the kind of people for foreign service who have the least talent for it. In the feeble light of such texts it is no wonder at all that a road in Jordan paid for by the United States and built only two years ago buckles and returns in bumpy stretches to the surrounding desert, if American aid has been administered by a corps that has been persuaded to come there in order to

1. From an article by Professor Walter Adams of Michigan State University reprinted in the Congressional Record, June 1, 1961, Appendix, 3950–52. I want to thank Professor J. Fred Rippy for calling this to my attention.

buy Scotch cheaply and to entertain more VIPs than they are accustomed to when they are at home. It may also be pointed out that near this road is one built during World War I by the British army which is still in good condition. Any hardship differentials seem to have gone into their work.

When the U-2 came down in the Soviet Union in mid-1960 the salary of the young pilot who had failed to destroy the plane was said to be in the neighborhood of twenty thousand dollars a year—a considerable sum for a young man in his twenties. It is not difficult to follow what must have been the reasoning of the officials who with knit brows set the high pay of young officers making such hazardous flights. Here in the United States, one can hear them say, a young man in industry, a sales manager perhaps, sitting in an office with a high index of comfort and safety, earns that much money—why shouldn't a pilot engaged in a task of momentous importance for his country, setting his life at stake, be paid on the same scale? The answer that courage and devotion have no scales must have seemed inconclusive to the decision makers, assuming such an answer was made at all. But the measure of their wrong evaluation goes further— the historical evidence is plainly against paying in the world's goods for recruiting the hero. If you look at the friezes and paintings celebrating remembered exploits, the hero is being rewarded with nothing more than laurel leaves although the Gods and Goddesses themselves are likely to be in attendance at the ceremony. It is not recorded that Nathan Hale was given a raise in his captain's pay, assuming that he got that, to go behind the British lines. And even in an abominable cause, that of the Nazis in the last war, the members of Skorzeny's group who plucked Mussolini from the mountain top of his Italian captors got nothing more than the brief thanks of the Fuehrer and perhaps a medal. In fact it may be argued that recruiting men for great exploits with offers of more money is bound to buy them too cheaply. The candidates for the job will be those who stand in line mainly for a paycheck, although we know human beings give their lives for other reasons. They spend them for other reasons too if they are serious scientists and scholars or military men.

Along with inappropriate economic rewards go equally inappropriate economic punishments. General Eisenhower, when he was in Germany soon after the war ended, is reported as having said, no doubt while still under the overwhelming impressions of Nazi atrocities, that he favored confiscating private German property in neutral countries. When it was pointed out that that would violate international law, the general merely asked if we weren't making law in Nuremberg. Actually, we were remaking it, not only in Nuremberg but in Washington, too, where the private property of Germans and Japanese held in this country was taken over by the Alien Property Custodian at the start of World War II and with a few exceptions hasn't been returned to this day. The United States thus created a precedent for Castro's confiscation of American property in Cuba almost twenty years before he was able to follow it. The confiscations were alleged to have been leveled at great German industries like I.G. Farben, which had been aiding Hitler's war, but regardless of the *Problematik* of such corporations or the rights and wrongs of their practices, thousands of individuals whose only crime was that they were German or Japanese owning property in the United States in 1941 had it taken from them.

On the other hand, the Russians worry very little about such relatively minor economic reprisals or the standard of living of the peoples in the satellite and underdeveloped countries. The East Germans live at a subsistence level; while their factories produce for a balance of trade with Russia and the other East bloc countries, the German worker and consumer get barely enough to keep themselves on the treadmill. The Soviet Union organizes a crusade for the minds, and on behalf of what they assert to be the wrongs of the populations they are wooing or coercing. They preach Peace or Native Independence, Freedom from Exploitation and Imperialism, and as Robert Jones showed some months ago in this magazine, what loans they make are political loans since the ruble can be depreciated or inflated as a barometer of Soviet approval of the behavior of the country receiving them. The standard of living of the worker interests Moscow not in the least, what the Soviets want is a quid pro quo as in the case of the anti-Western policy of Nasser, or moving down the line to the satellites, the production and puppet allegiances of the captive governments. And what the people in those countries are lavishly fed is propaganda with promises of a future which they know could scarcely be worse than the unrewarding living they now scrape together.

These exploited workers in East Germany and in Hungary sponta-neously revolted; they rose not only because of poor rations (the East German uprising started with comparatively well-paid construction work-ers) but because of the attempted crushing of their own integrity, because it became intolerable to them that the Communist slogans are only thin paint over the brute force of the secret police and the state it serves. But the propaganda deals with uprisings too; mistakes are publicly admitted, the noose around the necks of the subjugated people is loosened, a rapturous future is described in the space age controlled by the technical and moral superiorities of the Communist orbit. The Communist cadres believe this; they have to or the justification for their existence falls apart. The attack therefore is always made on the beliefs of the victims; the bank accounts, the take-home pay, the fringe benefits come second. And the men and women the Kremlin recruits for its multifarious foreign tasks are promised not cheap liquor and servants; what they are promised and what they give is a seven-day week and years of arduous preparation for their jobs. A man in Jordan at a party I attended said, in a group talking about the plight of their country, that what they needed for its salvation or even survival was three thousand disinterested citizens; people who wanted nothing for themselves in the way of villas or cars or the contracts that are passed around so freely among the in-group. If the United States wanted such a qualitative change among its academic recruits the American State Department bulletin could read something like this: "X is a place where you can learn a good deal and teach something of what you know. In a time when the United States and its allies are struggling to keep the area of freedom as wide and deep and viable as possible you would be doing a considerable service to your country and its cause if you went there and did the job you've been educated to do."

The other side of the coin of this perverse, primitive, anti-Communist Marxism is the private generosity of Americans. The people of no other country in the world—and many in the high- and middle-income brackets in South America, in Europe and elsewhere, could do the same if they elected to—provide such a flood of benefactions for the hungry, the destitute, the sick; for art and science as well as for inanities of all kinds. Here the standard of the checkbook, the free will donations of laboring men and farmhands as well as of the rich, have enabled millions of anonymous human beings throughout the world to survive. No European equivalent of this exists on a comparable scale and needless to say the Russian opportunities for producing creative work are limited to those who can regularly recite the party beatitudes. Even the greatest figures, if they stray from these limits, find their possibilities of writing and publishing disappearing. In most of Europe and South America the rich are too occupied with collecting things for their own account to bother with establishing research organizations or other aid to the general weal. The art museums are public, the opera and the theater are public, the concerts are subsidized—it is only in the United States where the general population and the producers expect private persons, and they expect themselves, to pay for the deficits. That many of these benefactions were given anonymously, long before a tax squeeze produced so much synthetic generosity, that in some instances it is even forbidden the recipient to thank publicly the foundation responsible for the appearance of the book or project it has made possible, is in the great tradition of self-denial on behalf of others. But the gulf between these two standards of the American ways is not to be bridged by private charity alone. The *clercs* and the other spokesmen for this culture can do more than repeat another's texts, some of them at least can speak up for the virtues of a society moved by its enterprises to standards of well-being undreamed in former generations or in other societies, but inspirited in the case of so many of its men of business, science, and scholarship by no motive whatever of private profit. It is this standard of probity in fact that might be distributed in this country and abroad, and it is absolutely free.

1962

Professor Toynbee and Madison Avenue

Arnold J. Toynbee is reported to have made the following remarks in an address at Williamsburg, Virginia, last June on the occasion of the celebration there of "The Prelude to Independence." It is especially worth reading them in the light of the articles on the public and private sector that are appearing in *Modern Age*. Professor Toynbee said:

> In the Western world of our day, the tempter's role, which in St. Francis's personal history was played by the saint's father, is being played, toward our society as a whole, by everything we sum up under the name of Madison Avenue and all that this label stands for. A considerable part of our ability, energy, time, and material resources is being spent today on inducing us to do hard labor in order to find the money for buying material goods that we should never have dreamed of wanting if we had been left to ourselves. The first assault on the cupidity that is latent in every one of us is made by Madison Avenue by finesse. The strategy is to try to captivate us without allowing us to become aware of what is being done to us. If this sly approach does not do the trick, Madison Avenue has further psychological weapons in its armory. If all else fails, it will resort to sheer bullying, and it will carry this, if necessary, to the third degree. Now this is the inner adversary with whom we heave to contend. And, just because he assails us from within, he is more formidable than any external opponent. And often we externalize our opponent when he is really within us. I would suggest that the destiny of our Western civilization turns on the issue of our struggle with all that Madison Avenue stands for more than it turns on the issue of our struggle with communism.

Toynbee is a philosopher whose historical erudition often wears thin as soon as it encounters his flinty determination to construct models closer to his heart's desire than the originals. A number of eminent historians have criticized him sharply, not for his brilliant and imaginative interpretations, but for the distortions he clings to. In this case he shares a common view of European and American intellectuals that the United States is made up of *Mass-Menschen*, of robots not a cut above the empty-headed vessels shown on the television screens in whose skulls hammers tap and springs unwind amid the loose screws that hold the victim miserably together until the fast, fast, fast pain relief readies him for his next headache. These are the people, undoubtedly, for whom the public sector must be broadened to protect them from buying what they want in the private sector.

The spreading of wares for sale is as old as barter, almost as old as human desires and temptation itself. It contrasts with tribal self-sufficiency and slave labor that can be merely handed its clothes and food and tools. This ancient method of distributing goods is still available in a somewhat more elaborate form. A worker I know in the Soviet zone of Germany saved up for a long time to get an overcoat. When it was brought home from the HO—the Peoples' Co-operative—store, the buyer discovered that it had a bad defect in the weaving. No recourse was possible—no exchange, no money back, because no mechanism exists in the bureaucracy against an arm of the state and of course no one outside the Ministry of Propaganda has any reason to win a citizen's goodwill. "Let the buyer beware" in the People's Democratic Republic, and let him keep what takes him many times as long to earn as it does his opposite number in the West.

For the majority of people the market has been the place not only of temptation but of hard decision among many needs. They were sometimes undoubtedly persuaded by fast talkers into buying something they didn't want or couldn't afford but when have people ever been separated from their follies? The value of luxuries, too, can best be measured by those who choose them for whatever aesthetic or other notion that may seem absurd to others. What "good" was the statue, the carved chalice, or the gold ornament, or the remote paintings on a high ceiling? Those who commissioned them believed they knew; these brought delight, a sense of awe or prestige, or another dimension to the daily scene. The public did not order such things, although it might admire them. The rise of technology and the mass market on the other hand commanded by the millions, has turned yesterday's articles of *luxe*, including even forms of art, into today's common possessions.

Who has been captivated without being allowed to know what is being done to him? The millions with a standard of living no other society has ever provided? Or Professor Toynbee? The buying waves of the last years in the United States have been conspicuously those that have had to do with the shift to the small car, to one-story houses, to television sets, to high fidelity and stereo radios and phonographs, to nylons and dacrons and drip-dry cottons and mixtures of all of them, to electric shaving and now perhaps electric toothbrushes, to more efficient cameras, washing and drying machines, deep freezers—every one of them inventions of technology, not of Madison Avenue. In fact, in the case of the small car no amount of advertising of the newer, longer, roomier, more *formidable* models had the slightest effect on the stubborn trend away from the big to the little. What is the evidence that people are bullied into buying by advertising? Madison Avenue seems to have been able to persuade Professor Toynbee that this is possible, but he has been an easy victim of the imaginary effects of its wiles and stratagems. Any publisher can testify how much money goes down the drain advertising a book the public doesn't want. Detroit explained over and over again to American car buyers that what they wanted was bigger cars with more power every year; but it was forced by the public to change its own ideas, plans, and production quotas. The Volkswagen, in fact, made its spectacular success in the United States with no advertising campaigns at all.

I suggest as a hypothesis that the Toynbees are far more affected by Madison Avenue than the main body of the population; the mass buyers of things are price conscious, more ready to fill in the gaps of their leisure, to offset, if you like, the sterilities of much of their lives by acquiring possessions that promise to make the day entertaining and exciting, without much effort on their part. That these devices may fail, or that they may merely extend the areas of banality, has little to do with Madison Avenue, but much with the deeper nature of the society. The low quality of most of the advertising on television is matched by the low quality of most of its dramatic productions; and if one feeds from the other, it is because they entertain the same spurious notion that the man with the hammer inside his skull is in fact their audience. But when during the World War magazines appeared for the benefit of the armed forces without advertising, a good deal was missing from the contents— coded news about the society perhaps, but still glimpses of what America finds beautiful along with the lotions of its discontent. The Toynbees are basically suspicious of the democracy of the market. *Panem et circenses*— what cannot befall the world if the voracious appetites of the masses are catered to or are secretly controlled or motivated by the slogans, sophistries, and measurements of the capitalist society. And how much more graceful and attractive a society has been when only a few people, those with good taste or with the public weal solely in mind, have made the decisions and not the coarse multitude of buyers themselves. Actually, Madison Avenue has not a fraction of the power Toynbee attributes to it. What it can do is to call attention to competing merchandise, to praise it, unroll it, shake it, spread it for sale. But these goods appear in a competitive market, where people choose bountifully among drinks, toothpastes, and pain killers. Madison Avenue did not invent thirst or teeth or pain; all it can do is cry the wares and the unmistakable trend toward more reliability in what is claimed for the virtues of the goods, for sale is itself a recognition of the long-term benefits of standards of quality. Some foreign manufacturers, I am told, could produce and sell thousands more of their cars each year, but have decided against the risks of increasing their plant capacity because it would also have meant a compromise with their standards. Ford, on the other hand, with his Model T changed the face of the country with mass production, and when this wonderful and indestructible car was forced by a change in public taste to give way to one with a gear shift, Madison Avenue had nothing whatever to do with the development, nor is it at all likely that it could have prevented it. As Professor van den Haag points out in his article,[1] the same company was unable, despite the lavish build-up, to persuade the public it wanted a dazzling new car of its devising.

The unconscious slaves of Madison Avenue are a figment of Mr. Toynbee's always lively imagination. Let us accept for the moment the dubious claim that this society induces us "to do hard labor to find the money for buying material goods we should never had dreamed of wanting if we had been left to ourselves"—whatever that may mean precisely. Where, in fact, is a man left to himself, and if he should be, what would he want that would not involve tastes and values of other men and women? But so be it. Let us say we work in the capitalist mines in order to buy those foolish cars, televisions, and FM sets—but what actual, contemporary society shall we compare with this one? The East Germans conducted what has been called a walking plebiscite on their preferences, and four million of them left everything they owned to start all over again, from the beginning, in the flourishing West, and we may surmise how many millions more from Eastern Europe and Russia itself would have gladly joined them. Yet the threat Mr. Toynbee finds is not with the system that drove these refugees and millions of others from their farms and homes but with Madison Avenue, which is trying to persuade people to have more of everything not less. A droll teatime story Mr. Toynbee has fashioned for himself and for a genuinely captivated audience, a story which could readily be followed by a pitch for a peaceful, uncoerced society by Uncle Nikita, after which, but not for long, the author would be able to resume his musings out loud.

---

1. "Private and Public Expenditures: A Reappraisal." *Modern Age* 6, no. 2 (spring 1962).

Alarms and Skirmishes

The creeping inflation—the kind that carries the price index up gently and steadily—has reached the postwar center of the European free market: West Germany. Prices are inching higher for clothes, food, furniture, cars, and almost everything else. The *Süddeutscher Zeitung* in May reported that a market basket of groceries had cost 15.96 marks in March 1960, and two years later, in March of this year, cost 18.19 marks; 62 percent of retail prices are up and 17 percent are lower. The automobile industry has raised its prices despite the entreaties of the government, and when the Volkswagen, that mighty symbol of Germany's recovery, announced higher prices ranging from $60-$125 for three of its models, Chancellor Adenauer's entire cabinet protested and then voted to reduce the tariff by 50 percent for competing foreign cars. Thus the high priests of the free market who since the currency reform of 1948 have opposed, in principle, political interference in its operations are moved not only to shake their fingers but to pick up a big stick.

For Germany has lived through two ruinous inflations, and the first sign of a wage-price spiral sends alarm signals through the web of the society. As a result of overemployment, 550,000 foreign workers have migrated to West Germany beginning with a trickle of 7,000 in 1957 that rose to more than 100,000 in 1960 and to 150,000 last year. Half of them are Italian, thousands come from Greece and Spain, and although no German labor commissions have journeyed to Yugoslavia as they have to the other countries, some 13,000 Yugoslavians, having heard of the promised land and the jobs to be had, have sought work in the Bundesrepublik. Some of them come "black," as political refugees from Tito, and must remain in camps until they get work; others obtain the proper visa from the French government, acting on behalf of West Germany in Belgrade. But getting a job in any event is no problem; workers of all trades are wanted: barbers, construction workers, household help, technicians, common laborers—and the real wages are the highest in Germany's history. But despite this spectacular effect of the operations of the free market, the Communist party in Italy has a special department to tell the Italian workers in West Germany how exploited they are, and the Czechoslovakian radio broadcasts a similar half-hour program in Italian beamed to them daily.

Across the border, East German soldiers are photographed goose-stepping in parade formations, wearing the uniform of the People's Democratic Republic that closely resembles the Russian, although in the early years of East German rearmament the helmet was that of the old German Wehrmacht. In West Germany the creeping inflation has not affected important diversions of the Bundeswehr. In one camp in Bavaria whose spare amenities German and American soldiers share, the German troops on a beer evening pay twenty pfennigs (five cents) for a stein of beer, or a sandwich, and they spend the time in convivial comradeship with the Americans, half of whom are Negro, restricted in telling one another their opinion of army life and discussing other common problems only by the speech barriers. Nothing like this, of course, occurs between the East German troops and those of their great ally Soviet Russia; the wall between them is higher than the one in Berlin. Nor is there a visible inflation in the East—there are only shortages, sometimes acute ones of food and clothing and of young people, hundreds of thousands of whom, while they could, fled to the West.

West Germany is the number two target of Soviet intelligence and propaganda; it comes second just after the United States. Berlin is only the most dramatic and visible center of the unrelenting pressure. Nothing can happen in Germany's relations with other countries that is unaffected by the Soviet offensive and sometimes even modest occasions show how intense and widespread it is. In late March a meeting of scholars, writers, and people in public life from Western Europe and the United States was held in Chicago to discuss the problem, "Berlin and the Future of Eastern Europe." Held under the combined auspices of the Foundation for Foreign Affairs, of Chicago, and of the Herder Institute, of Marburg, the purpose was to bring Polish, Czech, Hungarian, German, French, English, and American experts together to discover if it might not be possible to find a scholarly consensus on what the future of this fought-over area might be in the light of the political and economic realities of the 1960s. Papers were read by Poles who had taken part in the Warsaw rising against the Germans in 1944; by American scholars of many shades of political opinion as well as by German historians and members of the Bundestag, two of them from Chancellor Adenauer's CDU and one, the leader of the German delegations, Wenzel Jaksch, from the SPD. Jaksch before the war had been a member of the Czechoslovakian parliament and although a German, a Sudentenlander, he had opposed the Munich Agreement of 1938 because he was anti-Nazi. When Hitler took over the rest of Czechoslovakia Jaksch had escaped with the Czech government in London where he had spent the war years. Because he was as much anti-Communist as anti-Nazi, he did his best during their common exile to dissuade Beneš and his ministry from their ill-fated policy of postwar collaboration with Soviet Russia.

Like other participants in the conference, Jaksch spoke on behalf of a genuine new order in Europe, one that takes account of the ethnic and historic differences between its peoples but creates workable devices like NATO and the common market that bind them together for their self-preservation. The speakers in the conference were agreed that if such freely adopted, pan-European measures could be extended to Eastern Europe with the will to make them work, the animosities would begin to wither as they have in France and Germany where, for example, the historical woes of Alsace-Lorraine have simply disappeared. But in Eastern Europe the enmities are kept flourishing by the boundaries of the Iron Curtain and the propaganda of the Communist occupation, as well as by the professional ethnics of the exile movements whose accounts of the past are limited by the need to defend their own errors and whose hopes of the future would perpetuate them.

When the Chicago Conference was announced the Polish and Czech embassies in Washington protested to the State Department against the conference as such and against the presence of Jaksch, whom they denounced a revanchist. The State Department courteously and promptly rejected the protest, declaring the conference to be a meeting of scholars and Jaksch a proper member of it. Then the professional foreign bodies set to work; spokesmen among the émigré groups declaring it, among other things, to be unrepresentative. And Radio Warsaw in its broadcast of March 24 commented on the conference as follows:

The American journalist, Drew Pearson, gave the right evaluation of this revisionist enterprise . . . [writing]: "For the first time since the war a conference is taking place on American soil, at which a revision of the German frontier in accordance with Hitler's directives will be discussed. One of its participants, Jaksch, takes part most actively in a movement which demands that the Sudetenlands be separated from Czechoslovakia and Upper Silesia from Poland and both given to Germany. The occupation of the Sudetenlands by Hitler was the first signal that the Second World War was unavoidable and the occupation of Poland was the start of the Second World War. This is the reason why the peoples of Eastern Europe are so disturbed by the support given to the GFR [German Federal Republic] by the U.S. and why they are so opposed to giving West Germany any kind of nuclear weapons."

How that eminent authority on Eastern Europe, Mr. Pearson, obtained his information, or from whom, I do not know. But the purpose of the émigré spokesmen is easier to understand. They maintain their leadership in the organizations of nationalities by appealing to a sentimental, picture postcard view of the homeland. They preach a solidarity based on fixed and immovable prejudices, they are concerned not with a tradition, which is something living and creative, but with selective memories and antagonisms that confirm a minority in its need for existing as an entity in its uncertain self-esteem amid alien people. They have no cause to refresh the tradition by relating it to compelling facts, or broad perspectives of the contemporary world; on the contrary they thrive on illusions, the most unnourishing one that they themselves bear no responsibility for the plight of their countries; Fate or other nonethnic forces rolled the loaded dice. Thus the crimes of the Germans, the blunders of the Hungarians, of the Italians, the Romanians, the Bulgarians, etc., are preserved not only in the autobiographies but also in the character of the writing of much of the émigré press. The future is seen wholly in terms of this one-sided history. Enlightened editors certainly exist among these papers, some of them have written or will write in these pages; men who can move with the time and who share the sentiments that would like to make a new structure out of a wooden particularism that no more comports with the economic and political exigencies of these years than does the picture postcard vie with the moral ones. The Czechoslovakia that was itself divided into mutually suspicious, hostile, and frequently warring minorities, the Poland that joined Hitler in its partition, are now part of the Eastern bloc. As the Chicago Conference demonstrated, many of the observers coming from those countries are aware not only of the miscalculations of Hitler, whose criminal regime was unique in German history, but of those of their own leaders, whose mistakes arose from narrow policies fanatically pursued and to which many of the émigrés cling as stubbornly now as they did before they became exiles.

The problem for the West is how to turn to account the traditions of nationality, the pride in a history, in a common effort to reinvigorate a moral order that despite everything, the wars, the persecution, the concentration camps, the bombings, has persisted in Europe. In this effort West Germany is a key area, and this democratic Germany has tried to make amends, and properly so, for the Nazi past and sacrifices for the idea of Europe. But the existence of the Bundesrepublik does not diminish the importance of the captive nations nor is it a threat to them. Its army is under foreign command as are its chief military supplies; its economy and its purposes are European. The East Germans and the Poles, the Czechs and the Slovaks, the Hungarians, the Ruthenians, and the Ukrainians live not only under foreign domination but under a foreign weltanschauung that attempts to infiltrate into every activity. To oppose this more is needed than fanning the hatreds of the centuries that in part account for the predicament of those countries. As speakers at the conference pointed out, nationalism in the 1960s is taking forms that are no longer mainly linguistic. It is again possible for a European to travel from Scandinavia to the Mediterranean without a visa and to buy without irrational penalties the products of other countries and to sell to them, to seek work regardless of nationality where labor is in demand, to join in a common defense.

The troubles of the West are those of a society where imbalances caused by competing ideas and interests and pressures are in a constant process of adjustment. A traveler landing in the Munich airport in the summer of 1962 will find taxis available, as was not likely to be the case in 1961. Up to the present year the guild of taxi owners had been able, with the help of the Department of Public Order, to limit the number of cabs for the entire city to 850, and a suit was brought against the monopoly on the ground that it infringed individual freedom. The complainant won and as many taxis are available as the traffic will bear and the trade support. The case for the free market itself is not won; it perhaps can never be won unconditionally, but even in its imperfect form it is one of the formidable unifying elements in postwar Europe. And if the West will trouble itself to answer the propaganda, to enable its workers to compare not the blueprints, but the facts of life in the East and West, a comparison for which the testimony of hundreds of thousands of refugees who have fled the East is available, it will take a more powerful station than any the communist countries have yet built to convince these Italian, Yugoslavian, Greek, and Spanish workers they would be better off, more complete human beings behind the wall and the barbed wire put up by the other side to keep their workers in.

Seven-Eighths of a Man

What used to be called the Russian experiment is undoubtedly a success on a large, if limited and cumbersome, scale. A backward, agricultural country has become vastly industrialized, has survived both the onslaught of the military power that conquered the armies of Europe in a few weeks and the murderous internal politics of its own chief of state. Moscow in 1962 is a boom city with new buildings rising in every quarter, each with its neat pile of bricks allocated by a central planning committee that decided that this year bricks were more important than toothbrushes or razor blades—both of which were therefore out of stock in Moscow—or the labor and materials that would carve more heroic images into the labyrinths of the subway. The subways in Moscow and Leningrad are properly celebrated; they are as clean as those in West Berlin and far more handsome. But their well-crafted, pretentious decoration was added at the expense, for example, of housing that might have replaced the long rows of unpainted tumbledown shacks on the outskirts of the city where people have lived since long before the subways were planned.

New housing goes up rapidly and the familiar charge that it begins to show signs of disrepair almost immediately is evident from the most casual inspection. In Kiev, a new hotel that rose too quickly offers both rooms and baths but the doors often won't close and rust-colored water trickles in the tubs. In Moscow, after a light rain, mud puddles cover the depressions in the buckled sidewalks connecting the courts of the apartment houses. The apartments themselves are cheap when they are to be had, 13 or 15 rubles a month for two rooms, with a kitchen and bath that are shared with another family, but the waiting lists are long; in fact no one can move to the city without special permission because of the chronic housing shortage and the higher demands of the allocation of labor. This summer, prices of meat suddenly and uniformly went up 30 percent because farm managers cut down on livestock for which they were paid less by the government than they got for fodder crops. When I asked how the price increases would affect the diet of the ordinary worker I was told it would scarcely matter, that they ate very little meat in any case. But this was a fanciful reply, as were the dutiful letters in the papers praising the government for its wisdom in raising prices without anyone's mentioning Khrushchev's promise that by 1961 the Soviet people would consume as much meat and butter as the Americans. With wages in Moscow of 70 rubles a month for unskilled labor, 90 rubles for a truck driver, 100–120 rubles for building workers, 60 rubles for a young saleswoman, a healthy diet can be maintained on soup and bread and vegetables, but the average worker's household can't afford much, if any, meat, or butter, the price of which went up 25 percent.

In the Soviet Union, governed by theological principles, certain dogmas are *ab initio* true and may be neither questioned nor amended, only interpreted with new glosses. The indefatigable campaign to industrialize the farm, to turn the countryside into a complex of factories for raising crops and animals that has had so little success in the Soviet Union, its satellites, and imitators, is as fanatically continued today as it was in the thirties. In East Germany a stepped-up drive for collectivization was the chief cause not only of the food shortages but of the desperate flight to the West that continues despite the wall and the automatic rifles of the frontier guards. China, imitating the Russian experiment, is enduring one of the most disastrous crop failures of its history, and its refugees are beating at the doors of Hong Kong. As Karl Brandt wrote in his article in the summer issue of *Modern Age*, only 4 percent of the farmland of Soviet Russia may be used for private production, but this 4 percent raises 38 percent of the total crop. Yet the dogma of collectivization is untouched— what failed was not the ideology but the methods, the administration. The steppes are being plowed with only fair results, and as one American observer has pointed out, with a year or two of under-average rainfall (which is statistically likely) a dust bowl could take over what has been grassland adapted to the climate and soil.

The minds of the people are plowed day by day. The passion for culture that sends streams of adults and children through the museums into the theaters, the bookshops, the historic places, in part may spring from the drabness of daily life with its sparse gratifications, but it is nevertheless a striking symptom to the foreigner. People wait patiently in front of sold-out theaters and concert halls where a Benny Goodman or a ballet or a comedy of Marivaux is playing, in the hope of getting a last-minute seat; if need be they stand in line too for hours for books, for exhibitions as they have for food and clothing. But Soviet painting and sculpture is in the repetitive, academic tradition of Tsarist art, dull or worse; the Revolution changed nothing but its themes. The few pioneers of twentieth-century art such as Malevitch are kept in the reserves out of sight of the public. The architecture is uninspired whether in the building for domestic purposes, or exported to what used to be called Stalinallee in Berlin, or as a "gift" to the people of Warsaw in the form of the gray, neo-Gothic, Siamese-flavored mass sprouting towers and abutments that dominate the skyline of the city. The style of this hybrid structure is repeated seven times in Moscow starting with the Palace of Culture. In one of these, the somber Hotel Ukraina, where the no-tipping rule is more rigidly enforced than in other more agreeable hotels of the city, the mechanics of the building and the apathy of the personnel combine to bring the guest to a dead stop. Elevators serving the floors from the fourteenth to the gilded top are filled to bursting and they are likely to arrive at ten-minute intervals while the stairways are closed even to those guests who would be glad to use them at least for the descent. In the dining room anyone unlucky enough to choose a table that for reasons known only to the management is not in use will sit for a long time before an empty plate; no one will tell him he is out of bounds. Scarcely anything is beautiful or striking or merely pleasant in these cities unless it belongs to the past; trivial human courtesies are linked to it in hotels or taxicabs where the acknowledgment of a service may be accompanied by some practical token of it, and Leningrad's Winter Palace, the Peterhof, Tsarke Tselo now Pushkin, the monuments and the buildings are either old and handsome or new and commonplace or ugly.

The films that from time to time have assumed enough freedom, as in the case of the production of "Clear Skies," to suggest that the party does not always act without misjudgments, have their brief day and then are put back in their place by the ever-ready orthodoxy of the party critics. Thus in July, a leading article in *Pravda* told moving-picture producers they were not doing their job, which was to instruct Soviet citizens in the virtues of communism and the vices of the bourgeois societies. The film directors had failed to dramatize for the public the party struggle for fashioning a new world, to show the necessity for waging a merciless war against the Western ideologies. Another line of communication open for a brief period—Russian directors were making use of techniques and themes borrowed from Italian and French producers—is abruptly closed down as it was for Pasternak and for any others who have dared to question the ultimate wisdom of the party.

The Revolution solemnly continues to turn values upside down. The public is said to welcome higher prices, women to have contempt for bourgeois seductions, but lipstick, eye shadow, and perfumes are on sale and in use. A foreigner is immediately identifiable by the quality as well as the cut of his or her clothing, and the Russian women especially, who are decently but cheaply covered, are obviously fascinated by the differences. Whatever the party may tell them, they know that the goods in their shops are inferior and expensive. The ruble, for the tourist, has a highly inflated rate—mainly for reasons of prestige it is 1.04 to the dollar, officially, although the free market rate is 37 cents, so that a scarf selling in West Berlin for five dollars may be bought in Moscow for fifteen. But the actual economic practices in Russia do not go as far as to sustain the fiction of the parity of the currencies of East and West Germany. On the contrary, in a shop in Leningrad where only foreign money is accepted the West German mark is as readily used as the dollar or the pound, but the East German mark has no exchange value whatever—they won't take it. The satellites are permitted minor deviations from the main lines of policy with the exception of East Germany, where nothing is conceded. Czechoslovakia needs foreign exchange, and a tourist rate double the official one used for ordinary purposes enables the outlander to buy Czech goods at prices well below the Russian ones. Nevertheless, Czechoslovakia is kept under a tighter rein than Poland; in Warsaw the churches are open and filled and the door to the West is kept open wide enough to accept either American gifts or loans. Prague on the other hand is permitted to woo the foreign tourist and thus make its fourth contribution to the East bloc, but it was forced in Stalin's time to give up the Marshall Plan loan it had accepted and it is not likely it would fare better in this respect under Khrushchev.

But Prague has another unusual concession—a monument to Stalin; a huge, triangular mass of stone depicting the Generalissimo as he favored himself, in heroic proportions, at the apex of the triangle followed by a double line of faceless Russians sent to liberate the Czechs. This may be the only monument of Stalin to be seen in the satellite countries, or for that matter in Russia itself west of Georgia, which for special reasons is permitted to retain its relics of a native son. Why the monument remains in Prague is subject to interpretation; some say the vents for an air-raid shelter run through its masses, others that the problem of getting rid of it is greater than that of letting it stay. The street leading to it in any event is no longer named after Stalin, and in East Berlin too Stalinallee became overnight Karl Marxallee and there the statue of the once mightiest of men was pulled down and hauled off. In Russia the name of Stalin has disappeared from streets and boulevards, his likeness appears in no museum, not even that of the Red Army where great canvases record the valor of the Soviet soldiers and generals of World War II. No Stalin appears; he is *spurlos versenkt*. The city that once bore his name, in which the fate of the invading German armies was decided, has been renamed Volgograd. A wax Lenin lies in state alone in the Kremlin and some observers think he lies a little off center as though some faint ghost of Stalin remained alongside. But Stalin in memorium is nowhere to be seen; his grave in a row of well-known Soviet figures buried behind the Lenin mausoleum is indeed said to contain his mortal remains, but while the others sharing this plot have plinths with busts behind the stone slabs bearing their names, Stalin as yet has none. He has not suffered the fate of Trotsky, who commanded the troops of the Revolution and then simply disappeared from Russian history, but he moves toward those silences. Over and over I would ask someone old enough to have vivid memories of the man who was the law and the organizer of victory, as well as the high executioner of the Soviet Union, what had happened to him. Well, they would say, he represented the cult of personality; he was overvalued and he did some wrong things. Yes, I would persist, but he was commander in chief of the army and head of state and nothing is to be seen of him, not even a picture of a historic moment, say of his signing a document at Yalta or Moscow. Usually there was no answer at this point; a shrug of the shoulders. History, despite the talk of coexistence and the thin stream of cultural exchange, remains what it has been since the beginnings of the Soviet Union—that version of the past which is useful to the immediate policies and purposes of the men in charge. No foreign newspapers are on sale except the American and English *Daily Worker* and their equivalents from France and East Germany. Only in libraries and under special circumstances may a paper as heady as the *New York Times* be read.

The new middle class, of which David Dallin wrote in these pages, is certainly aware, uncomfortably aware sometimes, of this ceaseless assault on their opportunity to know what everyone in the free world is permitted to learn. The Russian as a human being is no more a robot than is the member of any other nationality; the Pioneers, the Consomols, what used to be called the Stakhanovites and now are known as the "shakers," the party cadrists, may fill their lives with the busy missions of the movement. But thousands of party members, too, know that despite Soviet technical achievements, the space missiles, and Aeroflot jets, they are not permitted to see the shape of the world or of the Soviet Union. From time to time, overnight they are told to revise their thinking. Suddenly the classroom lessons they had memorized for years are no longer true, and they realize that a line of communication open to other people is dead for them. They listen to foreign broadcasts, they repeat the anti-Western slogans, they are convinced that to go to college in the United States one must be rich, but doubts gnaw at them because they are not only Soviet citizens but also human beings. The question is basically the one Orwell posed in his *1984*: whether it is possible not only to make a man an obedient, salivating animal responding to the sound of the bell, but one who comes to love the sound of it. Will Soviet man one day, after the years of erosion of part of his humanity, rise against his keepers? The millions of Soviet prisoners the Germans captured in the first months of the war, the willingness of thousands of them to join "a Russian army of liberation," a recruitment that was thwarted only by the dogmas of another totalitarian society, the welcome in many parts of the Soviet Union given the German troops when they first arrived before the Einsatz groups and the SS taught the inhabitants they had exchanged a bad master for a worse one—these indicate the latent sources of revolt in a country where revolt seems impossible. But the human being, whether Russian, Ukrainian, Czech, Pole or East German, sees past his cage, learns to pronounce slogans without believing them, reaches out for the truth he knows has been denied him with whatever weapons he has. How long can a society last that shuts off its members not only from heresy but from its own history, that must continually abjure its teachings of the day before yesterday? How long can such a society make a successful assault against a West that for better or worse makes possible the use of the full energies of the free man? Can the seven-eighths of Soviet man replace the whole human being of the West compensating for the vacant places in his psyche with the solidarity of robots marching together? The answers to these questions will determine the history of what is left of the twentieth century.

Art for Everyone's Sake

Reading the posthumously published diary of Galeazzo Ciano with its references to the Italian version of the burning of the books I was again struck by the need of the dictatorship, even of the relatively ramshackle Italian variety, to bend the word and forms of the society to its purposes. Mussolini, like Hitler and Stalin, was sensitive not only to words that might conceal criticisms of his politics but to the painting and sculpture that would record the time in another way but one as dangerous apparently as that of the printing press. The Nazis some years after they took power put on an exhibition to illustrate the odiousness of what they called degenerate art, in Munich and Berlin, and in it were almost all the great painters of the twentieth century whose works were owned by German museums, from Picasso, Grosz, and Beckmann to Chagall. The paintings were later sold at auction in Switzerland with the exception of a few that could be hidden or filched as in the case of some canvases preempted by Goering for trading purposes. In the place of this "degenerate" art came romanticized and often outsize canvases—pictures showing the Fuehrer clad in armor with a banner in hand and mounted on a charger; the artist's mystique of the hero, adapted from beer hall murals, was proof even against Hitler's deep-seated aversion to horses. Or a family group might be shown as another proof of the healthy instinct of the race untouched by intellectual or foreign taints. For example, a picture of a trio of nudes on a sofa, a mother gazing into the distance while her young son with a sour expression plays on a flute and her little daughter morosely holds a flower. In Russia, too, any evidences of experimental art have long been removed from the galleries. The innovators, Russian or foreign, are stored away out of sight, the contemporary pictures shown are posters for the Revolution, and the emissaries of the Axis and of the Bolsheviks must have felt themselves comfortably at home as they visited the exhibitions in their respective capitals during the period of the friendship pacts.

Art gives rise to violent emotions even in cultures where it is not native but exists by means of collections gathered from somewhere else. In the closed society of the totalitarian states it takes the same forms, whatever the politics or ideology, and these are never in any sense revolutionary but on the contrary stale repetitions of the techniques and mannerisms of the past, differing from them only in the colors of the flags and the faces of the new leaders. It is reactionary art, as the regimes it serves are reactionary. It transfers the party slogans to a canvas. It is likely that artists somewhere in these vast areas are creating the plastic equivalent of a Dr. Zhivago but if so they must, like Pasternak, resign themselves to the studied rejection of the official institutions or the chance, sometime, of an appearance in the markets of the free world.[1]

In cultures like those of the American cities where art has been more often transplanted than homegrown it is always far from an inert ingredient. Whether the institution that shows it is privately or publicly controlled or a mixture of the two it continues to reflect the unsettled and often conflicting tastes of the community—of the boards composed of brokers, and bankers, and lawyers, and the men and women of affairs who for one reason or another feel called upon to spend a portion of their energies and money for what they intend to be the enrichment of the cultural life of the community. Their choices of what is to go into the collections are limited not so much by their political as by their aesthetic boundaries. When Yale was given the opportunity of getting the Jarves collection of Italian primitives for a relatively small sum its Corporation did not seize upon the opportunity as though released by an avalanche of long dammed-up passion, nor did Chicago's Art Institute promptly and gratefully accept the great collection of French post-impressionists that was offered to it. The trustees of such institutions are not likely to be (although there are brilliant exceptions) the native aestheticians who know in their bones what a good painting is, nor are they prone to pick and retain as trusted advisers the imaginative and often off-beat characters who can act boldly and intelligently for them. And yet, these boards too may lurch toward the truth; in both these cases the collections were accepted although by narrow margins.

Four main divisions of administering the display of paintings and sculpture, and indeed the higher learning in general to the public, have appeared in our day. One is that of the state institution in countries where the state is all-powerful. A second is that of the public institute or museum established within the democratic polity as in the case of postwar Germany, France, Italy, and the other countries west of the Iron Curtain,

---

1. Since these lines were written an article in the *New York Times* of December 2 reported as follows: "Premier Khrushchev inspected today one of the first exhibitions of Soviet abstract paintings and rejected the works as 'foreign to our people.'

"He personally scolded the assembled artists for breaking away from ideologically approved socialist realism. The Soviet leader thus apparently signaled the repression of a brief upsurge of freedom in the fields of Soviet painting and sculpture."

and to a limited degree in the United States. These, like their sister institutions, the state universities, may possess a good deal of professional autonomy in the way they are administered but in the long run, and in controversial fields especially, they may and in fact have often become subject to purely political pressures that have little to do with the truth or beauty of what they hang or teach. The third and largest group is that of the mixed institutes where private benefactions have made the collections possible but contributions in the form of land or buildings or services are made by the city or state. The last group is the purely private institution that accepts no grants-in-aid other than those rendered by tax exemption.

The first group, the institutions of the totalitarian state, has little or nothing to show for its years of activity outside its inheritance from other centuries and the additional contribution of the technicians who without risk to their jobs may restore and piece together as well as letter signs that now say, "Of our era," instead of "A.D." The second group has produced a competent corps of specialists and bureaucrats to run its shows and exhibits who, it should be noted, went over almost to a man to the new political order when their institutions came under the control of their respective leaders. They must have sorrowed over the loss of the great contemporary masters but they nevertheless took them down from the walls and hung the chromes of the revolution with the same care and devotion they had lavished on the masterpieces. These academicians and administrators went along, no doubt with longing and nostalgia for the past but with infinitely more concern for the exigent present and their pensions to come. The émigrés moved out with their own sorrows to embellish the scholarship of the free world.

The mixed institutes, universities and museums and the purely private ones operate with other advantages and hazards. Their trustees, whatever their human and entrepreneurial merits, are not of ten people whose temperaments and comprehension are tuned to the wavelengths of those broken surfaces and patterns that have characterized the painters of the twentieth century. Whether their motives are indeed those they proffer at their meetings and on public occasions, motives arising from a genuine desire to upgrade the tastes of the community, or whether they are in fact more closely related to forwarding in a polite form their own social or business advancement or merely their release from the blacks and reds of the balance sheets that occupy them daily, does not greatly affect the kinds of decisions they make. The world of art is essentially, for most of these people, mysterious and foreign; they feel themselves safe within it only so long as they are dealing with accepted names, and the professionals they employ must operate cautiously. Unless the directors and curators enjoy special prestige or have extraordinarily persuasive powers they must recommend pictures to be bought and shows to be hung that come within the range of the tastes and prejudices of the members of boards who are comfortable only with a good press and the approval of other people like themselves. But however ignorant, amateur, or genuinely talented the members of such boards may be, they have the possibility of bucking any official line, and in fact it was such a group of dissidents that backed the Armory show of 1913 against the officially entrenched, academic lifelessness.

It is actually by way of such or similar patronage that art has been nurtured and cultivated from the beginning of the Renaissance. These groups give the one indispensable condition to the survival of the artist and the one that is denied him in the Iron Curtain countries—the opportunity to exhibit. For nothing is trickier or more unpredictable than the modes of acceptance and rejection of art, and the words that describe them become as quickly historical as yesterday's slang. Nonrepresentational art, the wildness of the twenties, is the academic art of the sixties and the academic art of the early and mid–twentieth century, including Rockwell Kent, hangs in Soviet museums.

In the great periods of Italy and France, Holland and Spain, Germany and England, the individualist tribe of artists was also supported by patrons who themselves were more likely to be princes of the sword and purse than of the brush and palette or hammer and chisel. When writers moved out from the patronage of the man of power to the multiple decisions of the marketplace they did so through the medium of the printing press, a mechanism in general not adaptable to the production of works of art in media other than that of the pen. The painter and sculptor are still beholden to the much more restricted market of the collectors and museums who in turn are influenced by the specialists of the trade— the dealers and critics, and such specialists the public if it likes can ignore. With the affluence accompanying the postwar economic booms, the swollen budgets of the tax-exempt institutions together with the increasing shortage of works of art, even obscure rural institutions have added their share to the wave of inflation that has engulfed the art market. More and more people who never before were concerned with art have turned to it. And thus new problems arise to cloud the picture. In the race for materials to hang and show, in the flight to values that have both a price tag and evidences of the untagable human spirit, in the harried search for funds boards of trustees of the museums take refuge from their confusions in a public relations approach in their choice of both personnel and shows. They must impress the local donors, and the public at large, as well as one another. They must choose as directors people who get along in the community, something that artists themselves have rarely done, and rely on their recommendations as to what to buy without for the most part themselves knowing, unless the painting has a certified name, whether it is worth having or not. These boards are likely to be timid; their worst fear is adverse publicity, they want to buy the sure thing even if it costs more than two million dollars. But in the multiplicity of such boards there are always some who will brave the wrath of the press and put on exhibitions that have survived to convert their journalistic and other critics. Some of the museums, the institutes, despite the philistine pressures from within and without have managed to maintain a high level of taste and selection in what they have bought and displayed— higher for example than the purely public museums in France that in the nineteenth century bought the seemingly safe academic art in preference to the superb work of the innovators, much of which went instead to the grateful wilderness of America. Nor is the so-called avant garde immune from its own kind of fossilization—their cues are merely given by centers other than those of provincial acceptance.

What then is there to say of this chaos of money and opinion, of the conflict between the amateurs and the professionals? Perhaps that this is the very way art is sustained. The competition between museums, the open criticism of artists and writers on art as well as that of the few people in any community who are competent to judge, has provided among the institutions of private, and mixed private and public control, the constant scrutiny and exhortation to higher things that keep them from being merely the preservers of the records of other centuries, or what might well be the hyperaesthetic choices of the unfettered professionals. The professionals left to themselves can produce another kind of tyranny, as we see in the frozen liberal stances of our great universities where much the same uniformity is required in economics and politics as it is in the one-party countries. If the art institutes in the United States are not powerful forces in helping in the procreation of a new speech in art they are also far removed from the world described in the remarkable work of the Romanian writer, Petru Dumitriu, where as in the case of all the totalitarian societies every word, every gesture must be considered in the light of the political constellations of the day or week or month. The Western world is producing a deeper and more widely diffused art than the Eastern, a more revolutionary art and by way of its very conflicts and inconsistencies, its squares and jags and strange figures in inner and outer spaces, a more human one.

1963

The New Poor and the Old Baloney

A year or so ago I chanced to be talking to a judge from Abyssinia, a thoughtful young man who had studied law in England. We were discussing the death penalty, which I had told him I opposed, and he said he could understand this position with respect to Europe and the United States, but, he held, it would be impossible to abolish capital punishment in a country like his own. "Why," he said, "if we did we'd have an enormous increase in major crime just because the criminals could hope to be provided for at the state's expense for the rest of their lives."

We are so accustomed in the United States to the economic system that provides the essential commodities of life, like food and clothing, in such an outpouring of plenty the problem is how to get rid of it, that it is easy to forget that other societies have never come within hailing distance of such a state of affairs. The patched and battered pants and shirts and shreds of clothing for sale in the markets of Athens or one of the Italian cities, the slums of Cairo or Istanbul, the homeless lying in the doorways of Calcutta, and the human anthill of Hong Kong are signs of how thin the margins are for the simple triumph of survival on most of the planet. Things are thrown out in this country that are treasures over most of the world—empty sardine cans, worn-out rubber tires, an old hat, a threadbare dress, beat-up shoes, an umbrella that blows inside-out in a light breeze. Poverty here is of a different kind, even more gnawing perhaps in the dispirit that accompanies it but with its victims fed and clothed beyond the dreams of the peoples to the south and east of the United States. I have seen some of our needy drive up for their boxes of relief packages in taxis and late models of cars that would have been the transportation of the "exploiters" anywhere else in the world; if the occupants drove home to a slum, they came and went in style. They also got more butter, as the statistics show, than the cross section of the American population, for, as Karl Brandt and others among our contributors keep noting, we have a bottomless supply of that commodity that cannot be bought for less than sixty cents a pound although it may be given away. But the poor remain with us, and recent studies of their status and plight have rightly resulted in a good deal of discussion of who they are and what can be done about them.

One usually able reviewer in the *New Yorker* points out the anomaly that they are fat, eating too many foods with carbohydrates, he says, so the symbol of plenty throughout the world, the fat banker, the billowing dowager, has to be revised; the fat people in this country are the poor. But how true is this? Recent documentary films of the unemployed coal miners of eastern Pennsylvania and West Virginia, who are getting doles of government food, showed most of them both lean and obviously deeply troubled. But that some people manage to get fat on the relief payments and diets no one can doubt, although too many carbohydrates may not be the whole story. Among the poor are bound to be simply indolent feeders who gratefully accept what benefits may fall their way, just as some of the people in the new buildings that have taken the place of the rat-infested slums commit the same crimes they did before, but with more ease in the narrow corridors and lonely elevators of the high-rise structures.

We keep adjusting to such developments. The latest apartment buildings that are replacing the slums are constructed so that their elevators connect with outside balconies in public view, in the hope that this will discourage the assaults. They have not yet succeeded, however, in doing away with the corners and shafts where garbage and refuse may be tossed—although the technologists are doubtless working on that. And some of the adjustments are made in legal forms. In certain areas the rate of individual bankruptcy has gone up like a Jupiter missile to get rid of the accumulation of debts of the oversold or over-optimistic consumers. When the high-interest loans and the payments on everything get too far out of line with earnings, an enterprising and humanitarian law firm can arrange to pare them all down and to take its own fee in part on the installment plan. These are some of the defensive adaptations among the least affluent in this society.

Now the remedies for their predicament. The reviewer in the *New Yorker* says it is the weak and unorganized who suffer from low pay or none, that Roosevelt lost his nerve in 1937 and stopped spending and that is why the problem of the Depression was not solved; he tells of the low incomes on some farms, reminding us that the people in *Grapes of Wrath* are still with us, the displaced migratory workers and the farmers of the barren lands. The remedy obviously is to spend more—he thinks we should present each family with four thousand dollars a year, the arbitrary level set for the border of poverty in this country—for workers to organize. People who don't understand the need for these measures, according to the reviewer, predate Bismarck in their thinking, who had pioneered in the idea of government intervention on behalf of the standard of living of the German farmers and workers.

But the formula of *panem et circenses* (the latter are readily provided in these years of the supremacy of the entertainers) is an ancient one and has never worked to organize a society, but only to split it. A gift of four thousand dollars a year would freeze the imbalances in any economy. Competent economists have written studies analyzing the trends in our tightly unionized industries. Often liberals themselves, they have nevertheless pointed out that our developing economy was facing the danger of two in-groups with the power and resources to fortify their positions and to pick off the outsiders trying to get in. These are management and the great unions. It is enough in our image-preserving society for management to be able to keep the peace on the labor front and for union leaders to keep wages high and constantly increasing, even though more men are not hired by the enterprises they both represent. Labor-saving devices and methods of rationalization enable workers who have jobs to stay on them with shorter hours and more overtime pay, year by year to get more money for what they produce as long as prices of the companies' products remain competitive and their operations profitable. To this end a common purpose unites both management and labor regardless of its effect on unemployment and the rest of the economy. Prices and wages have gone up steadily, but neither production nor job opportunities have risen at the rate they might have had the goods been cheaper. In effect this has been a combination to keep the ins in and the outs out. In the prevailing corporate structure the managers who run the companies seldom own more than a minor share of the stock; industries are no longer run by the people who own them. The managers who are the executives of the amorphous owners want a happy annual stockholders' meeting; to be able to report that there have been no strikes, no labor troubles, no shutdowns. The union leaders in their turn want to present their constituents with a bigger take-home package, no matter who else goes without.

What this can also lead to we see in the constantly escalating demands: for a five- and four-hour day, for a built-in system for resetting advertisements that are already in type—a practice appropriately called bogus—for the extra stage hands who do no work, for the railroad telegraphers who take no messages. Year by year the irresponsible demands go up until finally they become insupportable—not only for the enterprises they put out of business, but for their fellow workers, the members of other unions and nonmembers, who had no complaints to make until, as the members of the newspaper guild have been, they were thrown out of their jobs.

This is an important cause of the unthawing unemployment. One of the men in the West Virginia documentary said he'd take any kind of work, from house painting to ditch digging. But he won't if the unions can help it: he would undercut the market for the overtime construction workers and for the house painters who with their narrow brushes and artificial scales help keep houses unpainted.

We have gotten used to the notion that this predominantly free economy can always support so much dead weight. But much of our unemployment has to do with our getting used to things. For example, with a minimum wage of $1.25 an hour a good many firms believe they should demand a high school diploma for a beginner to get a job with them. The work may not demand much book learning, but the requirement is one way of weeding out applicants. It and the minimum wage are also ways of keeping a boy from getting a job, adding him to the hundreds and thousands of young men who hang around street corners, fed adequately enough on their families' earnings or on government food packages, but understandably bitter and cynical and alien in their own society that rejects what they have to give.

The newspapers that have folded in these last years have been hit by the intolerably high costs of nonproduction, and the recent New York typographers' strike threatened to shut down permanently two or more for the same reasons. Neither an agreement between management and the rest of the staff nor the ingenuity of inventors and technicians together with any consideration of the public interest would calm the rage of the one union that was out to show its muscle. Members of other unions who up to then had been sympathetic enough to labor organization as such plainly saw the unprincipled drive for power this strike represented; one of them writing in the *Nation* said the issue was so obvious that the union's leadership would undoubtedly settle for some mere face-saving in its demands if it could get management to accept the crucial provision that it bargain first with the owners before the weaker guild makes its easier annual contract—so that year after year the cycle can start over again and the union can club out higher wages for less productive time.

Of the plight of the impoverished farmer we have heard much in these pages and will hear more from serious students of the problem. Many of the farms earning small incomes are owned as part-time ventures, kept to help out earning power by providing people who hold other jobs with food; others are retirement farms, secondary enterprises. But some farms are unmistakably submarginal, and, in the interest of the agricultural economy as well as of the people who own them, they should be given up for better ways of earning a living as the percentage of people needed to produce the food that can be distributed and consumed diminishes. Farming in the United States, as Professor Karl Brandt has pointed out, has done too well, not too poorly. American farms can produce far more than the country can eat or sell abroad, and they do it with less than 10 percent of the population compared with 90 percent in the nineteenth century and with 45 percent in contemporary Soviet Russia. Nevertheless, this leap forward still leaves us with the ill-paid and ill-fed farmers (if such there be) on the unproductive farms, with the Okies migrating from job to job, and with too many millions of unemployed, among them the boys who have quit high school and find no jobs because they have no diplomas. As Professor Brandt will argue in these pages,[1] the solution for the farm problem is the same one that would go a long way toward solving the problem of unemployment. It is to restore the mechanism of the free market wherever it can be restored. West Germany is a clear case history (and not only compared with the penal colony of East Germany) of the capacity of free enterprise to provide goods and work.

Other possibilities exist, having been used for centuries, and on the greatest scale in this one; the farmers could be ordered or driven off the land, as they have been in East Germany by government coercion; the coal miners of Pennsylvania and West Virginia can be forcibly resettled, as has been done with large groups for political and economic reasons in Russia; the unemployed boys can be drafted into labor brigades or the armed forces for such purposes as the government may one day see fit. Bismarck, who is favorably mentioned in the article published in the *New Yorker*, wanted social legislation and government responsibility for the workers' standard of living and for social services because he wished Germany to be a power among the great powers of Europe, and his welfarish and patriotic intentions had their logical and final fulfillment in Hitler. Once the government assumed responsibility for the welfare of part of the country it could—it must—prescribe how it is to be secured. If the United States really wants a recipe for preserving permanent unemployment, as it has for permanent food surpluses, it has only to keep its needy on a dole across which no bridge can be built to the comfortable millions of employed who with management have the power to distort the free enterprise system so that it no longer functions.

A wise economist once said to me as we were talking about a great slum clearance project: "This only looks like a solution, it is people who

1. Karl Brandt, "The Future of American Agriculture," *Modern Age* 7, no. 3 (summer 1963).

make slums." And so they do: out of the brand-new houses that they have sometimes been prematurely pitched into. If the needy in their despair or torpor get fat on relief foods, if they make a racket as some of them do of staying on relief or if they doggedly cling to farms and lands from which they no longer can make a living, this is not owing to automation, but to the choices they make in the partially paralyzed market mechanism. Only one kind of economy gives the worker the manifold choices of jobs and goods that are his (perhaps confused) own, or will give them to him when it has a chance to function and is not trussed up in the doctrinaire wrappings put on it by people who love their own ideas far better than their flesh and blood fellow men.

Richard Malcolm Weaver—Conservative

The spring issue of *Modern Age* opened with an article by Richard Weaver that was characteristic of his way of thinking. In it he compared two individualists. The first was Henry David Thoreau, a man universally acclaimed for his felicitous prose style as well as his bristling independence maintained against the persistent onslaughts of the state. The second was John Randolph, a stormy, deeply disturbed Southern politician, little referred to in the history books and a comparative stranger to the world of letters and ideas as taught in our universities. Without detracting from what Thoreau could do, which was to write with a flowing, elegant hand equally impressive to readers from Walden Pond to California as well as in Boston itself, Weaver showed how irresponsible Thoreau could be, self-righteously encapsulating himself from a society which he nevertheless made use of and to which he was to some extent indebted, defending his retreat with a loftiness that had more rhetoric than logic in it. Randolph, on the other hand, a slave-owner who freed his slaves but upheld the right of Missouri to extend the system he deplored, faced up to his dilemma; as Weaver said, he made his defense in depth, yielding where he had to, but fighting tooth and nail the war of principle. Randolph was not only the better dialectician but, as Weaver saw him, the more intuitive and by far the more responsible of the two. Thoreau's was a false ethic of individualism, for it was wholly one-sided: Thoreau took without giving; Randolph gave—not only freedom to the human beings he owned, but land to go with it and their means of subsistence. At the same time he defended the order (although he knew the necessity for changes within it) of which slavery was a part against the forces that he believed would overturn it and bring ruin and chaos with the revolution. This was a typical Weaverian distinction; it arose from concentrated reading and long pondering. What he wrote was designed to please no one's fancy but only to pursue his dialogue with the past, to make what he thought of as his modest contribution to the disclosing of a portion of the truth in which a system of values is embedded. It was to this end that Dick Weaver devoted his all too short life.

Not only his books and his conversation but everything he did evidenced his patient, stubborn battle on behalf of this core of values that he taught and by which he lived. Weaver had been a socialist in college—secretary of the local club he told us once in *Modern Age*—and had quit when the answers no longer seemed to him to fit the questions. His conservatism showed in all kinds of choices he made, whether spontaneous or deliberate. He flew only once in his life, from California to Chicago in a jet he had to take to meet a schedule. He said he enjoyed the trip and admired the Grand Canyon from the air—but he never flew again. He had written in *Ideas Have Consequences:* "We ignore the fact that space and matter are shock absorbers; the more we diminish them the more we reduce our privacy and security. Our planet is falling victim to a rigorism, so that what is done in any remote corner affects—nay menaces—the whole. Resiliency and tolerance are lost." He plowed his land in Weaverville, North Carolina, with a horse-drawn plow; he never used a tractor. He wrote his manuscripts by hand, typing them later on, for he needed, he said, the direct touch with the paper and not to be once removed from it by a machine when attacking a problem. A writer produced a manuscript, something written by a hand, not by a machine. Whatever over a long period of time had been humanized, brought into the life of the community, was always to be preferred to the merely new, however bright with chromium the new might be. It was not that a horse was to be preferred to a tractor for merely sentimental or aesthetic reasons; the horse had lived together with man for millennia—his ancestors' bones are found in the Western American plains of the Eocene, as are his own in ancient China. The relationship, in Weaver's book, was not lightly to be disregarded. As for the train, the iron horse, it too has been around for a century, has become part of the landscape, part of the language. That it is being replaced by the airplane was as clear to Weaver as to any other traveler; but he cast his vote for continuity even if it meant a long wait as he changed trains to and from Weaverville and Chicago. It was a sign of the mechanical, brainless reflex of the mob, he thought—in this time of leveling, where no center of authority any longer exists—to rush upon every technological advance as a means of transportation to the promised land.

Weaver did not believe much in promised lands, certainly not in any to be reached by technological means; he thought of a time like ours, with its shattering centrifugal forces, as a testing period demanding the full energies of conservatives if its humane culture was to be kept alive at all. Nor did he believe that the American habit of offering easy solutions gave to those who accepted them any more than they had had before. A group was talking one evening of the Negro in America, and someone asked why the crime rate for Negroes was higher in the North than in the South—

whether this might be owing to differences between rural and city areas, or the swift sanctions possible in a sparsely settled community, or differences in the methods of gathering statistics. Dick was silent for a while and then he said: "No, I doubt that any of these things are as important as the fact that the Negro is led to expect more in the North than he is given after he gets there." Dick was always suspicious of artificial constructs whether intended to be utopian or mere wholesale improvements on what had been before. He said one time: "The dialectic divorced from tradition is a menace to mankind." He was thinking, no doubt, of the plausible prospectuses so many glib minds have turned out: the racial pitch of the Nazis; the absurd nation of heroes of Mussolini; the dictatorship of the proletariat of the Soviets; all the simplifications that left out the burden of man's experience and turned his world into a cage.

But the dialectic, the entire rhetoric, in fact, in Weaver's hands was a gleaming, powerful instrument. He used it on the problems of English scholarship, on language, on politics, and when he was through something new had been established; outlines and interior relationships came into the light. His syllogisms were always humane. They had to do with teaching, not with pronouncements, with pointing a way, or destroying some piece of pernicious nonsense or blurred reasoning. Let us consider for a moment his chapter on the social sciences in *The Ethics of Rhetoric*. For many years critics had been attacking the poor writing and labored conclusions of the social scientists, but no one before Weaver had demonstrated why they did so badly. Weaver pointed out that they were dialecticians without a dialectic. A social scientist, Weaver said, can properly speak of a pile of bricks and metal, but 'slum' is a value word, a dialectical word, and in a few years places like Winnetka and Grosse Point may be called slums by those who live in more attractive places. "To say that a family has an income of $800 a year," he wrote, "is positive; to say that the same family is underprivileged is dialectical. It can be underprivileged only with reference to families which have more privileges . . . One could never arrive positivistically at a definition of a 'slum' because its meaning is contingent on judgment . . . The writer has passed with indifference from what is objectively true to what is morally or imaginatively true." Fundamentally, therefore, in Weaver's view the social scientists are melioristic; the natural scientists record, analyze, and interpret in a language describing primary things; the social scientists want to remake the society they observed. Their trouble is evident in their prose; having no real fulcrum to oppose to the weight of their subject they take refuge in polysyllables that leave the reader where he came in.

Everything is an elaborate beginning: "It is hoped that this will lead to . . ." as though they were waiting for the one additional, all-redeeming fact that would finally bring meaning to their ungrammar.

Weaver's concern for the word, for the free movement of the mind over the irregular surface of perceptions, was summed up in his notion of rhetoric that encompasses both logic and intuition. He wrote: " . . . Finally one's interest in rhetoric depends on how much poignancy one senses in existence." And to this he added a footnote: "Without rhetoric there seems no possibility of tragedy and, in turn, without the sense of tragedy, no possibility of taking an elevated view of life. The role of tragedy is to keep the human lot from being rendered as history. . . ." And, he went on: "Since we want not emancipation from impulse but clarification of impulse, the duty of rhetoric is to bring together action and understanding into a whole that is greater than scientific perception."

Weaver had no taste for compromise on the major issues—for the hopeful middle ways so popular in American thinking. "The heart of Lincoln's statesmanship," he wrote, "lay in his perception that on some matters one has to say 'Yes' or 'No,' that one has to accept an alternative to the total exclusion of the other, and that any weakness in being thus bold is a betrayal." The Lincoln Weaver so deeply admired was a conservative, far removed from the liberal do-gooder so many historians have doted upon. "The true conservative," Weaver wrote, "is one who sees the universe as a paradigm of essences, of which the phenomenology of the world is a sort of continuing approximation. Or, to put this in another way, in the real world he sees it as a set of definitions which are struggling to get themselves defined." Lincoln "found objectives in the moral idea of freedom and the political idea of union." Contrasting Lincoln's positions with the later ones of his party, Weaver wrote as follows:

> For thirty or forty years . . . [the Republican] party's case came to little more than this: we are the richest nation on earth with the most widely distributed prosperity; therefore the party advocates the status quo. . . . But when the circumstances of the status quo disappeared about 1930, the party's source of argument disappeared too, and no other has been found since. It became the party of frustration and hatred—and like the Whig party earlier, it clung to personalities . . . . They [the Republicans] persist with the argument from circumstance, which never wins any major issues, and sometimes, as we have noted, they are left without the circumstances.

"A grand source of ordering," Weaver thought, had departed from the world. A metaphysic had been lost and without it, he wrote in *Ideas Have*

Consequences, "our intensities turn to senseless affections and drain us, or to hatreds and consume us." The whole bourgeois belief in progress repelled him: "The mere notion of infinite progress is destructive. If the goal recedes forever, one point is no nearer to it than the last. All that we can do is to compare meaninglessly yesterday, today and tomorrow." In addition, he wrote, "since liberalism became a kind of official party line, we have been enjoined against saying things about races, religions, or national groups, for, after all, there is no categorical statement without its implication of value and values begin divisions among men. We must not define, subsume, or judge; we must rather rest on the periphery and display sensibility toward the cultural expression of all lands and peoples. This is a process of emasculation."

On the hopeful side, Weaver saw the revitalized conservative movement with its lonely academics (of which he was conspicuously one) refusing to go along with the liberal flood in their institutions of higher learning: the small group of economists who speak up for the free market, the poets who cherish the word, the philosophers with and without academic credentials who search for a metaphysical ideal that gives substance to a society and to a time, who search for the men and principles that may lead people to know what they mean when they say "democracy." "Democracy is a dialectical process," Weaver wrote, "and unless society can produce a group sufficiently indifferent to success to oppose the ruling group on principle rather than according to opportunity for success, the idea of opposition becomes discredited."

Dick Weaver lived as he wrote and thought, modestly, to himself, with his mind fixed on the far goal of a grand reordering of a splintered society. He took pleasure in occasional convivial gatherings with friends, and suffered uncomplainingly through the endless faculty discussions inevitably dominated by the liberals who thought rhetoric should simply be picked up by undergraduates—not taught to them—and who wanted to reform his courses or get rid of them. He was going to return for at least a year to the South, as a visiting professor at Vanderbilt University. Before then he would have been again in Weaverville for the plowing and harrowing and weeding of the land and of his own thinking. For despite his years in Chicago, Dick remained a countryman; he saw a design in nature uncorrupted by ideologies, and he saw one too in man's relationship to nature and to his own society. It was a relationship that demanded a metaphysic, piety, humility, and a structure, and in the writings he left behind these may be discerned together with the spirit that enlightened it.

The Challenge
of Our Time

The challenge has often been defined: it is essentially the problem of mastering the technological revolution that produces each year newer and more formidable weapons with which to subdue man's natural environment and also to destroy it, by means of the inherited responses—both social and psychological—that were barely adequate to cope with the relative simplicities of preceding centuries. The hand that drew the bow is the same human hand that can press the red button; the heads that made the decisions that in the Thirty Years' War reduced the population of much of Central Europe by two-thirds have not grown in size or cerebral capacities under the hats and caps of Washington, Bonn, Paris, London, Moscow, or Peking. The changes in political thinking that have occurred in the twentieth century have come out of this technological revolution and out of the reactions to the history that was, in part, of its making. The grandiose and sinister illusions of National Socialism were but one example of a marriage of a falsely construed history and an all too well understood order of the machines. And the Nazi state itself emerged because the statesmen of Europe and the United States had no sensible solutions for the problems of Europe after World War I. They too were unable to adjust their thinking and their decisions to the demands of a technology that helped to produce a worldwide depression or to the submerged longing of the peoples of Europe for an order with a deeper significance than the one that had brought on meaningless and devastating wars followed by vast unemployment. The deaths of millions of young men were not requited by the spurious world order of a League of Nations that was unable to restore the balances of the nineteenth century or to create the viable concepts and organizations that would make them unessential . . .

When President Kennedy came to Germany in the summer of 1963 and told his German and European audience that an attack on any part of their territory would be considered an attack on the United States he made a pronouncement that had a very mixed history. For this, of course, was a continuation of the doctrine of Woodrow Wilson and Henry Stimson, of Franklin Roosevelt and Wendell Willkie—to mention only a few of those in the United States who thought the One World had come much earlier than turned out to be the fact. These men lived and made their speeches in an era of lofty principles where self-determination was to be a cornerstone of a world made safe for democracy. It was, however, self-determination as a limited enterprise. It was a principle to be applied to Poles, to Czechs, to Slovaks, to Serbs and Croats, but not to the Sudeten Germans, or to the Austrians, or to the people who lived in Danzig, or Vilna, or Memel, for in these cases it clashed with the aspirations of those who had won the war. Words like "disarmament," "respect for obligations solemnly undertaken," "collective security," "open covenants openly arrived at," were used in a high rhetoric that covered the brute realities of a continent dominated as a result of American intervention by a weak France and its alliance of succession states. Words about democracy were conspicuous in the speeches and in declarations of the leaders of these newly created countries too, but the ancient oppressions of which they had so bitterly complained were as virulent as ever in the lives of their mixed peoples. Thus the Sudetenländer, presumably an integral part of the multinational state of Czechs, Slovaks, Ukrainians, and Hungarians, were discriminated against economically, politically, and socially by the ruling Czech hierarchy; when the Depression came, the Sudetenland was the most distressed area in Czechoslovakia. But no account of this catastrophe or of the vindictive political decisions that had helped to bring it about could eradicate the myth of a flaming Czechoslovakian center of democracy that had succeeded the feudal empire of the Austro-Hungarians. The legend remained fixed in the minds of the American statesmen who helped to found the country and then to perpetuate its mythology. The Polish Corridor too, although called by many leaders among the Allies themselves the likely origin of the next European war, became part of the system of legality. Henry Stimson, who had a compact solution for everything he regarded as a breach of international decorum, wanted the heads of countries that misbehaved or committed aggressions against this unstable order to be ignored in the councils of the powers as one might ignore a notorious transgressor or criminal if he turned up at a social gathering. Stimson would have preferred sterner sanctions than this social ostracism, but at the least he wanted to summon the moral forces of the twentieth century to maintain what he regarded as a world order. While the *Realpolitiker* moved deftly behind the slogans of international solidarity, the problems themselves remained . . .

Out of the nonorder that followed World War I, three major world-views competed for establishing the conditions their proponents declared essential to the welfare of the race or to a preferred section of it. The first was that of the neo-Wilsonians, who wanted to outlaw war, to adjust differences between nations by way of reason and juridical argumentation. The second was that of Soviet Russia, who with the appearance of Hitler quickly adopted the concept of the world alliance of peace-loving nations. These could, on suitable occasions, include friendly capitalist powers, for the just war in the Communist lexicon was defined as any war in which the Soviet Union took part and the peace-loving nations were either its allies or countries that would condone what actions, military or otherwise, she felt necessary to undertake on behalf of her security. The Russian state was based on a series of interpretations of the nature of the Industrial Revolution: an international order would be achieved when these dogmas were universally accepted. Nazi Germany, too, could easily identify the just war: it was the war on behalf of the race, against communism, against the international conspiracy dominating both the Soviet Union and the nations of the capitalist world—that of the Asiatic Jew who had been conspiring for centuries against the culture-bearers of the West.

Thus three imaginary worlds came into conflict, each of them exclusive—although for the brief interlude of the Hitler-Stalin pact it seemed as though the anti-democratic systems might range themselves against the Western powers in a powerful alliance of coerced populations, millions of whom accepted their bondage with enthusiasm, turning the vast technological resources of their countries into anything that served the state, whether they were ordered to manufacture tanks or automobiles or gas chambers. Before them were placed the perverted slogans of the machine age that were as appropriate to Soviet Russia as to Nazi Germany—"the common use before individual use," and over the concentration camps "Work brings freedom." When this short-lived alliance was disrupted by Hitler's attack of June 1941 the tattered banner of collective security was raised again, and on its behalf Roosevelt was ready to accept the sacrifice of entire populations, Poles, Germans, Czechs, and as it turned out the whole of Eastern Europe to the fantasy of the four policemen and the postwar collaboration of the great powers, one of which was to be the China of Chiang, that would have an identical interest in seeing to it that the peace of the world was kept. Neither Roosevelt nor Churchill would negotiate with the high-minded and courageous men of the German resistance, for part of the Anglo-American stereotype was the long-lived menace of Prussian militarism and the Junker caste they were believed to represent. The American and British leaders had only contempt for the idea that the army generals and the civilians who were risking their lives and those of their families against the Third Reich without any support whatever from the outside world could found a state that would be a long-range improvement over that of the Nazis. It was the German general staff, the prosecution kept telling the court at Nuremberg, that was the eternal enemy of the peace-loving nations, making and unmaking governments at will. The idea of dealing with its representatives to shorten the war and get rid of Hitler was waved aside as merely another crafty device to try to escape the consequences of the defeat.

But with the collapse of Germany and Japan the hollowness of the postwar design immediately became clear. Russia had no idea whatever that Hitler had been defeated in order to produce a "bourgeois" version of the four freedoms in which she too would play the role of protecting power. Nothing in Marx or Lenin or Stalin, excepting the latter's virtuous protestations to his Western colleagues on such occasions as those at Yalta or Teheran, could have given rise to such illusions. When Roosevelt at Yalta spoke of the need for free elections and a free press for Poland, Stalin told him briskly that those principles were well known, and went on to talk about something else. The notion that Stalin's postwar plans were the same as theirs was part of the interpretation of history placed upon his remarks by such men as Harry Hopkins and Joe Davies and the other busy emissaries who plied between Washington, London, and Moscow.

The image of the four policemen, however, faded slowly. The war in Greece, the Berlin blockade, the Korean War, the uprisings in East Germany, in Poland and Hungary, the building of the wall have played havoc with the myth that Prussian militarism was the chief danger to the peace of the world. They have brought an American president—who may not always have had the friendliest feelings for the Berliners of whom he unexpectedly proclaimed himself one—to declare himself the stoutest of champions for the maintenance of Allied strength in that city and to this date at least have prevented him from giving away the Oder-Neisse territories, a gesture believed desirable by so many of his advisers as well as by so many Germans. Treaty-breakers, the anathematized if somewhat sketchy outlaws of Cordell Hull, have been replaced by the unmistakable threat of the enemy coalition from Cuba to Laos. The brushfires that appear at intervals in Africa, or the Far East or the Mediterranean or near our own shores, are met in one form or another by an ad hoc coalition operating under the uneasy direction of the United Nations—surely a curious description of a body representing one of the great cleavages of history.

But the Western alliance is an inescapable necessity. In it both European and American policy at long last deal with realities from which much hypocrisy and many illusions have been burned away. We do not have One World, but we have working alliances of half a world that, in their power and well-being, remain a magnet for the oppressed millions of Europe and Asia. We have a nascent European and American order that has emerged not only from Hitler's diabolism but from its own failures. It is an order that corresponds to the material demands of mass production and mass consumption, an order in which each historical entity may take its place in a wider culture. It is an order in being and prospect, but it is far from complete. The challenges remain and they appear in many forms and places: unemployment in the United States and England, the farm problem wherever there are farms, the drive for equality among the colored races, the unreconciled differences in NATO and the Common Market, the continuing inflation, to mention a few of them. The European Economic Community has accomplished everything Speer had boasted the Nazis had done for Europe, without threats or violence, with no need to erect a wall to keep its workers from fleeing to the other side. . . . This collaboration of the West has nothing in common with the flimsy alliances and pretensions of post-Versailles Europe. The statements of its leaders about their common purposes and goals correspond to the realities of the need for defense both of territory and a culture. It is only a start: the alliance is threatened at many points from without and within, by the enemy at the perimeter and also by passivity and irresolution inside the fortress. But no matter how strong the French drive for a third force under the hegemony of Paris might be, what could this possibly come to in a time of genuine crisis? France has more than once called upon her friends for help when civilization—which her leaders always held to be coequivalent with the boundaries of France—was threatened. De Gaulle may sulk within his tents, but who can doubt where in the moment of crisis he or any successor must stand and whether he thinks he might better stand alone? But de Gaulle's moves toward more independence should be easily understandable to an American who believes the United States should have dealt resolutely and immediately with Castro's rocket pads because they represented an intolerable threat and calculated affront about which we could not debate either with our enemies or with our friends. And on this matter, it should be remembered, de Gaulle understood the need for taking action better than some of President Kennedy's own advisers. While every country must be the final judge of its vital interests, the overarching alliance of the West is an essential part of the vital interests of each of its members. France alone against Russia would be a lost cause; the United States without Western Europe, or Western Europe without the United States, would be fighting a last desperate struggle . . .

The loose confederations that have united the Western world since the war may not survive in their present forms; they need remodeling, to be adjusted to the growing strength of Europe, to the tactics demanded by the new weapons and to what we learn as we develop the common front. But the forces that brought these confederations into being remain the same; no one can secede from this history or stand alone in its stream.

Nevertheless, we are not the creatures of a dialectic. Although the forces making for union are powerful, they can be misdirected. A resourceful adversary will do his best to promote any differences that may be exploited in the alliance that keeps him from the mastery of the continent and of the world. But the Polaris submarines that disappear from the surface of the sea for two months at a time sail for us all, for de Gaulle as well as for Kennedy, and the German divisions on the front line are the divisions of the West. This is more than a military alliance, for the boundaries between the two world forces are far more ideological than geographical. . . . Reality has, in a sense, been simplified for us. Perhaps we can say that our capacity for coming to grips with it, our concept of it, corresponds more closely to its forms than was the case in the earlier part of the century. For we confront the naked question of survival—not only of physical survival but of that of the culture we have inherited and to which we have contributed. Is the nature of man with all its limitations and dead spaces such that he can learn to live, when he has the choice, in a disciplined freedom, to forego short-range advantages, to make sacrifices for the common cause—or is he rather in the age of technocracy the creature that needs to be handed the blueprints, to learn to recite in each generation a different version of a distorted history as one big brother succeeds the other and denies his works?

At least these basic changes have become manifest in the climate of the postwar years: the boundaries between states are losing their significance; the welfare of the people of Western Europe, even including the population of the Tyrol, is not felt to be at the mercy of the map makers as was the case after 1919. The causes of both World Wars are wholly lacking among the countries of the Western alliance: their cooperation is based both on necessity and on a consensus of purpose that is as widely shared as the spontaneous demonstrations in Germany for de Gaulle and for Kennedy would indicate. In the case of President Kennedy they had many significances, the chief of which was manifest in the shadow of the wall. The West needs to know its massed strength and to rely on it, to have the will to increase the flow not only of goods across its borders but of ideas as well, and to be as ready to sacrifice for this free community as are the zealots of the enemy cadres, to think beyond the local gain and privilege to the general purpose and to be ready to take risks on its behalf. For this is the first and last line of civilization. Either we will maintain it or the whole world will perish or—what is worse—be delivered to the men who have themselves become machines.

Black and White

The ingenuity of people is endless in finding ways to separate themselves from one another. If a declaration not of high purposes but of human practices were to be written, it would hold that all men are created unequal and different and the societies and infra-societies throughout the world thrive on the differences. North and south, highland and lowland, farm belt, cotton belt, wheat belt, the sides of the railroad track, neighborhoods, separate streets are enclaves, as are white and blue collars, earning power, religion, styles of dress and living, of education and thinking—the status symbols of every kind that mark the tribal and subtribal in-groups deployed against the outsider. Thus the tender growth of identity is sheltered and nourished—even language, the most common means of establishing the borders and unity of a people, is also the most common means employed to spot social, economic, and geographic differences within the linguistic area.

But easiest of all to mark human differences are color and race. When the Nazis took over, mainly from French and English sources, the doctrine of Nordic superiority and combined it with the dogma that anything that was useful to their own chosen people was good, and that damaged them evil, their embrace of racism became a kiss of death. South Africa alone, at the tip of a continent, remains a national survival of what had once been a doctrine accepted in one form or another by the people of the entire world but especially gratefully in the nineteenth century by the white races who dominated it. The doctrine had been a talisman for getting around the globe; moreover, as a system of tabus, rejections and acceptances, it simplified action: the traveler in a strange land took his place immediately in a hierarchy and his *mana* as a white man corresponded to the actual facts of power. The white race, as a result of its Judeo-Christian heritage as well as centuries of invention, warfare, and competitive struggle, had the moral and physical capital, the know-how and self-confidence that made for a culture of imperialism. Other races, of course, regarded themselves as superior too—China was the Middle Kingdom, the center of the universe; the Emperor of Japan was the son of Heaven—but it was the capitals of the West, in the nineteenth century, that made policy for the six continents; it was the white man who dominated them, and even the art of the African—his sculpture and carving—was often a subtle, if resentful, tribute to the white man's big medicine.

69

At the opposite pole from the Nazis in destroying the intellectual respectability of racism were the anthropologists. Like the linguists they had to assume the equal worth of the subject of their researches. Southern Piute or Menominee is as "good" a language as Greek or Latin if you are going to study their structures, and anthropologists no more than the linguists were to be put off by the literateurs who pointed out that the written language was something else than the spoken one and that the *Odyssey* was more than vowel and consonant clusters. In the liberal climate of the twentieth century the anthropologists and linguists won not only considerable victories with their disciplines over the mysteries of speeches and cultures, they also provided the intellectual substructure as well as a vocabulary for dealing evenhandedly with underdeveloped peoples that Europe and America in the nineteenth century had called primitive or thought of as "lesser breeds without the law." The hypothesis of equality was a fruitful one; no culture or language can be comprehended if it is approached as something quaint or as a regrettable deviation from the norms of Latin, or Whitehall or Kansas City. The comfortable myth that "primitive" people, whether in Africa or in the Middle West, have a vocabulary of a few hundred words was easily demolished, but new and uncomfortable myths sprouted in the place of the old.

Displaced from his eminence as the moral and temporal leader of the world, the white man in much of his own literature as well as in that of his nonwhite critics became an object of derision and contempt. In the extermination camps of the 1940s he lost his last claim to any kind of superiority, writes James Baldwin. "The Man," he says, in effect the abominable white man, is what American Negroes mainly discuss in the 1960s, and they are fed up with everything about him. The Black Muslims preach a holy war against him; Allah will destroy him, for he is the Devil, he is evil on two white legs and neither he nor his works will plague the blacks or the rest of the world he has corrupted for many more years. Even Baldwin, intelligent and highly gifted as he is, declares he has come close to the borders of this racism, so powerful is the anti-white phobia shared by this generation of Negroes and by many whites.

The danger to the Negro of what has been called the revolution of 1963 is far greater than it is to the white man. I do not mean merely that the Negro represents only 10 percent of the American population, or that he is everywhere at a disadvantage in the positions of prestige and power in the country, for neither of these latter statements is wholly true. If a Negro has any kind of superior ability, for example in the arts, he has a ready and mixed audience eager to celebrate his talents, and in the prevailing political structure he plays a considerable, even decisive role in key cities of key states both in presidential years and in run-of-the-mill elections. The danger is not mainly physical or economic, but moral. It is the always attractive notion that someone else is responsible for his woes; not only for his having the status of a Negro but also of a human being.

The Negro has come a long way in the last quarter of a century by virtue, to be sure, of his own efforts but also with the freely given help of whites who founded and provided much of the funds for the NAACP and other organizations of Negro protest. The tradition has shifted, its new forms have not made him white, but they have broken through a long row of caste barriers and more and more, in the growing sum of voluntary acts of recognition and friendship, a Negro has come to be judged as an individual, as a person in a predominantly white society in which he started at the bottom. He exerts large financial as well as political leverage, and the American society despite its inequalities and injustices has provided him with the means to prosper with it. Nowhere else has the Negro achieved the status and well-being he has reached in the United States. The countries run by Negroes—Haiti, Liberia, the underdeveloped states and tribal societies of Africa with their own sharply divided class systems, their segregation of ins and outs, their own brutalities—are no magnet for the American Negro, whatever he may think "The Man" has done to him. Nor are the Communist countries: not for the Negroes who have experienced their systems of segregation at first hand. It is true that the unemployment rate for the Negro in the United States is far too high, as are the dropouts of Negro high school students, and the latter in fact may be largely owing to the feeling of hopelessness the young Negro has about the chances of getting a job, but this is not the whole story. The Negro, despite discrimination, has multiplied and flourished in America; his birth rate in the decade 1950–1960 was 25 percent against 18 percent for the whites, and he is changing the color of Northern cities; he is now a majority in the city of Washington, where in the last ten years his increase has been more than three times that of the whites; in Chicago, a few years ago overwhelmingly white, there are now more Negro than white children in the grade schools; Manhattan, it has been calculated, if present trends continue will before long be a nonwhite island. Negro buying power in the United States has been estimated at $20 billion annually, more than that of many a white country of comparable numbers. Even on relief, where the luxuriant rackets have appalled Negroes as well as whites, the Negro has done well for himself when his standard of living is compared with that of people of any color in other parts of the world; nor is it in a purely physical sense a hardship standard in the United States. Not long ago a Chicago paper ran a story of a large Negro family that was getting some five thousand dollars a year legitimately in relief payments; it took some close figuring, the family spokesman said, to get along with so many mouths to feed, so many bodies to clothe and house, and that must be true, but still five thousand dollars is a large sum to be paid out to a family just for being there. Relief, of course, is not a racial problem, but when so many more Negroes than whites receive relief, when according to a reliable Negro writer like Louis Lomax more jobs have been turned up by the Urban League in "white" industry than there are qualified Negroes to fill them, these statistics reinforce the folk stereotype that a large proportion of the Negroes in America cannot or will not accept the full responsibilities of citizenship. Lomax writes: "There is a disturbing view held by many Negroes in high places that three hundred years of first slavery and then discrimination have destroyed the moral fiber of the American Negro masses: that perhaps they are spiritually incapable of becoming first-class citizens."

I do not see how we can afford to make such an assumption. It is a thesis that is the opposite side of the coin of welfarism: it holds that a man of any color is no more than a product of social and economic forces, that the individual himself bears a minor responsibility or none at all for what he is or becomes. It is a dangerous doctrine as well as an untrue one, for there were Negroes who came up from slavery itself to become both first-class citizens and first-class men and women in any spectrum of color. The most hopeless slavery is that which is self-inflicted, which would destroy any belief in the possibility of escape from it, which breeds on self-hatred and which would turn three hundred years of one part of the human heritage—a part that had great music and grace and kindness in it—into a wasteland of apathy and despair. It is characteristic of the pseudo-liberalism that is telling the Negro he has only to reach out to claim his heritage, that it produces the opposite of what it aims to do. It makes for frustration and bitterness when its alluringly easy goals recede; when the sit-downs open up a lunch counter but fuel the ancient prejudices so that whites strike out in return and the Negro is served desegregated coffee but behind another barrier of antagonism raised between the races. The white courts that in their zeal to break down segregation have made it possible for a new lawlessness to take the place of the old injustices have been tampering with the substance of a society, not only with traditional legal concepts of private property that may no longer be defended against trespass if color is involved, but against the hard-won peaceful coexistence, the increasing voluntary mingling of two peoples. Certainly in the United States there should be no segregation in the opportunity to learn, but for every school opened up with the force of bayonets for the admission of token Negro students, barriers are raised the higher against the development of a genuine interracial community. The goal in a democracy is to let all men and women be judged for what they are, to decategorize them, to let them appear by name instead of by race or region or accent: it is in this sense that they are created equal and it is this cause that has suffered a reverse in the liberal cajolement of the Negro which tells him that his time has come here and now, that he has only to organize and by direct action to lay hold on what is due him.

But what the Negro needs is to be integrated within an interracial community of consent, the voluntary help, for example, of unions and industry in training for jobs. No society in the mid–twentieth century can be a healthy one that excludes part of its constituents from the possibility of full membership in it. A ghetto breeds a ghetto mentality, both inside and outside its walls.

I once had occasion to read a half dozen manuscripts written by Negro economists and historians living in the Caribbean area—which has its own racial conflicts, unemployment, poverty, and diseases—by men who for the most part had attended British universities. Their manuscripts were not to be told apart from the work of white scholars; if anything they were above the American academic average in the competence of the research and writing. At the same time I chanced to read the manuscript of an American Negro teaching in a Southern Negro college, the product of a year's stay he had made, sponsored by the State Department, in an African country. This manuscript was illiterate and confused; it bore no resemblance to the studies written by the other Negroes living a few hundred miles away. The weight of the differences in these and many other examples is unmistakably on the side of the nonsegregated schools and universities, but on an integration that lies outside court decisions and the automatic rifles of the federal marshals and the army. It is an integration by voluntary association, by individual action, by way of self-discipline and by consent. The Negro in the United States has the same right and need to be judged and treated as an individual as anyone else, to attend, if he is qualified, the best schools and universities in the country, but he himself bears the responsibility for forwarding the changes in the segregationist tradition by his own performance, his own contribution to the society, and for this honorable goal he will have countless white allies.

1964

The Double Standard

A s Eliseo Vivas in this issue of *Modern Age* tells us,[1] every political and ideological movement needs its demons to account for the gaps in its ranks, as well as its failures. But neither Freud nor Darwin nor Marx ever made black magic on the minds of conservatives that compares with what the mere existence of the Right, whenever possible the extreme Right, does to the thinking of those who are called liberals. The tragic day of November 22, 1963, was an enormous apperception test conducted on a national scale, projected on television screens, reported in newspaper and magazine columns, with the themes of the commentators echoed and reechoed for the comfort of those who needed to believe them. "We are all guilty" was one of them; "the cult of hatred that lay behind the act" was another; and implicit or loud and clear in the explanations of the crime were the figures of the unreconstructed South and of the unreconstructed political opponents of the all-pervading liberal doctrine. An editorial writer in the *Nation* declared:

> Throughout the South, of recent years, there has been a steady build-up of violence, with more and more incidents, each a bit ghastlier than the ones before. Girls in a Birmingham Church are blown to fragments. A sniper kills a Negro from ambush. Mob violence disgraces a university campus. Acts of violence receive implicit sanction and approval by elected officials. Defiance of law and order is incited, through precept and example, by these same officials. And so it has gone. All of which suggests that it is not alone a mood of national "repentance" that is needed so much as it is a closer look at the "big picture" of war and preparation for war, of the steady preachment of violence in one form or another and the eclipse of social idealism. (*Nation*, December 14, 1963)

One writer in the *New York Times* called Oswald "politically eccentric," another recorded that the assassin to be sure had been identified by the Dallas police captain as "an adherent of the left-wing 'Fair Play for Cuba Committee,'" but added "there are also reports that Oswald, apparently politically erratic, had once tried to join anti-Castro forces." An editorial in the same paper on November 23 told of President Kennedy's efforts to

---

1. Eliseo Vivas, "On the Conservative Demonology," *Modern Age* 8, no. 2 (spring 1964).

curb violence in the United States: "And from the beginning to the end of his administration, he was trying to damp down the violence of the extremists of the right." The *New York Times* editorial of November 25 stated: "None of us can escape a share of the fault for the spiral of unreason and violence that has now found expression in the death by gunfire of our martyred President and the man being held for trial as his killer." A contributor to a review designed to give the American reader some straight criticism in the place of the neighings and stompings of the tame stable mates of the standard book sections wrote:

> It has been hard, these last two weeks, to feel much pride in being an American. Two assassinations, each ghastly in its own right and each uncovering still another side of our social pathology; callousness, maybe planned negligence on the part of the Dallas police; fourth grade children in the South cheering the news that a "nigger loving" president had been murdered.
> The author then goes on to sketch Oswald's type:
> A semi-intellectual, he picks up phrases and bits of ideology. . . . In one guise he is a man of "the left" and in another of the "right" . . . He is not a Communist, for that requires patience and discipline, nor is he a Marxist for that requires theoretical reflections . . . he finds his true moral home not with Khrushchev or Mao, who have begun to seem bureaucratic and settled, but with a hoked up vision of Castroism he has gotten from beguiled journalists. . . . But he is also a Southerner, a poor Southern boy burning with memories of class humiliation. The South because of its racist mania, is a violent society. . . . Lashed together by the delusion of superiority, the whites know violence to be a potent answer to threats from the dark. (Irving Howe, in the *New York Review of Books*, December 26, 1963)

But behind all this rhetoric, what were the facts so far as anyone knew them? The crime was not committed by an anti-Negro Southerner, or by a man who wanted to build up American armaments, or in any guise at all by a man of the Right. The evidence those reporters and editorialists had before them showed that Oswald called himself a Marxist, he had wanted to become a citizen of the Soviet Union, he had propagandized for Castro and according to his widow had tried to kill General Walker, who has never been noted for his leftist sympathies. Oswald was a psychopath, but of the left-wing branch of that order, and the talk linking him to right-wing Southern violence was a wish and fantasy. The ambushings and bomb throwings in the South are mainly done by other mentally disturbed people as are those committed in Chicago where Oswald's assassin came from. Obviously, many of these writers and commentators were bound to make the perpetrator into a man of the Right. An article late in January in the *Nation* advanced the hypothesis that he was in the pay of the FBI. He must be anything, a stool-pigeon, politically erratic or eccentric, anything but what he said he was—a leftist. The ideology the liberals created for him confirmed their ties and the existence of the demons who keep them always a step away from their private utopias. Oswald was no member of any states' rights cult of hatred and violence: a pro-Castro Marxist might be assumed to be motivated by precisely the contrary fixed ideas as those of his opposite numbers who bomb or ambush Negroes. So OK, if he didn't act as a trigger man for a rightist conspiracy, he's a stool pigeon for the FBI.

Collective guilt is an illusory charge against a people, another way of turning the event into an indictment of the whole United States. Did the Russian people kill the czar, murder the thousands of Kulaks, and those other thousands who died in the purges? Did they kill Trotsky with a pickax? These deeds, however, were official acts, acts committed on behalf of a regime that held the entire population by the throat. And what did some all-out professional liberals at the time have to say of that regime? I quote again:

> . . . in 1937 when the John Dewey Commission of Inquiry into the Soviet charges against Trotsky was being organized, a considerable number of prominent American intellectuals published a manifesto warning "all men of good will" against assisting the Commission and declaring that critics of the Moscow Trials were slandering the Soviet Union and "dealing a blow to the forces of progress." The manifesto was signed by Theodore Dreiser, Granville Hicks, Corliss Lamont, Max Lerner, Anna Louise Strong, Paul Sweezy and many other writers, artists and professors. (Philip Rahv, in the *New York Review of Books*, January 23, 1963)

It is this phenomenon that is the core of the problem. What the liberals of 1963 were doing when they repeated the charges that the world Communist press was making that the assassination of the president, despite the facts before them, was somehow owing to the Right was the product of a, by now, automatic reflex. Not many of them are likely to have taken their text from *Political Affairs*, which calls itself the "Theoretical Organ of the Communist Party, U.S.A.," which said in its December, 1963 issue:

> It [this crime] is the ultimate depravity of the pro-fascist ultra-Right forces—of the fiendish Dixiecrats and racists—who will stop at nothing to

destroy the democratic institutions of the country, to threaten the peace of the world . . .

It is the logical consequence of the repeated lynchings, bombings, and murders of Negro men, women and children in the Deep South at the hands of the Klan, the White Citizens Councils, the National States Rights Party, and of the organized Nazi and fascist hoodlums.

The Left for a large and much published number of intellectuals has never been guilty, not of the purges, or the murder of Trotsky or any of the unpleasant events denied in the official line. Only after Stalin was denounced by his successor for some of these acts was it possible in these circles to admit "the foes of the forces of Progress" were not slandering the Soviet Union when they said Stalin had been responsible for some pretty ghastly political murders.

But of course it is not just to identify the professional liberals with the far Left. They are not the same—they merely in this apperception test say the same things. They say them because they share the same demonology. In 1932 in Germany the chief demons for the Communists were not the Nazis but the Social Democrats. The line changed as the Soviet Union made its pact with Hitler and then won the war he had unleashed against it. The postwar enemies were the so-called imperialist powers, that is, those who wanted to stop Soviet expansion or, in the propaganda phrases, "the war mongers," "the lovers of violence." These lovers of violence for the liberals when the chips are down are the rightists, perhaps in certain untidy instances the Chinese Communists or conceivably the Castroites, but never Khrushchev, who promised to bury us. And nothing changes this persistent, cherished image of the Soviet Union nor its power to make its docile friends in the West echo its own interpretations. For not only are the demons the same for the Communist and liberal intellectuals; their heaven is the same. It is a place where the economic order is such that everyone has enough food and a job and the world has peace. The future is mastered by planning and by technology, competitive forces are mastered by the bureaucracy, an affluent society rejects its foolish individual choices and gratefully accepts the serious objects decreed in their place. Reactionaries stand in the way of progress toward these goals. They cling to tradition; backward agricultural areas are tradition-minded and status-ridden. When a deranged killer who appears to be the same man who shot at one of the most conspicuous segregationists in the South assassinates the president of the United States, the liberal commentators can no more accept the evidence before them than they can when they deal with economics. Their tropisms are by now ineradicable. Let us listen for a moment to Walter Lippmann writing in the *New York Herald Tribune* of November 26: "In his alienation Oswald turned to the Left. But that was incidental. Those who spat on Mr. Johnson and on Mr. Stevenson had turned to the Right. The common characteristic of all of them was their alienation, the loss of their ties, the rupture of the community."

Thus the Right gets into the act of murder committed by a self-avowed Marxist. In one sense, however, Mr. Lippmann is right, even if he is not far right. The extremes of Right and Left do indeed touch at the lunatic fringe—the most virulent of Nazi judges, the president of the Peoples' court who with shrieks of fury sentenced the men of the July 20 plot against Hitler to death, was a former Communist. The Eastern and Middle European countries now in the Soviet orbit have their former Nazi or Iron Guard or as they said "fascist" officials well represented in the successor Communist courts and administration. They have all, whichever side they were on, long been alienated from the Western tradition that has to do with, among other things, the search for truth.

Right and Left are measured with two different yardsticks by American liberals. Alger Hiss was invited some years back to talk to a group of students at Princeton University. A man of the Left, convicted of perjury, Hiss apparently supplied some form of nourishment otherwise lacking in the undergraduate diet. Gus Hall not long ago spoke to the students at Yale. Well and good, he is a leader of the Communist party and may properly be heard on political questions by those who wish to listen. Other students at Yale, however, wanted to invite Governor Wallace to talk to them, and this the university administration pointed out to them would be "offensive and unwise"—Governor Wallace would have spoken after the tragic bombing of the church in Birmingham. Nothing linked the governor to the bombing. It may well have been committed by criminal Southern segregationists but surely the governor of the state, who is a segregationist but not a criminal, may properly be heard in his cause, as properly as Gus Hall, whose party has been responsible for the murder of vast numbers of innocent people. Mr. Hall himself is undoubtedly free of any complicity in these murders, but the same thing may be said of Governor Wallace.

The samples could be endlessly multiplied. If the end can be expressed in vaguely humanitarian terms anything is justified. The liberals who denounce the cult of violence throw at us the propaganda picture of: "fourth grade children cheering the death of a 'nigger loving' president." Others among them not only defended the Soviet Union when its slave labor camps numbered ten or fifteen millions by saying the figures were invented, but also after the facts were well established and a new regime came to power openly acknowledging the very practices American liberals had so long denied, they cited the revelations as proof that Russia was evolving toward a new humanitarianism. The liberals now fitted Khrushchev as they had Stalin into their own image. When he said he intended to bury us he was merely enjoying a little joke while actually on his way to providing more substantial satisfactions for the good life in the Soviet Union. When he takes up the cause of Cuba or Panama against the United States, or his jet fighters shoot down an unarmed American plane, this has far less importance than his clear perception of the malefactions of the demons of the right.

It is true too much bitterness enters what should be debates among civilized intellectuals on the issues that divide them. Mr. Johnson's "Let us reason together" has been often quoted in the aftermath of the Kennedy assassination. To reason together means, if it is to work, to listen, to weigh, to take account of the evidence. It means among other things the simple capacity to call a confused Marxist and a psychopath and a Castroite by those names without invoking the enemy one would have liked to have committed the crime. It means soul-searching, which is not the same as brainwashing.

Behind the Soviet Show Windows

The ordinary visitor to Russia is on a continuously guided tour. He sees what his hosts think is good for him or good for them and, while he may wander on occasion about the showcase cities like Moscow and Leningrad, when he travels to or outside them he must follow an approved plan. Occasional exceptions, however, have to be made because the Soviet Union remains in need of technical assistance, and the report of one such traveler has just come to hand.[1] Published as a short pamphlet in Switzerland, it is written by a Swiss engineer, Paul Metzger, and recounts his experiences from November 1962 to July 1963 in trying to install automatic controls in a Russian chemical factory being built in Balakowo, about six hundred miles east-southeast of Moscow. The automatic installation was being made by the Swiss firm employing Herr Metzger; an Italian firm was in charge of building the factory.

The Swiss engineer, like everyone else visiting the Soviet Union, had to travel according to conditions prescribed for him: he had to take a night boat on the Volga from Saratov to Balakowo because foreigners are not allowed to travel by day. Neither on the boat nor on the train that brought him from Moscow to Saratov after a fifteen-hour trip was there any opportunity to get food or refreshments—Soviet citizens, knowing what's ahead of them, bring their own provisions. Mr. Metzger went without. In Balakowo his four-storied "hotel" had sixteen rooms, one of which he was entitled to sole occupancy according to his contract. He was put in what was called an apartment—a living room with a small bedroom attached—which he shared sometimes with one colleague and on occasion with two additional Germans who had come to work on the project. In the other dozen or so rooms of the hotel lived five Germans and up to twenty-eight Italians, five to a room in some cases. Two rooms served as dining rooms, and the commandant of the secret police who had charge of the hotel had a room reserved for his private use on the ground floor where he could observe the comings and goings of the guests. There were other guests in the rooms neither he nor anyone else in authority

1. Paul Metzger, *Sowjetrussland nach Schweizer Zeit* (Zurich: Aktion Freier Staats-buerger).

83

concerned themselves with—bugs that crawled over toothbrushes and towels and into closets and that shared the beds.

The workday bore little resemblance to the Soviet blueprint of the seven-hour day proclaimed in 1960 and the forty-hour week foreseen by the Soviet planners for 1963, which was to be followed after 1964 with the thirty-five and then the thirty-hour week. Metzger and his colleagues, excluding the Russians, worked forty-seven hours a week—the Russians worked longer—and no one was paid for overtime.

Metzger had had reason to believe the preparatory work for installing his equipment had been finished before he got in Balakowo, but he was mistaken. Although his Swiss firm had been repeatedly assured by telegraph that everything was ready and all that was lacking was Herr Metzger, when he got to the factory everything was topsy-turvy. Some of the equipment had been installed in the wrong places, electrical wiring was lacking, and many items that had been shipped were simply missing. No one knew what had become of the delicate machines, the synchromotors, the time relays and such: they had vanished. The spare parts that were supposed to have been delivered were also missing. It was all very mysterious until the Swiss engineer noted what happened when deliveries were made after he arrived. Truck drivers, paying no attention to lettering that said "precision instruments," simply dumped their loads near the factory, and the unpaved roads when it rained in Balakowo turned into mud holes. No one bothered about the contents, and Metzger found that half the glass parts of the deliveries he did receive were broken, and any steel was badly rusted. Much of the equipment had been buried in the winter under the snow and when that melted away it lay under water. Metzger believed that crate after crate had simply been bounced out of the trucks, and the small boxes either were buried as the big ones fell on them or were broken up by the bulldozers and cranes that were eventually used to pull the accumulated deliveries out of the mud.

The Soviet workers assigned to the project did not approach Western European standards. A Soviet engineer, Metzger found, had the training of a skilled Swiss worker, and a skilled Soviet worker had the training of an unskilled Swiss. People he talked with, foreigners who had worked in other parts of Russia, said they had observed the same differences.

In addition, the planning bedeviled them all. If a pipe had to be laid, the workers—twenty to thirty women—dug the ditch and laid the pipe (men were called in only for the hardest physical labor). But if something went wrong, if either the pipe could not be sunk on time or the ditch not filled, the crew had to go somewhere else to another assignment—in this fashion the planning office never missed its schedule and was never penalized as it would have been if the workers had finished their job. But as a result open ditches crisscrossed the city. Metzger gives another example: six women had the job of constructing a partition with bricks and cement on the second story of a building where he worked. The bricks and the cement were brought to them by other women workers on planks about a yard long—one plank for every two women. These materials were kept on the ground floor and they had to be brought a distance of about two hundred yards to where the wall was being built. Back and forth the women went, each carrying some twenty bricks and a couple of clumps of cement on their plank, and while the material was on the way no work was done on the wall; the women bricklayers simply waited for the materials. When the bricks and cement came the women put them in place by hand and they spread the cement by hand; they worked without trowels, wheelbarrows, or shovels. Women routinely performed hard labor of all kinds and Metzger noted that even those digging ditches in the freezing weather hummed songs to themselves—Russian songs of old sorrow.

The rules were strict. Each month and at Christmas foreign workers were theoretically allowed to receive one package, which had to be sent from private persons, not from a firm; the packages could be valued at no more than ten dollars nor weigh more than two kilos (4.4 pounds) and they had to be packed so they could be repeatedly opened for inspection. German workers who heard from home that as many as five packages had been sent to them told Metzger they received only one of them and it after months had gone by. What worked to perfection was the surveillance. The militiamen detailed for the job of keeping an eye on the foreign workers were everywhere, at the doors of the hotel and factory, in the corridors and at every corner. The translators who worked with the foreigners and often were alone with them reported every week to these authorities on their conversations. Never, said Metzger, were the authorities' suspicions of the foreigners abated; they remained at least the potential "instigators, spies and saboteurs."

These suspicions under the conditions of work could be easily confirmed. A chemical factory has its dangers in the best of circumstances and in those of Soviet Russia the dangers were multiplied. Quicksilver was carelessly spilled from container after container, so that pounds of it accumulated on the factory floor that could not be recovered with the implements at hand. As the room temperature rose both the Russians and the foreigners came down with severe headaches, dizziness, nose-bleeds, and fatigue symptoms until they could work no longer. They had developed quicksilver poisoning that came from the fumes. the Soviet engineers knew no antidote to this but Metzger's wife, who had been an assistant in a dentist's office, wrote him that zinc dust applied to the room's surfaces made the quicksilver harmless. Her letter was held up a number of weeks by the censorship and another fourteen days went by before the Russians were able to take the countermeasures. These too were inadequate: instead of using zinc dust they put clumps of zinc on the floor. but the quicksilver fumes were not the only danger. Carbonic disulfide, which is used in liquid form for the manufacture of viscose, was poured out in overgenerous amounts by the inexperienced Soviet workers. When its vapors mix with air at high temperatures it explodes. Before that, however, the fumes when breathed damage the mucous membranes of the human stomach, then other organs become involved, leading to impairment of reflexes, muscle fatigue, loss of memory, and eventually brain damage. Metzger showed serious signs of illness but despite the efforts of his Swiss firm and of the Swiss ambassador in Moscow he was not allowed to go home to be treated and to recuperate until the chief physician of the hospital to which he was sent said either he must be given a furlough or he would die. Only then did his exit permit come through.

Metzger returned to Switzerland, and then went back to fulfill his contract to Balakowo, this time loaded with food to supplement the tedious Russian fare of cabbage soup and warmed-over potatoes. Both the Russians and the foreigners expressed their astonishment at seeing him after two month's freedom and he found the same disorder at the plant as when he had left. His ten installations could have been readied for their proper operation within a matter of days; with their fully automatic circuits in use, the danger of explosion would have been completely avoided, the quality of the product improved, and fewer workers used. But the heads of the plant were afraid to make the shift; they feared their quotas might not be reached and Metzger had to cool his heels for three weeks until chance played into his hands. Owing to the ineptness of a Soviet worker an explosion occurred in one of the mixing machines. Sabotage was immediately suspected, but Metzger managed to convince the authorities that such accidents were bound to happen through human failure and that the remedy lay not in the secret police but in putting the machines on their automatic circuits. He finally got permission to go ahead and in three weeks could finish his work.

The city of Balakowo has no places of amusement whatever, no hotels, no restaurants, no theaters, no pubs. It has wide unpaved streets, a community well at each street corner; the sixty thousand inhabitants get their water in this fashion. The houses are made of wood, and, judging from the photographs that Herr Metzger managed to smuggle out, are in considerable need of repair. But the most important thing in the Soviet economy where a plant is going up is to fulfill quotas, not to repair houses. The plan, as Metzger observes, is mightier than the attrition of human forces. That is why the number of plant accidents is so high—the goal has to be accomplished in the midst of this fantastic confusion. Soviet workers wage a daily struggle against the norms, and it is carried out in the blare of incessant radio propaganda piped through the plant that never stops during either work or meals. The Russian worker is modest; he makes few demands and expects little enough; he appears passive, to accept his fate with the indifference of those who are up against an impersonal, immovable higher authority. From time to time a rosy future is predicted for him. A commentary to the Seven Year Plan of 1958 told him the Soviet Union had come to the decisive phase in the competition with capitalism, and that by 1965 the Soviet Union would have overtaken the United States in per capita production. "Then," the statement said, "the Soviet Union will have the highest living standard in the world." When Metzger showed his Russian colleagues pictures of his family and of his Swiss house and car they would not believe that people could really live in such a fashion. They thought his photographs were stills from a moving-picture film that had been sent to Russia as propaganda. The Russian worker numbs himself with such explanations and meanwhile he uncomplainingly continues at his monotonous job. Metzger did, however, detect some difference in the younger workers—those between fifteen and twenty-five; they seemed to him more alert, owing to the intensive training they were getting in technical subjects and a broader education in special evening schools.

What Herr Metzger has written is borne out by the evidence of many others, including even casual visitors to Russia. David Dallin once told me that in his childhood in Russia the snow-covered streets of a village used to be flattened by a primitive scraping apparatus drawn by horses so they could be made passable, and that the same method is still being used. The space capsules take off with the help of the German technicians the Soviets captured at the end of the war, the jets copied from American models crisscross the Soviet skies, but behind them, decades if not centuries behind them, is the daily life of the ordinary townsman or villager. This is not, to be sure, the whole story. Soviet technicians and scientists and plant managers do on occasion manage to break through the heavy red tape. Soviet surgeons have pioneered new developments in stapled sutures; during the war none other than Heinrich Himmler paid tribute to the ingenuity of the Russian army and the partisans; in many cases, especially as the war went on, their arms and techniques were superior to those of the Germans. The weapons were more simply designed, and the soldiers and partisans were schooled to make use of every possible device in defense and attack as they operated behind the German lines. But the dead weight of the planning apparatus, with its need for an excess of caution, for not being too successful lest the next year's plan make impossible demands, above all the Kafkaesque world of brooding suspicion in the dreary round of the long week has not changed since Stalin or, for that matter, since Lenin.

The Revolt of the West

N o matter what the outcome of the election [in the United States] on November 3 it will have served an essential purpose of the democratic process. For the forces behind the candidacy of a critic of the prevailing liberal doctrines have been long a'building. Since the election of 1940 a considerable portion of the electorate has regarded itself as being partly disenfranchised; it has regularly had no chance to vote for a presidential candidate of whose political principles it thoroughly approved or, putting it another way around, who uncompromisingly represented its ideas of what American foreign and domestic policies should be. Franklin D. Roosevelt, who had made plain to many—both friends and foes—that he was likely to involve the United States in the European war, was opposed not by the anti-interventionist Senator Taft but by another internationalist, the author-to-be of a book called One World. Wholly devoted to the liberal dogma of collective security, both Mr. Roosevelt and Mr. Willkie clearly saw the danger to civilization and to the United States of Adolf Hitler, but neither was ever able to perceive the all too similar shadow cast by the Soviet Union. The American voter in 1940, in an election dominated by issues of foreign policy, was given no choice between moderation and extremism, between war and peace or between the goals of the America First Committee or the Committee to Defend America by Aiding the Allies. Both candidates piously promised to stay out of the war and both demanded measures that could only lead to American intervention.

In 1944 there could be no contrasting views in either domestic or foreign policies. Governor Dewey in the course of the campaign was given hitherto secret Pearl Harbor material from sources close to Admiral Kimmel that at the least threw some doubt on President Roosevelt's qualifications as commander-in-chief of the armed forces and at the most laid him open to the charge of inciting the Japanese attack. Mr. Dewey, understandably enough in the midst of a bitter war, chose not to make an issue of the president's conduct. He also made none with regard to his major policies.

In 1948, following the "can't lose" techniques provided by regional polls, questionnaires, and automatic calculators, Mr. Dewey presented not much more than a somewhat colorless alternative to Harry Truman.

Mr. Truman, having played the piano for Marshal Stalin and signed his name at Potsdam, had slowly but resolutely come to see that the Soviet Union was unaccountably and belligerently not following the prescriptions written for it by American liberals, that it was having no part of the peace forces of the one postwar world. By the time the election came around both candidates could compete with one another mainly in their denunciations of Soviet wickedness and in their promises to provide a thriving domestic economy by way of both government and private enterprise. A choice between them was a matter of taste.

In 1952 the Republican party again, as in 1940, had the chance to nominate a conservative whose views ran counter to those of the Democrats. Robert Taft had spoken and voted against President Roosevelt's policies both domestic and foreign; he had opposed the Nuremberg trials, the great symbol of a postwar collaboration of the peace-loving victors, because he thought they were political trials, and he had led the Senate fight to prevent President Truman from putting striking railroad workers into the army because, he said, this would amount to forced labor. A man of principle and courage who had spent his life in politics, Taft was sidetracked and defeated by the same "liberal" forces in the Republican party that had prevented his nomination or that of anyone of similar views in 1940. Those who had supported Mr. Taft could vote in the 1952 election for an eminent and charismatic general whose candidacy had also been proposed, a few years before, by a Democratic president, but not for the man whose words and deeds had for long years separated him from the Democratic opposition and who presented an alternative policy on almost every important issue. The one aspect of Mr. Eisenhower's regime of grave, head-shaking concern to the liberals of both parties had to do with his secretary of state. It was true that under Secretary Dulles no great blocks of territory were lost to Communist imperialism, but Dulles' brinkmanship, his notion that communism might even be rolled back, set off the only serious, concerted, and long-lived attacks on Eisenhower's foreign policy or indeed on his administration.

In 1960 Mr. Nixon, during his first debate with Mr. Kennedy, assured his television audience that both he and his opponent had the same purposes. There followed a discussion of the "image" of the United States, which Mr. Kennedy thought had suffered under the Eisenhower administration, a calumny which Mr. Nixon indignantly denied. But again it was not easy to separate what precisely the one candidate would do differently from the other and why. Both men committed themselves boldly to a defense of the free world: Mr. Nixon had spoken up heatedly to Premier

Khrushchev and Mr. Kennedy would certainly do the same should he be given the opportunity.

The Republicans and the Democrats wooing the party free market of the 1960 electorate were for the same things and said the same things. Everyone in the approved seats of power said the same things—the major columnists, the great foundations, the professors, and the former students of the professors in the Eastern universities who were now signing the checks for the coffers of both parties. They all repeated precisely and as a matter of course the same texts as the loftiest among the liberal writers.

Not unknown to them, but vastly underestimated and held in contempt and derision, were the exiles from the leading councils, exiles with a very different reading of recent history and with other ideas of how four or more freedoms could be preserved in the United States and possibly other countries as well. They had their intellectual roots in men the liberals had long since disposed of—in an international group of scholars and writers who had plowed their own stubborn way against the liberal tide—Charles Beard, Ludwig von Mises, Wilhelm Roepke, Richard Weaver, a school of economics in the University of Chicago and a scattering of other colleges and universities, a few historians and political scientists, philosophers and literary men. And then along with these leading revoltés were thousands of college students who exercised their biological right to attack the fixed ideas of another generation that had led them or their elder brothers into a war and then into a twilight zone of never-ending hostilities. They formed clubs and discussion groups and, more articulate than their elders of a generation before, they founded papers and magazines and talked back to their professors except to the handful who despite the academic and social penalties were ready to act as their advisers.

What they believed in was the intellectual bankruptcy of the liberals who had been writing for students and one another for these many decades and who had finally come to occupy virtually all the places of power in a society of managers. They ran the Eastern press, the broadcasting systems, the major foundations and universities; their ideas dominated the decision making of both parties. It was a hierarchy concentrated in the East; its chief opponents were the descendants of the old isolationists, of an individualistic tradition that has remained vigorous in the West and Middle West. But the division was far more philosophical than geographic; the East too had its Conservative Clubs, the West a full measure of interventionists.

The pendulum had begun slowly to swing back after Taft was defeated for the Republican nomination in 1952, but the liberals were too preoccupied with one another's ideas to note any change. When the Republicans met in the Cow Palace in 1964 the Eastern press was unable to offer any coherent account of what happened. One writer in the *New York Times* thought the situation resembled that in Lebanon, where offices are apportioned according to religion. The choice of the Catholic Mr. Miller as Goldwater's running mate, he thought, might be the beginning of a similar system in the United States. A usually sophisticated observer, he now seemed ready to believe that the Protestant Lyndon B. Johnson had been brought to the 1960 Democratic convention as Mr. Kennedy's running mate by a stork that chanced to be in the neighborhood. Grim articles were written on the migration of folding money from the East Coast to the West and Middle West, on the bucolic fanaticism of Mr. Goldwater's supporters and their possible connection with "hate groups." The liberal press saw what ideologues easily see—a conspiracy—this one of the chronically disenchanted, of those who have been bypassed by the potent streams of contemporary thinking, of those who are no more than nostalgic for another and simpler time. The bad guys they had shot down over and over again had unaccountably won.

But in fact the revolt has other origins—it stemmed primarily from the abject failure of the liberals to fashion not only one world but any coherent view of society that matches the realities. In their belief in such formulas as collective security, the punishment of aggression everywhere, in government action to secure racial equality, in government intervention to secure economic justice, the liberals have introduced a hodgepodge of ad hoc measures that have produced the opposite of what they sought. For the promise of Soviet cooperation a third of a world was delivered to communism; for the illusion of racial equality to be enforced by the central government a painfully emerging harmony coming about through individual and voluntary acts of understanding and friendship has been replaced with a massive and growing group hostility based not on the qualities of the person but on his color. In the places of prices produced by supply and demand, of wages determined by productivity, appear a suffocating accumulation of unused farm products together with artificially high prices for what is consumed, and labor monopolies that enforce their demands for constantly higher wages at the expense of all the rest of the community.

The liberals, because they are ideologues, arrive at new stances only by way of bitter experience or political expediency. They have never understood the dynamics of communism: they have lived in a love-hate ambivalence that makes their decisions whimsical and dangerous. Dean

Acheson, who once left South Korea out of the list of the territories the United States intended to defend, now like a rejected lover regularly denounces the Soviet Union and all its works, and perches among the war hawks of his party. President Johnson, who in the spring of 1964 declared that he could understand Russian fear of Germany (although none other than Khrushchev had boasted that the Soviet Union could destroy the Bundesrepublik with five or six bombs), orders, with at least one eye on the coming election, a heavy retaliatory attack on North Vietnam harbors without previously consulting either Congress or his allies. The late President Kennedy was of one mind when the invasion in the Bay of Pigs took place and of another when the rocket pads in Cuba were being built. In both instances he was forced to act: in the one case against the success of an invasion he had however reluctantly approved, in the other for the demolition of enemy bases that had become in the opinion of a small majority of his advisers an intolerable threat to the United States. The bases were destroyed, the Soviet technicians remained.

The liberals live continually in the hope that this time the Soviet Union will live up to their aspirations for it; it is an illusion they have cherished for fifty years as the Soviet zigs have followed the zags. Stalin at Yalta promised Roosevelt that Poland would have free elections; freedom of the press and of the ballot, he told the president, were well-known principles and he accepted them as a matter of course. Roosevelt was delighted; he said the atmosphere on the gala occasion in the Yussupov palace, where forty-five toasts were drunk on the night of February 8, 1945, to celebrate the success of the deliberations, was that of a family dinner. He and Harry Hopkins left the conference in the glow of the new day that had dawned; the first great victory for world cooperation had been won; peace was assured as far as the eye of man could see. Roosevelt was so convinced of Marshal Stalin's goodwill that he was impatient to meet with him alone without the burdensome presence of Winston Churchill, who now seemed to the liberals, who had loved him dearly, a reactionary and an obstacle to the all-important understanding with Stalin. The pattern does not change; Khrushchev's ceaseless efforts to split the Western alliance are rewarded by President Johnson's repeating Russian propaganda about the military threat of one of our chief allies.

It was this endemic "Liberalism" that many Democrats and the Republican convention at San Francisco rejected. Goldwater has not been the leader of the revolt that rejected it but one of its products. How durable a product he is will be shown as he develops his case. He undoubtedly shares the main principles of its intellectual progenitors and he has shown courage and consistency in representing them. He wants a free market economy, decentralization of the increasing power exerted from Washington, a clearer, more consistent and firmer policy toward Communist expansion; he seeks to strengthen the alliance of the anti-Communist powers and he refused to attempt to be all things to all men when he voted against the racial equality measure. Not everything he has said would be considered sound doctrine by conservative thinkers who counseled moderation in the place of extremism, who believe that the job of military men is to carry out the decisions made by the responsible civilian authorities. But on the whole he presents for the first time in at least twenty-five years a clear choice to the American voter. If the two-party system is to continue to have meaning in a time when bloc voting threatens to replace individual balloting, this must come about by giving the voter such an alternative in the place of the spurious differences that Mr. Willkie attributed to campaign oratory. Mr. Goldwater, however great the other differences may be, has restored to the American electorate the same kind of choice that Abraham Lincoln made possible for them to make a hundred years ago. When the critical question was raised it had to be answered by principles not by expediency, regardless of whether or not they were popular at the moment. The Republican party under Goldwater at long last has attached itself to a set of principles, it has turned to the electorate for a decision on whether they are shared or rejected. As in the case of the free market of commodities the voter has been offered a labeled alternative instead of a nonchoice determined by those who know what is politically stylish. The 1964 election has marked the return to a two-party system: in the long run, because ideas eventually determine events, that can be far more important than who is president.

What about History?

In time of war it has often been observed that phalanxes of historians, like journalists and preachers, rush to take their places in the front of the propaganda warriors. All that is left is the stance of objectivity, the apparatus of research, the skeleton of footnotes, references to documents and occasions—the facade of scholarship. But the texts of the wartime historians like to tell of the congenital malformations of the enemy's character, of his brute and belligerent inheritance, or his paranoia, his incurable lust for aggression, his deafness to the reason that motivates the ardors of the inhabitants of the country to which the writer belongs and of those, of course, of his allies. Then after the dust of battle settles, the new books and articles appear, sometimes written by the same authors, sometimes by their revisionist successors; and it turns out that matters weren't so simple after all. War guilt is reapportioned, atrocities are reappraised and sometimes acknowledged as having also been perpetrated by the country of the writer. History is returned again to the hands of the peacetime historians—until the next crisis.

This is the pattern for what might be called historic wars—for conflicts like those of the eighteenth and nineteenth centuries—and which held its form, as far as the Western powers were concerned, through the First World War. But from the beginning the case of the Soviet Union has been different; not only for the historians who write in the Soviet Union but for many of those in other countries the USSR must be defended in both war and peace.

During the war, for example, David Dallin wrote a book about the Soviet Union and mentioned the defection of the Russian General Vlasov. He said that this was the same General Vlasov who had been so highly praised as a great Soviet hero by Eve Curie in her book *Journey among Warriors*. Mlle. Curie had traveled to Russia during the war, and Dallin quoted her encomium of Vlasov that had appeared in the first edition of her book. By the time the second edition had appeared, however, Vlasov had gone over to the Germans and Mlle. Curie had written that the defecting general was a different Vlasov from the man she had encountered and thought so highly of. That is chapter one of a curious story. Chapter two: a teacher at one of the eastern colleges, a political scientist, reviewing the Dallin book and disliking it heartily, objected to Mr. Dallin's quotation from Mlle. Curie's book, saying she had disavowed meeting the defector and that she had stated explicitly that the Vlasov she had interviewed was quite a different character. Chapter three: Mr. Dallin's careful researches had disclosed that there seemed to be but one General Vlasov and that was the man who, believing that Stalin had senselessly sacrificed the lives of thousands of Russian soldiers, had defected to the Germans after his surrender and declared his willingness to lead an army against the regime he felt was destroying Mother Russia. "Both" Vlasovs, Mr. Dallin pointed out, had the same initials, "A. A.," when they were mentioned in the press as well as in Mlle. Curie's book, "both" were reported as being in command of the same sector of the Russian front. Chapter four: I wrote to the professor of political science, pointing out that when Dallin's book was published the only edition in print of Mlle. Curie's book had been the one in which she had praised General Vlasov, that the quotation was accurate, and his attack on Dallin completely unfounded. The professor, waving aside this plain evidence of fact and chronology, wrote back citing the lines in Mlle. Curie's second edition, which had come out some months after Dallin's book, and said that any quarrel was between Mr. Dallin and me.

This was a wartime episode, but as far as the apologists for the Soviet Union are concerned the war has never ended. As long as Stalin lived he was described within the Soviet Union as the "great Stalin," outside it any reference to the purge trials as being faked, or to the forced labor on which his economic system depended, promptly found a posse of academic defenders of his ways who denounced not the tyrant but the writers of books who dared to spread such calumnies. These acolytes of the Word, of the Truth, of history as it really happened, took the relativist view—history was not only in its nature time-bound and colored by the prejudices or class background of the writer, it must serve a pragmatic purpose whether it was called advancing the cause of peace, furthering the goal of coexistence, or merely exposing anti-Soviet machinations. All kinds of hypotheses were proposed to account for Stalin's failure to live up to the American dream. One professor of history at another eastern university thought Stalin had acted in such a belligerently anti-American fashion because of the twenty-year treaty of alliance he had signed with the British in the course of the war. Others said Stalin was a prisoner of the Politburo, still others that he could not trust Molotov who kept doing things behind Stalin's back.

Then came the reign of Khrushchev; after the memorable speech of the new leader denouncing the old, the historians inside the Soviet Union reversed their fields. Now they said they had not been free to tell the truth or even to know it, and down came the icons and the monuments and off in the opposite direction went the historical writers, with a new hero in the main role and opposite him a brand-new villain whose name had to be taken down from dozens of broad avenues as well as from the city that was the very symbol of the Soviet victory in the Great War. Outside Russia, precisely the same thing happened. Now it appeared there had after all been wholesale purges of innocent people; millions of slave laborers, despite the manifestos of American liberals, had actually been used—but that was all under the reign of the bad Stalin. Those days were dead and gone; Khrushchev was the apostle of peaceful coexistence, a man who wanted more goods—something the liberals doted on—for the common man in the Soviet Union; such forays into *Machtpolitik* as the building of the rocket pads in Cuba were readily explained away by Khrushchev's bowing to the demand that he agree to remove them.

But now Khrushchev is gone from his seat of power, denounced in his turn by a new regime whose attack on him appears in *Pravda* and also in serious journals of opinion in the West. One such revisionist statement has just appeared in the *Nation*. In an article published in the issue of October 5, 1964, before it had been announced that Khrushchev had been deposed, Alexander Werth reported on his two-month visit last summer to the Soviet Union. Werth quoted from an article that had appeared in the *London Sunday Times* by Lord Thomson, who also had visited the USSR and traveled to Kazakhstan with Khrushchev. Thomson had written: "I came away from my visit to the Soviet Union convinced that the Russians are making a more rapid industrial advance than is generally realized in the West and . . . I am disturbed by this progress . . ." Thomson had then gone on to talk about Khrushchev: "What a salesman! I think one of the world's greatest. He projects his views to his people so forcefully that it is little wonder that his leadership is so accepted. . . . They admire and respect, and yet are in no way cowed by him. Rather it is the pride and affection of a perhaps humble family toward a member who had made good in a big way." Werth commented cautiously: "All this, though correct up to a point, is rather an over-simplification." He then recorded his own impression during an earlier visit he had made in 1959–1960: "that Russia was sitting on top of the world; that prosperity was steadily growing, that everybody was highly optimistic about coexistence with the West, and that Khrushchev was immensely popular for both international and domestic reasons." Since then, Mr. Werth wrote, many Russians would agree with what Palmiro Togliatti had written in his political testament: "It is wrong to speak of the socialist countries . . . as

if everything were always right in those countries. . . . Nothing is worse
than to create the impression that all is well and then, suddenly, to have to
start explaining new difficulties . . . and which are not necessarily isolated
phenomena." And, Werth commented, although it might be argued that
"the disastrous Russian harvest of 1963 was an isolated phenomenon . . .
it continues to affect the Russian standard of living and the general
mood of the country." He went on to tell of the many admirable aspects
of everyday life, the free medical services, the low rents, the excellent
transport system in Leningrad, which, however, had a grievance—many
of its best writers, artists, and signers move to Moscow. Also prices were up,
food and clothing were very expensive—for example, butter at two dollars
a pound, a simple cotton shirt cost four or five dollars. Thus, "It may,"
wrote Werth, "be a sign of greater freedom, but there is certainly a good
deal of angry grumbling, not least among the working class. It is directed
even at Khrushchev himself, whose optimistic forecasts of only a few years
ago are now quoted against him. Some of the more irresponsible young
people go as far as to claim that 'things were better under Stalin.'" Farm
income was up at the expense of the city workers and "The 1964 harvest
has been very uneven. If Khrushchev has effectively demonstrated that
the virgin lands, far from being the 'dust bowl' they are supposed by the
Western press to have become, remain one of the very largest sources . . .
of grain . . . [t]he fact remains that Northwest and Central Russia have
again suffered severely from drought."

"For these reasons, perhaps," wrote Mr. Werth,

> Khrushchev appears to be less popular with the industrial working class than
> with some sections of the peasantry, who compare their present condition
> with the ruthless exploitation they knew under Stalin. On the other hand, he
> is well regarded by the intellectuals. Engineers and technicians of every kind
> consider themselves a privileged elite; . . . Scientists are also pro-Khrushchev
> because he allows them considerable freedom of discussion. . . . The artistic
> and literary world also appreciates its greater freedom (though it may not show
> much respect for Khrushchev as a critic) . . . The artists and film makers no
> doubt realize that some ex-Stalinist hatchet men are still keeping a vigilant
> eye on them, but the feeling prevalent among these people . . . is: "For God's
> sake, let Khrushchev stay; anyone else might be much worse." . . . As Olga
> Bergholz put it to me: "Khrushchev may not be a great literary critic but, hell,
> so long as he's there I know at least that I shall never go to jail as I did in
> 1938 under Stalin."
>
> But the new freedom is only one part of the story. If nobody is worried
> anymore about his personal security "so long as Nikita is there," everybody
> in Russia is sharply worried about the way the world is going.

They were worried, wrote Mr. Werth, about "That guy Goldwater" who would mean

> not only a possible war, but a *probable* war. . . . a Goldwater victory would mean the end of the policy symbolized by the test-ban treaty, which is also looked upon as the real cornerstone of Khrushchev's foreign policy. These Russians want to live in peace with everybody. They are intensely patriotic and even nationalistic, but are singularly free . . . from any missionary spirit with world pretensions. . . . this very widespread public sentiment is largely reflected in Khrushchev's increasingly cautious foreign policy. Although, as it were, honor bound to defend Cuba in the event of an American invasion . . .

Thus writes Mr. Werth, whose recent book on the Russian German war has been hailed by the *New York Times* as "one of the most important books to come out about World War II." It may be so; I have not read his history, but it is possible to say something about Mr. Werth as a historian. For on November 2, after Khrushchev had been deposed, Mr. Werth had another article in the *Nation,* and lo, three weeks after his first article he was writing about a different Khrushchev and a different public response to him in Soviet Russia. Mr. Werth starts out his second piece with some self-praise. He writes: "In 'Russia in 1964,' reporting on my summer visit to the USSR, I indicated that Khrushchev's stock had fallen low in his own country. This was particularly true among the industrial workers, who blamed him for shortages, the high cost of living and the mess in agriculture." Then Mr. Werth went on to revisit his visit to Soviet Russia:

> The working class openly attacked Khrushchev as a "windbag." . . . An industrial executive in Moscow went so far as to tell me in August: "You have no idea how our workers hate Khrushchev." Another thing which rankled was his Cuba fiasco. Many people tended to agree with the Chinese that the whole stunt of setting up missile bases in Cuba and then withdrawing them was a mixture of adventurism and capitalism . . . No doubt, as I wrote in my previous report, his determination to give first attention to improving relations with the United States and the West was popular in the country at large; yet in party circles this "excessive" pro-Western and anti-Chinese orientation seems to have been causing more and more disquiet. I could feel it everywhere I went.

Why, if Mr. Werth ran into this sentiment of unease wherever he went, did he fail to mention it in his first article? In that report Khrushchev merely appeared to be less popular with the working class than with some sections of the peasantry. And in that article, too, Lord Thomson was quoted on the admiration and respect, pride and affection, the Russian people had for Khrushchev, who was one of the world's greatest salesmen. "Rather an oversimplification," said Werth, but still obviously worth quoting. And Werth from his own observation tells how highly the intellectuals—technicians, scientists, artists, and filmmakers—regarded Khrushchev. They had to deal before with the Stalinist hatchet men and one of them at least had gone to jail under Stalin; but that was 1938 and long ago—before the reign of the good Khrushchev—as of October 5, 1964. The only reference to Cuba in the first article tells of the patriotic Russians being honor bound to defend that country in the event the United States should attack. In the second piece, the Khrushchev Cuba policy is a "fiasco" and attributable to a man who "mixed adventurism and capitalism." It may be doubted that those suddenly revisionist words— should he ever read them—would be taken amiss by Khrushchev, for he was brought up in the rough-and-tumble view of history that the winner takes all—the offices, the appointments, and the adulation of the historians. He in fact made his own signal contribution to this view when he made his memorable attack on Stalin and began the demolition work on that legend. For him now to be the victim of the next revision might pain but would certainly not surprise him.

"I pity," writes Mr. Werth further, "the Soviet historians who will have to rewrite the hundreds of volumes of 'Khrushchevite' history, with its absurd magnification of the part played by Khrushchev in the 'winning of World War II.'" Mr. Werth wonders if there may not be at least a partial rehabilitation of Stalin: "perhaps some of the more absurd manifestations of Khrushchev's pathological anti-Stalinism will be corrected . . ."

It is probably too early for even one as knowledgeable as Mr. Werth to do other than ask questions as to how the new party line will develop. But one thing is certain: whoever directs it and whoever propounds its theses will find its echoes not only in the Soviet press but also among the liberal historians.

Just as the great Stalin became in due course the employer of hatchet men after he was succeeded by the jovial Khrushchev, admired and re-spected by all save some angry grumblers and irresponsible young people, so is this same Khrushchev turned overnight into the man the workers hated. For this school of history the only crime a Russian statesman can commit is to lose or die.

1965

The West German Statute of Limitations

On May 8 of this year, unless the law is changed, the statute of limitations for all crimes, including murder, committed during the period of Hitler's National Socialist regime will come into effect in the Bundesrepublik. The statutory limit in West Germany for the prosecution of felonies which may be punished by a sentence of life imprisonment (no death penalty exists in the Bundesrepublik) runs for twenty years as it has for major crimes since the adoption of the Criminal Code of 1871. This is usual practice on the continent of Europe, although in England and the United States murder and a few other crimes, such as bigamy, may always be prosecuted. In this country only the state of New Mexico has a statute of limitations for murder (it runs for ten years); in all the rest of the American states, however, murder may always be prosecuted.

The law of 1871 was continued under the new constitution adopted in 1949 while the country was still under occupation, and the reaffirmation of the provision of the pre-Hitler criminal codes of both the Weimar and Wilhelminian periods was not owing to chance. The new constitution or Basic Law, as it was called, also did away with the death penalty: the founders of the new state to be had witnessed more than enough of legal and illegal killings; the power of the state was henceforth to be whittled down as far as possible where it could do violence to the citizen. The West Germans wanted a society where the state exists for the benefit of the individual and not, as under Hitler, the individual for the state.

After the collapse of National Socialism the victorious powers, and later the German courts, had an enormous job on their hands in dealing with Nazi criminals. The military tribunals of the Western allies tried more than five thousand cases and sentenced some eight hundred to death, of whom more than half were eventually executed. Trials were held throughout the countries the Reich had occupied, including those behind the Iron Curtain—Rudolf Hoess, the commandant of Auschwitz, was executed in Poland, other Nazi hangmen and their helpers were tried in countries of both the West and East. Not all the sentences were for acts still held to be crimes after war passions had cooled. The sentence of Field Marshal Kesselring, for example, who was condemned by a British court in Venice, was first commuted to life imprisonment and then was annulled when his responsibility for the Ardeatine massacre was later reassessed. Such instances occurred in a sizable number of cases, especially in those involving German military leaders. Of another kind, however, were the incontestable Nazi crimes committed on a scale never possible before: genocide, though it was no twentieth-century innovation, was brought to new heights of efficiency, for no other period had the technological skills to produce the beltline factories that could murder and cremate thousands of people a day for months on end.

The German courts, which directly after the defeat of the Reich had only secondary jurisdiction over such crimes—the Allies reserving to themselves the conduct of trials of major criminals—nevertheless found 5,445 Nazi criminals guilty and sentenced twelve of them to death before the death penalty was abolished. It became clear, however, during the many trials that were held after the Bundesrepublik became a sovereign state, and as in the course of each new trial new defendants were involved when witnesses implicated them or they implicated themselves, that many men who had taken part in the exterminations were still at large either in West Germany or outside its borders. Therefore, in 1958 a center was established in Ludwigsburg whose purpose it was to screen every piece of evidence that came to hand to discover the names and whereabouts of Nazi criminals who were still at large. Mainly through this center, German judges have been provided with the names of men who are still wanted, and it is sufficient under German law for a judge merely to note such a name for the statute of limitations to be interrupted and to run for an additional twenty years. Thus it is not true that if Martin Bormann, who was sentenced to death in absentia by the Nuremberg Tribunal, were to appear after May 8 he would go free under German law. His name and those of other specialists in the apparatus of extermination such as Hans Eisele, Josef Mengele, Gerhard Bohne, Heinrich Mueller, and hundreds more have been duly inscribed on judicial blotters; assuming no other jurisdiction took over first they would be tried under German law anytime they are found. As a result of the researches of the Ludwigsburg Center and of other investigatory bodies, 750 cases involving thousands of persons are still to be tried before German courts—enough to keep the courts busy for four years.

Nevertheless, the approach of the May 8 deadline has set off both in and outside the Bundesrepublik a storm of protest. The minister of justice, Ewald Bucher, has declared that in his opinion the law cannot be changed without an amendment to the constitution, a view which is contested by others who maintain that no more than a vote of the

Bundestag is needed. The Bundestag, which has three times, the last in 1960, decided against prolonging the statue of limitations, has called on the Justice Department to ask the Ludwigsburg Center to intensify its investigations and review the complete file of documentary material on acts of murder committed during the Nazi period from German and all other sources and to report by March 1. The Bundestag will then review together with the federal government the question of extending the statute of limitations. The German government has called on everyone who has additional information about any Nazi criminals in any country of the world to supply their names. As a result of the accelerated search, names have been forthcoming from the Berlin Document Center, still under American control, the Centre de Documentation Juive in Paris, from Norway, from the Wiener Library in London, and from at least one individual in the Soviet Union.

None of this subdues the hue and cry. The governments of the countries behind the Iron Curtain, for which everything has its higher political purposes, have from the beginning accused the West German government of being the historical continuation of the Hitler regime. They take a self-righteous satisfaction in releasing information from their captured files on anyone whose denunciation would in any way embarrass the Bundesrepublik and confirm the Communist propaganda thesis. Often the files in their possession have produced a dossier on which the West German government has acted; such information is sometimes true but it is not designed for a judicial purpose. The Iron Curtain countries have their own highly placed former Nazis and Iron Guardists who immediately changed the color of their shirts; when official accusations are brought forward they are made entirely for political maneuver. If the East Zone Communists had wanted justice they could have had it sooner without waiting for a politically opportune time. May 8 will paradoxically, if the statute of limitations is not prolonged, very likely produce more documents from the East than if the criminals might still be legally punished.

Not for the first time are the Germans on the long horns of a dilemma. Those who oppose a change in the law say, among other things, that they have had enough of retroactive law, of laws designed to fit political occasions, under National Socialism. They say too that it is highly unlikely that many unknown perpetrators of crimes are still at large—people who have not been tried or whose names remain unlisted. The Ministry of Justice has pointed out that 90 percent of the cases tried by German authorities were heard before 1953; after the subsequent trials and the additional names on the blotters of those still being sought, not many Nazi murderers could now possibly escape prosecution should they be discovered; not enough to justify the tactic of changing the law in the fashion of the Nazis.

One may suspect that the real reason behind the disinclination to prolong the law is that the Germans, although overwhelmingly anti-Nazi, are tired of the subject, tired of the denunciations of Germans and non-Germans, and would greatly prefer to put the past behind them, to forget it whenever possible. As it is, they say, the trials will go on for at least another four years with the cases already scheduled to be heard; is there to be no end to this dark chapter of their history? Furthermore, the arguments go: Who else besides Germans has ever been tried? Whoever stood before a court because of the destruction of the undefended city of Dresden, where more than a hundred thousand[1] noncombatants were killed in a single night; or for the rape and plunder of German cities by the Soviet army; or for Hiroshima and Nagasaki?

The critics of such views look at the matter with an inward and outward eye. For one thing, they point out, these were no ordinary crimes: six million human beings done to death in extermination camps, pseudo-scientific experiments designed only to torture or kill the victims; Einsatz squads organized to hunt down and "cleanse" Europe of the Jew; transports organized in which people traveled without food and water so that cadavers tumbled out of the freight cars when they arrived at whatever terrible destination they had been shipped to; no statute of limitations should exist to prevent the trial of a single one of the men who committed crimes such as these. Furthermore, the argument about the one-sidedness of the punishments for war crimes does not apply in these cases. People who are being sought now are not those who committed alleged war crimes but those who took part in calculated mass murder. It may be true that Allied nationals were guilty of heinous crimes, that the decision to bombard population centers was an atrocity both of those who gave the orders and of those who carried them out, and the same thing was true when Allied commandos were told to act like criminals and did. Morally, no doubt, such men on the Allied side should have been tried too. But in a world where war still exists, no heads of victorious states and no victorious generals who have been fighting against a criminal regime can be tried for having won their war or for overstepping the blurred boundaries between legality and illegality in some of the methods they

1. Recent information offers a much lower figure, twenty-five thousand killed and tens of thousands wounded.

used. In any event the discussion in the case of the statute of limitations has little to do with matters that might be called reprisals, or means, however savage, of conducting total war—it has to do with crimes that are considered such throughout the civilized and uncivilized worlds. To make it impossible to prosecute even a small number of murderers who might be able to reappear with legal immunity in Germany because no judicial action had been taken is grotesque.

It seems to this writer that the arguments of the latter group are well founded. These were certainly no ordinary crimes, and the trial of even a lost handful of those who committed them should not be prevented. Retroactive law and such legal shenanigans as were practiced by the Nazis were devices against the innocent, against people who had offended no law but only "the health sense of the Volk," or were believed in some sly way to be damaging the party and state. But murder, especially mass murder, is not in this category—to make possible the prosecution of anyone who has committed it does not endanger or weaken the structure of law. Practical considerations, as the Bonn Foreign Office has undoubtedly informed the government, are not to be ignored either. In the same issue of the *Bonn Bulletin* from which I have taken some of the figures given here are headlines about the common fate of the free world, the necessity of thinking of the whole Western community. Stubbornly going their own way in a matter that has left the entire civilized community aghast is not likely to further such high purposes.

The Germans had a long way to go before they got rid of their pariah status. Thanks to men like Konrad Adenauer, Ernst Reuter, Ludwig Erhard, Theodor Heuss, Kurt Schumacher, those who revolted on July 20, 1944, and thousands like them, as well as the universal revulsion, once the facts were known, of the German people themselves against the regime that had ruled them, West Germany has gradually been welcomed both as an ally and friend of the other peoples of Europe and the West. The German state has voluntarily made amends that were open to it to Israel and to individual victims of the Nazi period. Thousands of Germans have volunteered to work on behalf of reconciliation and it is likely that less anti-Semitism exists in Germany than in any country of the world outside of Israel. But always behind the scenes other forces are evident. An insignificant core still exists of old and new Nazis who, under no nationalist disguise, have been able to muster enough votes to keep a party on the slate in Germany, but who nevertheless manage to publish a few insignificant newspapers and to remind people that Hitler too started from small beginnings. Other states and peoples as well as

Germans are violently allergic to such manifestations even when they seem to have been diluted to legalistic argumentation; the time is past, as no one knows better than the Bonn government and the German intellectuals, when the country can pursue its own self-regarding policies without concerning itself with the reactions of foreigners. Germany has a valid case for reunification, for the adjudication of her claims for territories that have been German for centuries and were taken from her as ruthlessly as Hitler took land from his neighbors. None of these legitimate German goals may be secured without the help of others, and while the foreign policy of states is not made by moral sentiments they nevertheless play their role in democratic states where public opinion is heard from.

Nevertheless, the case against changing the law is a strong one. Under the West German Constitution, where, as under the American Constitution, every citizen is equal before the law, prolonging the statute of limitations must affect anyone suspected of murder, not only former Nazis. Thus what has long been regarded on the Continent as a basic principle of justice would be changed largely in response to foreign pressure. What effect is this likely to have on the new German democracy? And if the Bundestag votes to prolong the statute and the courts hold the act unconstitutional, what then? Won't Germany's image before the world be as tarnished as if the attempt had never been made to change the law? Furthermore, any remaining major criminals are still subject to trial; only minor culprits, and not many of those, would possibly be affected by an amendment of the statute.

It is a repetition of history worth noting that it is almost as hard to be a conscientious and well-regarded German in the post-Hitler world as it was to be a conscientious and well-regarded Jew in Germany in 1933.

On the Cold
Conservatives

O ne of the charges often leveled against conservatives is that they lack a fellow feeling for the underprivileged, that they defend a traditional society whose beneficiaries they are, leaving the others to pick up any crumbs they can find. Conservatives, in a word, lack compassion, and when their ideas are fleshed out in political terms they are successful only where people still live in the past, still cling to an outmoded set of notions that have nothing to say to the modern world except *sauve qui peut*. One example of this view has just appeared in the course of a criticism of two recent books by conservatives. The reviewer writes:

These books have more rational content than conservatives usually allow themselves. Nevertheless, the authors still shiver in the cold sweat of original sin, still fear the sin of pride in men's attempts to improve their conditions. They sit, shielded by their creature comforts, their status, and their religion against the problems of poverty, ignorance, disease and unemployment that make others too uncomfortable to be conservative. They have not yet faced the question, asked long ago by Lester Ward, as to why, if individual effort be so efficacious as Spencer and Summer said, collective effort must be so deleterious. Or the question, how, if man be too sinful to be trusted with governmental power over others, he can be trusted with unrestrained economic power over others. Or why, in thus setting their ideas above the prevailing opinions of the past 30 years—or 200 years, they are not themselves guilty of *hubris*.[1]

Another writer discussing the books of philosophic scientists refers to the conviction of the German physicist Weizsaecker that the social message of Jesus must not be forgotten; "The forces of conservatism and inhumanity are already too strong, without that," writes the critic.[2]

It cannot be said that conservatism has become a dirty word because dirty words are in vogue; it becomes something else. It means "square" and "heavy" and "backward looking" and "inhumane." Since we in the United States are given to love-hate syndromes and since many of the

1. Thornton Anderson, *American Political Science Review* (December 1964): 988–89.
2. Stephen Toulmin, "The Physicist as Philosopher," *New York Review of Books*, April 22, 1965.

current nostrums being served up to cure our sicknesses are, to say the most for them, no more than shots in the arm, the connotations of "conservative" will certainly change. But why should it have this pejorative meaning among intellectuals—do accusations like these have to do with certain conservative writers, or with essential conservatism, or the preconceptions of the critics? How true are they? Let us look at some of the practices of our contemporary societies in a century when it has seemed possible to free mankind from ancient burdens of toil and trouble.

First it may be noted that it has not been the society dominated by the free market in our day that has been oblivious of the plight of minorities, of the underprivileged. The sustained acts of terror, the crimes against humanity have not been those committed by the representatives of any traditional order but by the revolutionaries; the expulsion of the kulaks, the system of slave labor, the mass murders have been the work of the Stalins and Hitlers who did not hesitate to concern themselves with the problems of ignorance, disease, and unemployment. Even in the United States, during the war, thousands of innocent American citizens were shut in well-run concentration camps because they happened to be of Japanese ancestry—the victims of an American administration dedicated to solving the problems of poverty and unemployment, to taking care of the forgotten man.

None of these acts was the act of a conservative nor would they be likely to occur under any conservative administration. Conservatives in the United States speak of decentralization, of the inalienable rights of individuals for whom the state exists and of a balance of powers to maintain these rights. Every demagogue laments the plight of the poor; it is from them that he gets his mass following and the ploy is an international one from South America to Siberia passing on its way through many North American cities. And yet it may be observed that only one society has obliterated the kind of grinding poverty and back-breaking labor that until recently was endemic in every country of the world, and that is not the society of the dictatorship of the proletariat, of the racial comrades, or of government enterprise, but the open society of the capitalistic exploiters.

It is a society that not only can afford to be generous but whose mores demand generosity even of the most reluctant giver. The Rockefeller who carefully doled out dimes felt it necessary to hand out millions through a foundation bearing his name, not because of the income taxes of those years but because it is not enough in the capitalist society to own oil wells and to live it up in the capitals of the world in the sporty fashion of princely oil magnates from other societies. It is precisely this needful concern for public opinion that distinguishes the free-enterprise society from the states that are alleged to be projections of the hitherto disinherited proletariat or of an exploited race. And since the free-enterprisers are the arch-conservatives of these latter years and the society they activate has produced the matrix of technology and affluence that has opened up the almost unlimited possibility of individual development on terms chosen by the individuals rather than by their leaders or their governments, every ill that flesh is heir to may be ascribed to them. In an unfree society the goals are plain: to stay alive, to get an apartment, to be pleasing to the authorities, and the effort to achieve them leaves little room for daydreaming about utopia. West Germany does not preach a crusade against poverty, ignorance, disease, and unemployment. It is East Germany who does that and puts up a wall to prevent mass escape to the capitalist jungle where all sixteen million of its people would rather be. The results of this German experiment of the collective as against the individualist society could scarcely be clearer—therefore they must be explained away by our contemporary ideologists by introducing other factors. So must the Hungarian and Polish revolts. Or when these have been clubbed down then a theory of social evolution is called upon to describe the immanent and permanent change in the compassionate revolution that lies just ahead.

Conservatives are mistrustful of governmental power because unlike private economic power it cannot be offset by counter forces. The American-born Japanese had no possible recourse against being put into concentration camps. When the government ordered their arrest and transportation and the Supreme Court held this incredible act legal, that was that. No remotely parallel private economic power exists, and if it did conservatives would oppose it. Private enterprise is hedged round by competition, by public acceptance of its products, by labor unions, by laws, by the readiness of its people to work for it. No unrestrained economic power exists in the private sector of this society. Only government has the unrestrained power to tax and inflate; to determine how much money may be kept by a citizen and the rate of attrition of his savings.

No conservative believes a collective effort as such to be deleterious. Technology of itself imposes a highly articulated common effort on industrial and farm complexes, on transportation, on almost every byway and activity of contemporary life in an industrial society.

But there is a vast difference between the voluntary cooperation of individuals who remain persons in their economic and political life and the faceless *Massenmenschen* who are assigned their jobs and who shout their slogans, sign the political memorials handed to them, and mechanically vote one ticket. What conservatives are trying to do is to increase the chances for maximum development of each person in his own right to become as complete a human being as it is possible for him to be. Good or virtuous collective action for the conservative is action that is freely chosen. It has nothing to do with the staged demonstrations, the allegedly spontaneous resolutions of protest and approval or with the automatic voting that is solely conditioned by party edict or color or religion or income bracket.

Generations of tyrants as well as city bosses in the United States have wept for the poor and done their best to organize the ignorant and the unemployed. Were they more endowed with compassion than the conservative free-enterprisers who, when they had the opportunity, provided jobs and wages and goods in an affluent flood the like of which had never been seen before? If by their oratory you shall judge them then the tyrants and the city bosses, and sometimes their betters, have been filled with the utmost compassion; but if by their works you shall judge that is something else again. The poor remain poor, many of them ignorant and in want; they have merely been given handouts to tide them over.

It is interesting in this connection to take a look at the urban renewal program in the United States. A recent article by a liberal writer declares it a failure; he reports that the rentals on the new dwelling units erected under the program in New York are now running to some $192 a month and that the former slum dwellers, who are a long way from being able to afford such sums, are moving to new slums.[3] Conservative critics have long pointed to the obvious flaws in this grandiose program, not because they like slums or poverty but because they are dubious of a government program to eradicate them by a bulldozing operation. To be sure, this attitude may seem on the surface to be lacking in compassion, but here are the words of the author of the article mentioned above:

> Suppose that the government decided that jalopies were a menace to public safety and a blight on the beauty of our highways, and therefore took them away from their drivers. Suppose, then, that to replenish the supply of automobiles, it gave these drivers a hundred dollars each to buy a good used car and also made special grants to General Motors, Ford, and Chrysler to lower the cost—although not necessarily the price of Cadillacs, Lincolns, and Imperials by a few hundred dollars. Absurd as this may sound, change the

3. Herbert J. Gans, "The Failure of Urban Renewal," *Commentary* (April 1965).

jalopies to slum housing, and I have described with only slight poetic license, the fifteen years of a federal program called urban renewal.

Conservatives were not arguing for slums when they made similar criticisms some years back; they just didn't believe that government planning could get rid of them in this fashion. Nor do they believe that more young people are made employable by a minimum wage that keeps them from being employed. Or that union monopoly is a better and more humane variety than that of the cartel. Nor is their view of the future possibility of a better world limited to that of a favored race or class. It is conservative economists who preach the need for free trading areas that encompass as many countries as care to join, a work force that is free to move where the jobs and pay are best, and it is conservative writers who fight the collectivist ideological tide that threatens to drown any opposition. Protesting their own interests? Not in the present academic climate in the United States. Universities and the great foundations don't like the idea of forwarding the teaching of "conservatism and inhumanity."

Yet it is the conservative with his notions of prudence and moderation and balance of power who has steadily opposed the radicals and the dictatorships of the Right and Left, who believes in the ability of men to choose the good or the less evil without having the choice made for him. It is he who has sought slum clearance, not by forcible removals but by way of creating economic opportunity and the desire not to live in a slum; who has fostered the conquest of ignorance by attempting to educate individuals to use their intellectual resources as far as they can go; who for years has made possible the attack on disease by way of free research without resorting to publicity campaigns to dazzle Congress, or driving five hundred doctors a year to emigrate as has happened in Great Britain. It is the conservative who has wanted unemployment to be conquered by increasing productivity and jobs; as for compassion, he believes that is manifest in the relationship between persons. On a political scale it becomes little more than occupational hand-wringing and the buying of votes.

Camus has called this the age of servitude, a sweeping characterization that could all too easily describe it within a short period. The technological resources are at hand to make the kind of nightmare world that Orwell foresaw, and those intellectuals who run in packs are its advance guard. Big Brother loves all his people but on the great plans for transmuting the lot of the impoverished and ignorant he builds his state.

After the Night of
the Long Knives

In this issue of *Modern Age*, Ernest van den Haag has drawn up a legal bill of rights which, like all bills of rights, is intended to apply to the entire citizenry without undue regard to color or race.[1] One suspects, however, that any such legalistic statement, no matter how compelling its logic, will evoke little enthusiasm among the crusading whites and Negroes who are the dynamic forces of the Negro revolution. Revolutions in their nature are extremist; they feed on sentiments and emotions and they have small use for any logic or scientific observation that cannot be turned to account for the conquest of the next objective of their struggle—in this case the goal of absolute equality.

What we have been experiencing, not only in our own society but throughout the world, is the end of a political and technological apprenticeship of the underdeveloped colored races, especially of the Negro. Over a period of some hundreds of years the Negro in Africa, in the Caribbean, in South America as well as in the United States learned the language and the ceremonies of the white man; he learned to use his science and technology, his medicine, his machines, his way of living, his way of thinking. But for the most part he learned to master the use of these things, not how to invent or create their new forms. That kind of thinking, on a considerable scale, must doubtless come in the new phase which is upon us. Up to now the Negro has been largely a manipulator either of what he has earned the right to have or of what has been given him, and as a result of this history, whatever the Supreme Court may say, he is not in his own mind or in that of the white community a full-fledged member of the predominantly white culture.

One of the bitterest books to be written by a Negro in these last years, *The Wretched of the Earth*, has come from the pen of an Algerian Negro, Franz Fanon, a doctor with psychiatric training obtained in Paris. Dr. Fanon attacks the white race with its own weapons of higher learning; he is filled with hatred of the white race as such, of its delusions of superiority, of its imperialism, its contempt, its brutality, its lust for power.

---

1. Ernest van den Haag, "Negroes and Whites: Claims, Rights and Prospects." *Modern Age* 9, no. 4 (fall 1965).

His heroes are the oppressed, the exploited, the victims of the *Herrenrasse* delusion, and to qualify for a place in this category they must be colored; no white man is eligible. The publisher's biographical sketch of Dr. Fanon tells us that when he was taken ill in his mid-thirties with an incurable cancer he was brought to a hospital in Washington which, although it could not save his life, was obviously the best he could turn to with its accumulation of medical lore and instruments that had been developed in Europe and the Orient and among the Arabs, but very little among the Negroes. This he made use of in his hour of need as he had used the white man's psychiatry; but for a Negro who considered the whites a race of devils the hospital's medicines must have been especially hard to swallow.

A similar kind of ambivalent rejection may be observed in James Baldwin's *Another Country*. Baldwin's characters, however, whether black or white detest one another; they may have remissions when for a short time they rejoin a quasi-normal society that includes friendship and affection, but mainly they come together only briefly, bisexually or homosexually, whether in miscegenation or with their own race, to end in a fury of hostility. Everything is permitted in Baldwin's world and everything turns into a horror for it takes place in a society that remains balefully dominated by the white man no matter how hard the Negro pounds against its walls.

Such books are far removed from their predecessors of only a short time ago; the resolute and sympathetic Negroes of Joyce Cary's and Alan Paton's Africa, the prewar American Negro autobiographies and commentaries, the novels by both blacks and whites of that period. I mention Baldwin's and Fanon's books because they are an erudite and eloquent statement of the emotions of the Negro revolution that we have witnessed in these last few years. They are as uncompromising in their way as the Black Muslims in theirs, as extreme as the riots and the passions of the mobs, and they well out of the same sources.

The Negroes and the whites who crusade with them essentially want history to begin afresh, to be recorded on a new tape; they want the white man in a huge act of penitence to redress the past, to undo it, to unmake the Negro everywhere from what he has been in his apprenticeship stage into the copartners of the entire white community, of its status groups, of its leadership. Nowhere do they hold the Negro to account for his own failures or transgressions because it is solely the white society that has degraded him, kept him from assuming his full stature. Atrocities in the Congo, acts of violence committed by Negroes in the American subways or on city streets are the white man's fault, the fault of a society that has only exploited and humiliated the Negro and made it impossible for him to forget that he is of another color. It is the white man's atrocious behavior that accounts for the low estate of mankind. As Baldwin, I believe it was, wrote some time ago, the gas ovens of Auschwitz took away for all time any claim of the white race to moral superiority.

And it is undoubtedly true that Adolf Hitler has made his contribution to the Negro revolution. The notion of biological racial inequality could not possibly survive the millions of deaths that could be ascribed to it.

But in any event, revolutionists have no time for self-criticism; their cause has exploded out of an accumulation of grievances both real and imagined and they move outward against the barricades and toward their vision. The children of the revolution can do no wrong; only the enemy is guilty. When in the nineteenth century the African Negro looked at the white man and characterized him in sculpture and drawings he made plain his mixed admiration and fear of the white man's *mana;* the guns are there, the bearers carrying their white burden, but at the same time the Negro ridiculed the white man, caricatured him for his absurd and prestigious ways. It was for the most part amiable criticism, the white man was of another inscrutable world, he could be brought down to the African earth with satirical strokes of the chisel or brush but he remained a being whom it was sensible to placate. The Negro, however, was learning to use the guns and the books the white man brought, he was learning the language of the white man's power. In the United States another kind of adaptation occurred. The American Negro in the back-to-Africa movement of the twenties, to be sure a crackpot affair, asserted his Negro qualities by rejecting the white man's civilization lock, stock, and barrel, as some years later the Black Muslims would do in another context, or he demanded to be like the white man. Negro newspapers were poor carbon copies of the white ones with advertisements for hair straighteners taking the place of those for lotions against uncurled hair, otherwise they were written on more or less the same pattern from social notes to politics. The actual life of the Negro communities was far richer, it had more laughter and affection and style to it than was recorded in its press, but when the Negro returned home it was to a segregated society and it was there thousands of Negroes preferred to be. Carl Van Vechten's famous novel about a Harlem that three decades later would be regularly labeled a ghetto was called *Nigger Heaven* because Harlem for Negroes throughout America was a promised land. The Negro lived in a world that was separate from that of the white man and where they intersected he accepted the white man's standards. That was as true in Africa and the Caribbean as it was in the United States.

The wave of rebellion, of revolution, is to be understood as something churned up by demagogues and political opportunists. It is too massive, too powerful for that. City bosses, political candidates of all descriptions may make use of it, but it gathers its strength and power apart from any local geography. South Africa has imposed its own solution on the Negro rising, a solution that is based on a continuation of the apprenticeship stage, but we have yet to see how successful that can be in the face of the stirrings and upheavals in the rest of Africa and the resistance to the apartheid measures among many whites both in South Africa and the rest of the world.

It appears in fact that this revolution was inevitable; once the techniques of the white man were available to the Negro, and they had to be made available both for his own sake and the white man's purposes, the Negro would only need so much time to master them. And once he had mastered them he would demand that the wages for his mastery would entail desegregation of the edges of the political and social world in the same fashion that much of the realm of technology had been desegregated. As Professor van den Haag points out, however, it is not enough to demand; for a marriage the consent of both parties is needed and the consent of the white man is, aside from the crusaders, only partial and restricted, a segregated consent. So-called Fair Housing is voted down 2-1 in California—and this before the August riots; the Negro must depend on the courts and on a minority of intellectuals to carry that phase of the battle for equality further.

But essentially the next phase depends largely on the Negro. It is he, with his vastly increased access in higher learning, his political and economic power, who must take the next big step toward a de facto equality. The chances may be multiplied by the kind of action that van den Haag describes on the part of the whites who go out of their way to find places in the universities and in business for qualified Negroes, but the qualifications must be supplied by the Negroes themselves. Only thus will they take an equal part in the second cycle of their acclimatization to the white culture. They must contribute now to its genesis, its range of intellectual disciplines, to its political and social integrity as well as to its music and literature.

Are there signs that they are capable of doing this? Far more signs, I believe, than one would detect in the violence and bitterness of the mobs and in the writings of the intellectuals. These indications make no headlines but they are evident in large and small affairs. A Negro is one of the best students in a good private school for which he has been tutored by volunteers among its alumni. Another young Negro is a competent architect but until he was granted a special scholarship arranged for him he was working as a janitor like his father before him. As Professor van den Haag points out, employment opportunities are fewer for Negroes; architect or janitor, there was nothing between. Further, the quality of writing, of research of a purely intellectual kind is demonstrably higher in the last few years in communities where the Negro has had freer access to first-rate universities. I have already told the story in these pages of the dissertations written in the Caribbean by Negroes who had gone to British universities and how superior they were to material in the same field from American Negroes in the South. Such a degree of professional competence can only be developed by capable men who have been given at least the same opportunity to develop their talents as their white contemporaries have had. These men had mastered the techniques, they were doing precisely the same kind of original investigations as their white colleagues and it was of the same quality. Whoever had granted those Negroes their degrees had made no gesture of condescension; the Negroes had earned them on the same terms as had the white men in their universities, although it may have taken far more effort to get them into the universities.

The Negro revolt has made plain the stereotyped inequalities, the massive indifference to the Negro as an individual when it came to being admitted to a restaurant or hotel or to a school or polling booth. These barriers are now down but those that remain are far more formidable, for no law except the role of Christian charity declares that you must accept the Negro on his merits as a person because you want him to be a full-fledged member of the society in which you live and work. As Professor van den Haag says, to be judged as an individual is what every Negro wants and that is what he is entitled to in the American society of the 1960s.

The Baldwins and the Fanons have expressed their disgust with the white man but they have done no more than to project the negative qualities of human beings of every color onto the whites. The defects of the Negro and of the white man are poured into this witches' brew. And yet the process of acculturation goes on; the unpretentious efforts of Negroes and whites who are giving their energies to developing the Negro to participate in the creative processes of the technological society are bearing fruit. Negroes are doing research, they are taking part in the business, scientific, and university world as well as in the arts; as they continue in increasing numbers to do this and as they accept the responsibility for being what they are, the invisible barriers will go down too.

Where the
Twain Do Meet

The United States has been fortunate in some of its enemies, and it may also be said that its late enemies may rejoice in having had the United States at hand in the days of their reconstruction. For while American foreign policy for a considerable time was made under the illusion that with the defeat of the two chronically aggressive powers, Germany and Japan, a new world order of peace-loving nations would emerge, it soon had to take account of the harsh realities of the postwar world; and once it did the United States helped rebuild these countries with almost the same energy and enthusiasm it had given their destruction. Both Japan and Germany bear witness to the wisdom of the policy of generosity; they are admiring allies, far more sympathetic to American purposes than is, for example, the France of de Gaulle, and they reject what may be called their un-American past as thoroughly as does the United States.

The economic recovery of Japan, nourished by American aid, has been even more spectacular than the Bundesrepublik's. Starting from zero in 1945, Japan by 1965 was one of the great industrial powers of the world; the third-largest producer of steel behind only the United States and the Soviet Union; the world's fourth-largest automobile manufacturer, the fourth-largest producer of electrical power and the third-largest importer of oil. Its shipbuilding industry, accounting for 58 percent of Japanese plant exports, is the first in the world—even shipping companies in West Germany, long a center of maritime construction, have given contracts to Japanese shipyards. Japan ranks fifth in gross national product following the United States, West Germany, the United Kingdom, and France. Its growth rate of industrial production has been steadily higher than that of any other nation, increasing at an average of some 10 percent a year— and in the next years when the expansion is expected to taper off it is projected at 7 percent, or double that of the United States.

The American contribution to this phenomenal recovery was not only the $2 billion of direct aid and credits plus huge procurement orders; it was also an increment of the American presence, of the American desire to make things work as God and the founding fathers intended them to. In addition, of course, there was a new enemy abroad, more formidable

119

than the old. The United States demanded no indemnities of Japan; Americans in the occupation were forbidden to buy land or shares in Japanese companies and the American armed forces provided for the security of Japan's frontiers without the Japanese having to pay taxes to maintain a large army, navy, or air force. Japan spends some 8 percent of her national budget on defense, a figure that compares with 40 percent before the war and 75 percent in 1941. Land reform initiated by the Americans has virtually eliminated tenant farming, largely by abolishing absentee ownership—tenant farming has gone down from 50 percent before the war to 10 percent; universal suffrage was introduced as was a free trade union movement that has organized some 36 percent of the labor force.

Up to 1948 the United States was bent on reforming Japan through a social and political revolution that would take power and prestige from the groups that had formerly held it and spread their benefits and the wealth of the country among the peasants, workers, and middle classes— a program as revolutionary as any originating in Moscow. In Japan as in Germany in the early days of the occupation the Left was favored; former bureaucrats and big businessmen were purged and imprisoned; Communists and others who had been in jail for political reasons were immediately released and often given preferred jobs. In both Japan and Germany big business was held responsible by American policy makers for the military aggression of the former governments of those countries; not only did all high *Zaibatsu* (big business) executives lose their jobs but they were also subject to a capital levy that in the case of the great fortunes rose to 90 percent. The Americans first planned, as they had in Germany, to break up all the largest industrial companies, but this proved impracticable and only a few out of three hundred were "decartelized."

Many influential Americans, including "liberals" such as Dean Acheson and Elmer Davis, demanded, before the end of war, the abdication of the emperor, and there was considerable sentiment favoring his trial as a major war criminal; but because a few conservatives such as former Ambassador Joseph Grew and the present Ambassador Edwin Reischauer knew the situation in Japan and fought for their views, "unconditional surrender" was modified and the Mikado was permitted to remain on the throne as a constitutional monarch. The new constitution drawn up by the Japanese under American guidance confirmed the emperor's renunciation of any claim to divinity that he had made on New Year's Day of 1946; it declared that the emperor derived his position "from the will of the people with whom resides sovereign power."

The Diet elected by universal suffrage was declared the sole lawmaking body; the former hereditary and appointive House of Peers was abolished and replaced by an elected House of Councilors second in importance in its legislative functions to the more broadly based House of Representatives. The constitution not only provided for the formal balance of forces that American democracy regards as fundamental to its purposes, including an independent judiciary under a Supreme Court, but also provided that the membership of the Supreme Court be submitted to a popular vote every ten years.

It went further; it added rights that have not yet appeared in many Western constitutions—for example, "the right to maintain the minimum standards of wholesome and cultured living," "the right to receive an equal education and the right and obligation to work." Compulsory education was extended from six to nine years, and while the American-sponsored reforms of the school system, designed to make it conform more closely to practices in the United States, caused, as they did in occupied West Germany, considerable confusion, they also helped spread more formal education among more people than ever before in Japan.

Thus the plus side of the balance sheet is a large one. Under the influence of the crushing defeat and the uplifting American ideals for other countries the Japanese in their constitution solemnly renounced war "as a sovereign right of the nation" and declared they would do forever without land, sea, and air forces. For a time, almost everything the Americans wanted them to think or do the Japanese thought and did. They were accustomed to authority and now they dutifully set out to make themselves respectable and successful like the Americans. Citizens of any Western nation traveling in Japan are automatically considered American until it can be proved otherwise. To be American means to be progressive, up-to-date, it means being self-confident and prosperous, and the desire to attain these virtues leads to emulation, to study of American mores, habits, and methods, as well as to envy and resentment.

The Japanese have always borrowed heavily from other cultures—from China, from Korea, and from the West—and the Industrial Revolution was made to order for their talents. A disciplined people, working frictionlessly together in large groups, gifted technicians and scientists, they could readily turn their energies released from feudal and militaristic bonds to the skills and payoffs of the American way of life. With real wages increasing every year, with a standard of living much higher than that of any other oriental nation and by the 1960s close to that of Italy, the principle of "prosperity through peace," through following the lead of the United States, had demonstrated its magic. Some of the prosperity had nothing to do with peace; on the contrary it was a result of war, for it was during the Korean War that the United States turned to Japan with huge procurement orders as well as with an invitation to consider changing her position with regard to her own defense.

And it was at this point that Japanese policy began to show serious signs of diverging from that of the United States. Japan had had more than enough of war; her people had been repeatedly told by their conquerors that her army and navy and her big business had been responsible for the catastrophe that had befallen her, and since business, including big business, was manifestly doing well by the country the Japanese concentrated their passion for peace on political resistance to any attempts to rearm or to become involved in any armed conflict. Reluctantly, they have increased what they call the "self-defense forces," for it would not be peace-loving enough to have merely "defense forces," to some 280,000 men in the three branches of the armed services, but they want no more than such modest numbers nor do they want those forces to be used outside the country. The security treaty with the United States that was passed by the Diet over bitter opposition led to the downfall of the Kishi cabinet; the American use of Okinawa as a military base is such an explosive political issue that when Prime Minister Eisako Sato visited there in the autumn of 1965, he had to take refuge in an American guest house against the demonstrators protesting the status of the island. It was owing to the violence of the mobs shouting against the signing of the security treaty that the Japanese government felt it necessary to withdraw its invitation to President Eisenhower to visit the country in 1960; and again in the autumn of 1965 the protests and demonstrations of Japanese farmers and others imported from the cities succeeded in stopping the firing tests of American missiles with atomic warheads on the Mt. Fuji practice range.

At least a large minority of the population is represented in these demonstrations. The conservative, Liberal-Democratic Party has some 60 percent of the seats in the Diet—the Socialists and other left-wing parties share the rest. The labile Japanese intellectuals on whom the Americans in the beginning had cast a benign eye are mainly left wing; newspaper articles in major papers are often thinly veiled Communist propaganda. But while the left wing, with its appeal to young people still revolting against the conservatism of their elders, gains about 1 percent a year in the balloting, it is sharply divided on every issue but the campaign for the "peace front." The small Communist party has been taken over by the Red Chinese faction, although an unreconstructed Moscow wing remains.

The moderate left are strong supporters of parliamentary democracy and the gradations run from these people to those who want to destroy it.

It is not easy to see how it can be destroyed so long as prosperity continues, along with an exhilarating freedom of thought and a standard of living unprecedented in Japanese history or in that of any other Asian country. Since 1963, however, there has been some economic recession; small enterprises working on borrowed capital have been squeezed out of the competitive race; wages have risen but so has the cost of living, which goes up at the rate of 6.4 percent a year. Japan has an inflation not far behind its rate of industrial growth. Nevertheless, she has transformed her economy, producing first-rate products competing with the best of those from Europe and the United States, and her rapid industrialization has turned her lovely countryside wherever it is level and habitable into an almost continuous chain of dusty, towering, conglomerate cities. Despite this urbanization, by virtue of her scientific agriculture, she is almost self-sufficient in food and the formerly explosive birth rate has fallen to one of the lowest in the world. The population increase is now slightly more than 1 percent a year, and the downward trend permits the prediction that the population will soon stabilize at a hundred million, a number the islands can support in reasonable comfort.

Thus the Japanese recovery, both physical and psychological, is a remarkable one. The Japanese alone among the peoples of Asia have solved their birth control problem; they have achieved a standard of living that is not only the highest in Asia but that may be compared with Europe's, they have democratized their society and politics, and they are at peace with the world. They are foot-dragging allies of the United States when the peace is threatened; although a large section of the population understands American reasons for armed intervention against Communist expansion, much nonsense is written about American "aggression" in Vietnam and there is no sentiment for sending any Japanese self-defense forces to that country to help out. The bombing of Hiroshima, however, is attributed not to American brutality as the Communists tell them, but to the blindness of their own military leaders. In 1970 the security treaty with the United States will come up for renewal and the concerted aim of the left-wing parties will be to prevent by all the means at their command its being continued. Resting securely in their enclave behind the Seventh Fleet, the American air bases, and the American army, the moderates among the Japanese left can indulge themselves in dreams of neutralism while Red China hurls its threats against imperialists that include their own nation. The members of the far left can prepare for the glorious day when Mao Tse-tung or his successor liberates Japan from its full rice bowls and soaring wages, and its "subservience" to the United States, which absorbs more than 27 percent of Japan's exports, and in their place imposes the controlled economy that drove Hong Kong to close its borders against the hordes of Chinese daily attempting to flee.

Nevertheless, Japan of the mid-1960s is a boom country, turning eagerly to American styles real or imaginary, to jazz, sandwiches and hot dogs, and advertising signs leading to their places of natural and man-made beauty. Japan's traditional, delicate patina is rapidly disappearing in an anonymous international style. "Moon watching" on the hills, "poetry washing" in the neighborhood of the shrines is submerged by Hollywood's cowboy TV and movies. The crime rate is up as is juvenile delinquency; a good many drunks are to be seen on the streets. A few may even occasionally manage to stagger up the steps to the austere Shinto shrines where the Japanese sense of form and mystery has for centuries made a place of abiding and sober communication between the gods and their people. Reverence, awe, these too have diminished.

What would the Japanese do in the event of a serious economic depression? Dependent as ever on foreign trade for their life, would they turn to the East if punitive tariffs or a depression cut down their Western markets? China hasn't much available to export that Japan needs, but Japan has almost everything that China needs to develop her planned economy. Could China, could the Soviet Union provide alternatives to the West? Communist foreign policies conform more to political than economic needs—witness the Russians in Cuba, the Red Chinese in Africa—and they would make considerable economic sacrifices to penetrate Japan. The Japanese are not a fickle people; devotion to a leader and a cause is an ancient tradition celebrated in their history and drama and they have good reason to be devoted to the United States; although good reasons, too, could be found and have been by the left wing to be critical of wartime bombings that can be said to have gone far beyond military targets. Japan has been revolutionized on an American pattern with a marked loss of grace and aesthetic sensitivity, but with more vitality released in a far more open society than she or any other Asian country has ever known in the past. Like the West Germans, the Japanese were struck to the ground and raised again by the hand that had smitten them, raised despite *dirigiste* policies that if long pursued with a less resourceful people might have turned them into a welfare state. This is an unusual event among nations and one that is unlikely to be repeated should the Red Chinese or Moscow ever get the opportunity to try their hands.

1966

The Chinese and the Human Sea

The Chinese have long dealt in metaphors; literateurs like Ezra Pound have thought this poetic practice to be connected with the form of the written language where the character, the so-called ideograph, is not as far removed from the object as is the case in Western writing. However dubious this interpretation may be linguistically, the observation is nevertheless accurate so far as it has to do with a Chinese way of communicating with one another and with foreign peoples. The proclamation of "the Three Red Banners" under which "The Great Leap Forward" was to take place in Red China in 1958 followed the speech of the chief of the propaganda department on the "Harmonious Blooming of a Hundred Flowers," wherein criticism was to be encouraged and party differences were to be acknowledged and reconciled. None of these metaphors worked out in precise terms. A totalitarian system cannot tolerate for long any differences of opinion, whether or not they be likened to the flowers of the field, and the proclamation, after spectacular gains had been made in heavy industry in the Great Leap Forward, was followed by a catastrophic famine and huge industrial losses. Steel production, which between 1953 and 1957 had gone up over 200 percent, plunged down 40 percent in 1960—and between April 1960 and November 1961 ten million people died of starvation. Although harvests have improved since then, the failure of the agrarian revolution may be measured in part by the food China has had to buy abroad ever since 1961, food, may it be noted, that came entirely from capitalist countries. It has been estimated that each Chinese in this last year received some sixteen hundred calories a day, a considerable improvement on the figures of a few years ago, but still 20 percent under those of 1933.

The human toll has been high, not only from natural causes and the failure of the blueprints to work but by the deliberate hand of the party; some ten to twelve million people were executed between 1949 and 1958; an additional fifteen million were sent to forced-labor camps.[1] Nevertheless, the revolution lurches ahead; landlords have been expropriated and

1. Jürgen Domes, *Politik and Herrschaft in Rotchina* (Stuttgart, Berlin, Köln, Mainz: Kohlhammer Verlag, 1965).

127

liquidated, the traditional family system has been replaced by communes; revolts of the despairing peasants have been crushed, but production in the mainly stagnant economy of these last years has risen in electricity and oil, fertilizers, and farm equipment. Minor concessions have been made to the peasants: in 1962 farmers in the People's Communes were given permission to cultivate small plots of land for their own use and to sell the produce on the free market, but immediately the noose was tightened again; 60 percent, it was decreed, of any profit from such sales must go to the state and part of the produce must be sold to the commune at fixed prices.

The people live and die under the iron rule of a fanatical ideology, its barbarous methods and its poetry. They are "the human sea" that nothing can withstand—130 million more Chinese were alive in 1963 than a decade before. Since Red China, despite the explosions of her atomic bombs, lacks everything in comparison to the industrialized nations, the Chinese metaphors bridge the gap. It is people and not the machinery of war that count; machines may destroy and kill, but the human sea is indestructible and it will engulf its enemies.

Chief among these enemies is the United States. The Chinese minister of war, Lin Piao, has rung changes on the metaphor: China is organizing the forces of an agrarian world against the cities; China is the leader of the peoples of Asia, Africa, and Latin America who can tear apart the United States "piece by piece, some striking at its head, some at its feet." Early in 1966 the army was told it must be prepared to carry out orders to fight the imperialists "even if this involves climbing a mountain of pointed swords and crossing an ocean of flames." Thus the war is to be waged on many fronts and with every means: in Vietnam, in Africa, in the Balkans; and the internecine struggle with Soviet Russia for leadership in the Communist world is based on the Red Chinese refusal to wait for the processes of history to accomplish the final defeat of its imperialist enemies. The war in Vietnam is not only a just war, it is a useful war from the point of view of Red China: it is a war where the enormous technological superiority of the United States cannot be fully brought to bear; where immemorial discontents and the slogans of the revolution against imperialism are powerful not only among the peoples of Asia and Africa but in Europe and the United States as well. It is a conflict made to order for the wolf pack circling around the preserves of its future victims.

These are the metaphors, but bleak realities are near at hand. Red China has taken over Tibet and invaded India but not only has she been unable to capture the islands of Quemoy and Matsu, she has been forced to witness the transformation of the island of Formosa, under the arch-enemy Chiang Kai-shek, into an anti-Communist bastion second only to Japan in the Far East in its well-being and rate of economic growth. With American aid the government of the Republic of China has accomplished a revolution nearly as striking in its success as Japan's. It is in Formosa—Taiwan—that the great leap forward has taken place. Taiwan has the second-highest living standard in Asia. Tenant farming has been reduced from 40 percent to 14 percent, and where twelve years before 36 farmers out of every 100 had owned their own land and 25 percent were part-owners, in 1964 the number was 66 and 21 percent were part-owners. Between 1949 and 1964 agricultural production went up 74 percent and industrial output 304 percent. Rice, the basic crop, was up 43 percent in the same period, the production of timber has more than doubled, fisheries produce more than four times what they did a decade ago, and new crops have been introduced. The number of factories has also more than doubled as new industries have been started manufacturing lamps, plate glass, rayon, pharmaceuticals, refrigerators, and television sets. Exports are up 287 percent over 1952 while imports have risen 98 percent. Formosa's growth rate has been twice that of its neighboring states, excluding Japan, Australia, and New Zealand, despite the fact that defense spending takes up half the budgets of the central and provincial governments.

As was the case in Japan, this American-sponsored revolution has been on the whole a beneficent one. Landlords were not expropriated, they were paid in land bonds and stock of government industrial enterprises; farmer buyers amortized their loans over a period of ten years paying at about the same rate they would have as tenants. Before the land reform, tenants had turned over as high as 70 percent of their harvests to the landlords; beginning in 1949 a maximum payment of 37.5 percent was permitted. In 1951 about 230,000 acres of public land was transferred to individual farmers, and beginning in 1953 the government bought large tracts of land from absentee owners which were then sold to some 195,000 tenant families who in the course of ten years received full title to the property. In all almost six million acres of land were turned over to former tenants. Because of the lower rate of payments and the incentive of working on their own behalf the farmers have put money into buying fertilizers; they have groomed their land intensively and the yields have gone up accordingly.

In Red China 90 percent of the production is controlled by the state; in Formosa the government is steadily withdrawing from business.

State industries predominated in the early period of the nationalist administration of the island when Japanese property was sequestered after the war. The national and provincial governments still own a large share in some industries, the Taiwan Sugar Company and a pioneer aluminum company, for example, but they have sold the stocks of other companies to private investors. Whereas in 1952 39.5 percent of Taiwan's industrial production came from privately owned industries, in 1964 31.1 percent came from the public sector. Incentives to private industry have been offered through tax benefits, loans, and technical assistance.

Since 1951 the United States has poured almost a billion and a half dollars into the Formosan economy, into the production and distribution of electricity, communications, mining and industrial construction, transportation, and port facilities. So successful has the operation been that it could be ended in 1965—a rare event in aid to underdeveloped countries.

Taiwan has absorbed more than two million people who came to it from the mainland after the victory of communism, and the population now stands at something over twelve million who have to be supported on an island of some thirteen thousand square miles with only four thousand square miles of arable land, since two-thirds of the country is mountainous. Thus even including the mountains it has a population density of 770 people per square mile. The population growth has been high, 3.6 per thousand, but it is turning downward as a result of a birth control campaign similar to that of Japan. The island, however, is more than self-sufficient in food—agricultural production has better than doubled in the last fifteen years.

Formosa is a one-party state as far as the real power is concerned, but political life dominated by the Kuomintang and especially by the person of Chiang Kai-shek is nevertheless relatively free by Asian standards. Two parties exist outside the Kuomintang; the Young China Party and the Social Democratic Party, but they elect members mainly to local offices, and the central government is controlled by the Kuomintang. Although within the party there may be a fairly wide range of political opinion—from liberal socialist views to those of the extreme right—the Kuomintang is controlled by Chiang and his hierarchy. Neither criticism of Chiang nor any pro-Communist propaganda is permitted in Taiwan; but aside from such general prescriptions the political restraints are not to be compared with those of the mainland. A longtime enemy of the regime who once proclaimed himself Provisional President of the Government of Formosa, Thomas Liao, has returned to the island and described in a propaganda leaflet why he decided to make his peace with Chiang; Liao has been treated generously, he said, and he or for that matter any ex-Communist, providing he is ex, can return there and take part in the life of the community without reprisals. But they cannot preach separatism or cast any doubt on the legitimacy of Chiang's government. Professor Peng Ming-min of National Taiwan University was sentenced to eight years in prison for alleged activities on behalf of an independent Formosa. While the island's policy is far from that of the democratic processes of the West, Taiwan is an orderly and well-regulated state by the standards of its neighboring countries. It is also a state at war; a state at the frontier of the Communist orbit, open to infiltration by Red agents; its outermost islands have been under the attack of the mainland guns, its ships have successfully fought against the ships of Red China.

Still, it is a peaceful island. For centuries Chinese painters from the mainland traveled to Formosa, the Beautiful, to paint its landscapes, and it remains one of the garden spots of the world. A city like Taipei is not well lighted, especially when seen after the dazzling electrical displays of Japan, but it is safe. You may walk through the dark streets or a park late at night and nothing more than the importunities of the ladies of the evening or their male assistants will disturb you. Children may leave their homes to go to the late movies and neither coming nor going will they be slugged by their teenage contemporaries or by any other gangs. It is not that the police are so much in evidence; the streets are safe because the population is not given to violence.

The native Taiwanese, Chinese in race except for an aboriginal population of some 150,000 of Indonesian stock, saw the main government jobs taken over by the refugees from the mainland and have understandably resented the newcomers. American observers have reported considerable disaffection among these older inhabitants, but the native Taiwanese have certainly shared in the prosperity of the island, which flourishes as never before either under Japanese or Chinese rule. The fact is that Chiang and the officials of his mainland government who managed to come to Formosa after the defeat on the continent have had to learn from their bitter experience. The bureaucracy has been cut down, no opulent buildings have been constructed, for Taipei is merely the provisional capital. The government does not wish to waste money on building there; it hopes one day to return to Nanking. Until the Korean War, the nationalist leaders had little encouragement or aid from the United States. They were dispirited survivors of those who had ruled over half a billion people and they had gone down under the attacks of the human sea that had been swollen by many of their own followers. Their mistakes were patent, but it should be noted that they were not the only ones to make them. The miscalculation of American "liberals" about the nature of Mao's communism or despite the knowledge, the deliberate aid to him, are still evident: at least three of the foreign advisers now in Peking aiding the Mao government are Americans; two of them former members of the staff of the then Secretary of the Treasury, Henry Morgenthau, another Anna Louise Strong, who once edited *Soviet Russia Today.*

Many causes may be found for Chiang's failure to achieve on the continent of Asia what he has been able to accomplish in Formosa—the land reform, the agricultural and industrial progress, the political stability, the improvement in education—95 percent of the eligible children are enrolled in the elementary schools of Taiwan. Chiang was at war on the mainland against Japan and against internal enemies, and even assuming the subsequent know-how and desire to achieve basic reforms he had small opportunity to pursue them. And it may parenthetically be noted that one of the main charges made against his regime—its alleged corruption—has been often repeated in Communist China, leveled by the Communists themselves, when plans went wrong, against the Red bureaucracy.

That the free world of Hong Kong and the partly free one of Formosa are magnets for thousands of mainlanders cannot be doubted. Defectors appear in the offshore islands of Formosa, and in 1962 seventy thousand refugees went over the border to Hong Kong, a mass flight like that which led to the erection of the Berlin wall. Only in the case of the Chinese it was not alone the threat of dire punishment for attempted escapes that stemmed the tide but also the fact that Hong Kong felt compelled to send back a large proportion of those who had fled. Life is hard for the refugee in Hong Kong, but obviously not as hard as in his native land, and while he could he came over in droves. It is this discontent that makes Chiang and his advisers confident they will be able one day to return to the continent. Widespread revolts have taken place on the mainland, in parts of Hupei, Yunnan, Shensi, Kiansi, Chekiang, and Kiangsu that could be put down only after a bitter struggle. From the refusal of large numbers of Chinese soldiers to return home after they were captured in the Korean War, from intelligence reports, and from defectors, the nationalist government, like other exile governments, gets the news that leads it to hope that if one day it could land again on the mainland the countryside would rise to join it. Like Winston Churchill in 1940, with its army of a half million men the Formosan government says to the United States: "give us the tools and we will finish the job." By the tools it means transportation to the mainland, for the Taiwanese are already armed with American weapons. To an outsider the strategy seems largely composed of wishful thinking; the Nationalist army may be a good one but it is a fraction of the size of the land forces of Red China and it is easy to exaggerate the degree of disaffection in a Communist country. But it is also easy to minimize it and whatever the internal situation may be at a given time, the existence of the Formosan government is always seen as a major threat by Peking. The Republic of China lives a precarious diplomatic life; the recognition of Mao's government by France in 1964 was a heavy blow, and year after year the admission of Red China to the United Nations looms as a more likely possibility. But here, too, the battle is joined; Formosa also sends its technical advisers to Southeast Asia, the African countries, and to South America to compete with the emissaries of the Soviet Union and Red China; and above all it takes its vital place in the chain of defense in the East, in the war of which only one local manifestation is to be seen in Vietnam. It is a prospering and unsinkable island off the coast where the human sea rages against its enemies.

The Condition
Contrary to Fact

S ome years ago I read an account of an attempt on the part of a foreign-aid group from the United States to improve the lot of fishermen and the local population in one of the seacoast areas of China. The time was after World War II and before Mao Tse-Tung had completely taken power, when there was talk of a Chinese coalition government and Washington was eager to bring American know-how, goodwill, and resources to help solve the manifold problems of a country whose economy and politics were obviously in need of wholesale repair. For centuries Chinese fishermen had sailed from their harbors in boats designed for coastal waters, not for the deep sea; they had brought back their catches after a few days' fishing in nearby waters and sold their hauls on the docks. Sometimes the catch was poor, and the American teams sent out to produce plans for assuaging China's ancient troubles had a promising idea that was promptly acted upon. The Chinese fishermen were provided with efficient new boats and equipment with which they could range far beyond the former coastal limits to where the waters were no longer fished out and where they could find a dependable supply of protein to help feed the teeming population of the coastal area and the hinterland. But things didn't work out according to the blueprints. The fishermen caught more fish with their wider-ranging craft, many more fish. So many in fact that the catches piled up on the docks and the price of fish that could be sold plunged to such levels that the fishermen could not make a living. The American planners had forgotten that this part of China had no railroads, highways, or refrigeration; no way existed of transporting the surplus fish to the countryside where it could be sold and the people in the immediate area could not possibly deal with the mountains of fish that had to be consumed quickly if it was to be edible. Part of the population gratefully stuffed itself with cheap fish but the rest rotted on the docks and the fishermen cursed their benefactors.

You do not have to go as far as China to see the results of such incongruities between simplistic theory and reality. The Urban Renewal Program designed to provide low-cost housing mainly for the benefit of the Negro ghettos has been called the Negro Removal Program; it has destroyed thousands more dwelling places than it has built and

134

has often priced the new apartments out of the market of the poor, thus merely displacing the inhabitants of the former ghettos to other slums, farther away. A Rental Aid Program with similar high purposes is designed to break through ghetto walls and send people who otherwise could not afford to live there to neighborhoods where they can be integrated into a non-slum environment. It proposes to provide its clients with the additional funds necessary to pay for such accommodations after the recipients have paid out one-quarter of their salaries for rent. Like the majority of the present Supreme Court the planners obviously believe that the desirable end is what counts and the ingenious means must be contrived to bring the benefits of the affluent society to everyone. And yet the rent supplements under the proposed law are not to be paid directly to the tenants in their new neighborhoods but to the landlords. The framers of the law evidently have some knowledge of the experience of welfare agencies, which have found that paying out sums of money directly to the beneficiaries does not always result in their being used for the purposes the government intended. At any rate, the supplemental rent in this case is to be paid by the federal government to the owner of the building. And in the experimental projects where the plan has been tried out it is reported that the landlords or their agents make regular visits to the apartments where the new tenants live to make sure they are showing no signs of re-creating a slum in the environment to which they have been transplanted.

What is this experiment likely to do to the families who are moved to their more spacious apartments and neighborhoods? A television program showing some of the people installed in their new quarters near Washington filmed a family (obviously a large one) where the little girls and little boys may now have separate rooms instead of being always crowded together, and a landlord who declared that some of his subsidized tenants were so delighted with their quarters they were repainting them at their own expense. A pleasant scene, and one in contrast to the Chicago slum where Martin Luther King was televised carrying out a basket of debris from a ramshackle house. But one camera shot does not tell the whole story, or not at once. A few weeks after Dr. King was shown toting his basket down the stairs, the same house was again filmed, and in the course of that sequence the lawn was shown to be covered with garbage that had been thrown around three large, empty garbage cans. When one of the tenants who had been protesting against the sorry state of the house was asked who had dumped the garbage, she said she didn't know. This method, air mailing as it is called in Harlem, of treating garbage, is unlikely to be adopted or continued in the case of families moved to non-slum areas—to combat such habits is apparently one of the main purposes of providing the supplementary rent. But there are other matters that television cameras do not show. What is the effect of paying the supplementary rent directly to the landlord? Will it be taken as a sign of mistrust by the subsidized tenants? Is that the way the other people on the block pay their rent? And since every house, or apartment, is part of a community which has its mores and habits and values, however absurd they may seem to those of other communities, what about the mores and habits of the newcomers? Will they dress in the same way as the other people around them, share their standards, speak the same language, and have the same kinds of friends? If not, is there a supplement to provide them? A news item in the *New York Times* of April 16 reported that Negroes in the City College of New York, traditionally one of the most liberal of institutions with regard to racial, ethnic, or religious background, prefer to eat by themselves and to have Negroes as friends. One of the reasons given by the Negro students interviewed was that they felt more comfortable with Negroes than with whites; out of school hours they had different friends and during school they also preferred to be with one another. City College was never segregated, it never excluded Negroes from its student body on any pretext, and yet there is self-imposed segregation.

What are the well-meaning drafters of the rent supplement bill doing to the Negroes who accept its benefits? A society is a network of relationships—the people who live in a neighborhood not only pay about the same amounts for rent, they have usually saved and gone without and worked and striven to be there. The neighborhood represents their place on the totem pole. Are they likely to welcome or accept people who join them by way of supplements paid their landlords? And what will the arrangement do to the self-regard of the people who receive the benefits? One of the things they want, and rightly so, is to be accepted for what they are, essentially, as individuals; will they feel themselves to be interlopers, or citizens like all the others? If they are moving into a white neighborhood their status may not be enviable. A Negro family that tenaciously withstood the animosity of its white neighbors for a number of years in an eastern suburb has recently decided to move out and according to the newspaper reports the husband has been in the care of a psychiatrist. The white couple who adopted a Negro baby in California, finding its neighbors a bristling phalanx of antagonists, felt they had to give up the child. The attitudes of the neighbors aroused against the presence in their midst of a two-year-old child is undoubtedly deplorable but it is such prejudices and values, paltry as they are by more generous standards, that make a community what it is. Every society and sub-society in the world has its in-ways by which it distinguishes itself from outsiders, and nowhere will it be easier to distinguish the outsider than in the case of people who are ticketed from the beginning as different from all their neighbors in choosing to live where they do.

In this issue of *Modern Age*, William Henry Chamberlin tells of events in the New York suburb of Mount Vernon and in Boston as compulsory integration by busing and predetermined notions of a desirable percentage of racial balance have aroused the white citizenry.[1] Mount Vernon and Boston are by no means the only centers of violent protest. Other New York suburbs, the *New York Times* reports, are seething with a counter-revolt of the whites against proposed school mergers. In Hartsdale, for instance, the word "nigger" is being used for the first time in what the *Times* calls a sophisticated community where the word has long been taboo.

At the same meeting of conservatives to which another contributor to this issue of *Modern Age*, Professor Hutt, refers in his article,[2] a Negro scholar spoke on race relations. He told them what the audience clearly was ready to hear—that when a Negro has managed by his own efforts to break out of the ghetto, to join the American middle class, it would be heartening to find a welcome among them and a recognition of the all-out effort it had taken to get him there. Since he was talking to conservatives who believe in the supreme worth of the individual he was given just such a welcome, and it seemed to me he touched upon the heart of the matter. It is not through welfare and food packages and handouts or rent supplements that human beings of any color get their self-respect, their acceptance, their sense of belonging to a neighborhood, a community, a nation. On the contrary, handouts may be the source of the hopelessness and the hostility, the alienation we have seen so much evidence of, in part because they are never enough. Abject poverty, the hungry belly, must be alleviated in a society that will not tolerate them and that has the means to alleviate them, but handouts do not feed self-respect nor do they produce equality or first-class citizenship. In another recent outbreak that took place near Washington, Negro boys rioted at an amusement park and then damaged houses on their way home, even breaking the

1. William Henry Chamberlin, "Pitfalls of Forced Integration." *Modern Age* 10, no. 3 (summer 1966).
2. "Civil Rights and Young Conservatives." *Modern Age* 10, no. 3 (summer 1966).

windows of ambulances sent out to rescue some of those who had been injured. As Arthur Krock reported in the New York Times, these were not boys without money looking on at things they could not buy. They had money enough to be able to take over the rides of the amusement park they first were visiting and then were breaking up. They were spoiling to show "whitey" where he stood. They were boys brought up to believe they had implacable grievances that, as Martin Luther King had told them, gave them a right to break the law. It would take dedicatedly "liberal" or sadistic parents to want to send their children to school with them.

It is instructive to compare such behavior and the hostilities evident on both sides with reports of what has happened in the integrated units in Vietnam where Negroes are slightly higher in proportion to their white comrades than they are in the general population. Many a white boy has learned to respect the Negroes and many a Negro boy the whites who fight alongside him in a way that is only paralleled in civilian life in the field of sports. In battle Negroes lead mixed groups or take their places in ranks under white soldiers without resentment, and with, in many cases, a completely different sense of the worth of the other race than they have ever had in their lives before. Nor is the mutual respect, the comradeship, according to reports, limited to the combat areas; in their free time, too, the soldiers of both races often choose to be together.

The differences between this situation and the one at City College are owing in large part to the shared dangers, the ultimate test of men of any color in battle, the mutual trust and dependence that develop in an effective combat team. But this is surely not all. The relations are stripped of cant and traumas and the antics of both races. The soldiers do not react to one another by virtue of color but as men. On the domestic scene, on the other hand, blacks and whites are more than ever race-conscious. One may suspect that the drive on the schools, the demonstrations, the riots, the incessant demands, and the unruly behavior of Negro mobs in the United States have had their effect in shifting a hitherto friendly attitude on the part of many whites toward the Negro to a far more critical one. One may ask whether such a violent reaction to the presence of a two-year-old child in the midst of a white community in California would have occurred before the riots at Watts had taken place. Or whether the people of Boston, that center of abolitionist sentiment at the time of the Civil War, would have made any issue at all of an integration that was not imposed upon them under a dubious theory of a healthy racial balance to be achieved at the expense of all their traditions clustering about the neighborhood school.

The rightfulness of much of the Negro protest is beyond dispute. To read the autobiographies of Malcolm X and Claude Brown[3] is to see how two bright young men were cut off from the mainstream of American society because they were Negroes. The white eighth-grade schoolteacher of the intelligent Malcolm X told him he should give up any idea of being a lawyer and concentrate instead on becoming a carpenter. The teacher apparently did not know that it was harder in many parts of the country for a Negro to become a carpenter against union resistance than to be a lawyer. But it was a white staff member of a reform school who gave Claude Brown the first notion he ever had that there might be something in the world besides dope and sex and hipstering. The hatred Malcolm X worked up against the white race is the rage of the gifted outsider who finds no way to get in. Malcolm X lived in white neighborhoods, went to an integrated school; what he needed is what Professor Hutt suggests may be the main solution to the Negro problem: not rent supplements, but the opportunities of the really open society of the capitalist marketplace where he could get any job and the training for any job he was competent to do, regardless of the prejudices of eighth-grade teachers or of trade unions. The chance for the Negro lies in his being given an equal opportunity to earn his full place in the American society, and this can never be done by rent subsidies or handouts. On the contrary, they are structured to fix his special status, to keep him as a special case within the white man's domain. What the Negro needs in order to feel like a first-class citizen as he apparently does in Vietnam and in specific American communities—business, artistic, academic, and scientific—is to earn the title after he is given every chance and perhaps a little bit more. But the handout, the supplement is not a genuine way of life; it creates its own portable ghetto wherever it becomes one.

3. *The Autobiography of Malcolm X*, with the assistance of Alex Haley (New York: Grove Press, 1965). Claude Brown, *Manchild in the Promised Land* (New York: Macmillan, 1965).

The Wave of the Past

When in the summer of 1914 the young men of Europe marched forth to war from under the flowers that had been showered upon them by their exultant fellow countrymen and countrywomen, swept along by their own conviction of the righteousness of their cause and their longing to rescue the fatherland from its peril, neither they nor their leaders had any idea of the kind of war it would turn out to be. Uhlans rode into battle with their lances, poilus in the bright uniforms of another century; it was the cut and thrust and headlong charge on the bloody but glorious field of battle depicted on the canvases that filled the museums and the history books that they saw before them— not the fields of mud, the mechanical mass slaughter of the trenches. Learned books have been written on the failure of the generals not only to foresee what would happen, but also, after the war started, to learn from what had happened; of the generals' clinging to historical habits of thought and practice while hundreds of thousands of men died of their arteriosclerosis. The preparations for World War II were far more adaptable, in part no doubt because of the criticisms that had been made of what had occurred in World War I, and the lessons that were drawn from the experimental battlefield in Spain. But even so, the Poles again sent lancers into the field and a more advanced military theory, attempting to wrench itself free of past errors, envisaged such a wide range of possibilities that almost nothing was left out. It was the German army more than any other that in 1939 selected and combined from among the vast choices presented by these theories the mechanized, motorized, and airborne army of specialists and foot-sloggers that produced the blitzkrieg. It was the then current blueprint of the National Socialist revolution that made it impossible to turn these victories into anything more than armed occupations, under military force and a secret police, that imposed the necessity to expand further. But the ineptitudes, as in the case of World War I, were international. The French had more tanks on the western front in 1939 than did the Germans, they had more troops, and they had the world's most renowned system of fortifications, which had been superimposed on the world's most renowned system of alliances— a massing in the early and mid-thirties of the forces of Europe against the German Reich so overwhelming as to represent, on paper at least, the greatest coalition of all time: Russia, Czechoslovakia, Poland, Great Britain, Belgium, Yugoslavia. It was a formidable array, and it fell apart in a matter of months.

Wrong and stupid judgments, miscalculations, brainlessness can have more deadly consequences more quickly in the twentieth century than they had in the nineteenth or in the centuries before it. It is one thing to misdirect an army and lose a great battle in which a few thousand men are deployed, after which a peace treaty shifts the lines of states that were changed before and will be changed again as the luck or the genius of battle changes and the fortunes of states ebb and flow in the accepted context of a Western order; it was another thing to make a similar miscalculation in 1914 and again in 1939 and it is still another in the late 1960s. When Adolf Hitler mistook his paranoid, fanatical, parochial view of history for a worldview and imposed his rule of violence and illegality on his own people first and then on the major part of the continent of Europe it was to have effects far beyond the twelve years of his tyranny. When Franklin Roosevelt failed to grasp the essential realities of Soviet Russia and put all his cards on the postwar collaboration of the USSR with the United States and the other "peace-loving" nations of the world, the effects of such incomprehension were far more long-lived than when he thought the China of Chiang Kai-shek should be one of four policemen putting down aggressors in the postwar international society of his imaginings. The two men are not otherwise easily to be compared—what is comparable is the long-range effect of decisions made on the basis of their private worlds, the one filled with terror and concentration camps for the pariah races or for those who resisted him, the other created in humanitarianism, in cherishing the forgotten man and all those lacking the four freedoms. But the laws governing nations and human societies doubtless work as surely as those of nature and we still bear, as we will for years to come, the burden of the violence and hatreds Hitler unleashed and the fatuous concepts of the nature of communism held by Mr. Roosevelt.

It is easy to understand the desire on the part of de Gaulle and many others less intransigent than he for a third force. American policies, like those of other states, are made in part with domestic politics in mind and in addition a long frontier has to be taken into consideration that must be maintained far beyond the borders and immediate interests of the European states. The crises in Korea, in Cuba, in Vietnam were farther away in the judgment of many European observers than even the remote quarrel Mr. Chamberlain alluded to when he was speaking to the British people in 1938 of the Reich and Czechoslovakia. American policy has often seemed unduly belligerent in these postwar years to many foreign observers, although what has seemed to be an over-bold or even aggressive American posture has depended on the nationality and political orientation of the critics and the circumstances that gave rise to their criticism. Thus in 1948 and later when the Russians again seemed intent on causing a showdown, many good people maintained that it was impossible to hold Berlin. Berlin lay in the middle of Soviet-held territory, the mistakes had been made at Potsdam and earlier in dividing the city, now it must in one way or another be acknowledged a victim of its present allies and the inscrutable conqueror. The Berliners themselves violently disagreed with this view of their situation, but I have heard such defeatist notions uttered by other Germans, including a professor in a well-known university who told me West Berlin should be acknowledged as lost and a new Berlin rebuilt somewhere in West Germany. We need not go through in detail the entire list of invitations the United States has been tendered to withdraw from its commitments or in refrain from undertaking new ones. Greece in 1947, Korea in 1950, the offshore islands of Formosa and then Formosa itself, the ultimatum to Cuba, the intervention in Santo Domingo, in Vietnam, all the acts taken to resolve the crises in these areas have been denounced in succession as war-breeding or immoral or both, and they dealt mainly with crises seemingly far removed from those of a divided Germany and a comfortable Europe. Not only traditional diplomacy but long experience have taught statesmen to ask, what's in it for us, what can we gain and what do we not stand to lose by being drawn into the folly of war, of utter destruction through the whims of a foreign power intent on its own concerns?

The answers to such questions must depend in large measure on our view of the nature of the enemy. First let it be pointed out that in no case that I have cited has the attack come from the West or from the United States. I do not like to use the word "aggressor" because it has come to have no precise meaning; the aggressor is always the other side and the Soviet Union and Red China have known for years in advance who the aggressor is and what constitutes a just war to defeat him. So I speak of an attack, of the attack made on the Greek government by Communist forces inside the country with infiltrated aid from the then pro-Soviet government of Yugoslavia; of the attack on West Berlin by means of blockade; of the attack against South Korea mounted by the North; of the attack by the Red Chinese on the offshore islands of Formosa; of the preparations for an attack on the United States directly by the installation of missile sites in Cuba; of the attempt to extend by civil and guerrilla warfare the Castro branch of Soviet imperialism in Santo Domingo and other Latin American countries; of the attack of the North Vietnamese on the South. What were we to do about these? Retreat from each one separately as so many Americans and Europeans have urged as each crisis arose? Retreat from some of the areas and stay in others depending on their strategic importance to the continental United States or to its allies? The latter would be called a flexible strategy, which is what all strategy should be. But where do we retreat to? Let us begin, as we might have, with Quemoy and Matsu, the offshore islands. Even Mr. Kennedy when he was a presidential candidate suggested that these islands might well be the subject of negotiations. Had we persuaded the government of Chiang Kai-shek to surrender the islands, what then? Would this have appeased Red China, caused her to accept the fact that Formosa is in non-Communist hands and to withdraw her claim to that island? Or might it not have whetted the appetite of the government of Peking which, like the governments of the rest of the postwar Communist countries, establishes its boundaries as deep in other people's territories as its power or its threats can move them? And had Greece, or West Berlin, or Formosa been surrendered, would that have appeased the dynamic forces of world communism? Would Soviet Russia then have settled down to negotiate the reunion of East Germany and the Bundesrepublik and Red China renounced its further claims to the leadership of a world revolution and the territory of its neighbors and of the imperialist enemy? Was it not the refusal to surrender—despite the demonstrations that in one form or another withdrawal was the prudent and the moral course—that has kept the peace, that has in fact produced the détente that enables General de Gaulle to journey to Moscow and to indulge himself in the illusion that he is aiding the forces of security and of French prestige when he leaves his place in the alliance that has sheltered the recovery of France and Europe—and its extensions in Japan?

It would be folly to miss the opportunity that has been presented to us. We have in being an association of nations representing a breakthrough from the past, from the wicked past of useless slaughter for ends that are now trivial for this society. We not only have a military alliance in being but a moral alliance, and to foster it means treating its members as equals, as partners in a defensive network, who can also be the source of a future system of security that might at some ripe time exclude no one.

Before long atomic bombs will be produced by nations other than France and Red China; our system of security must be alert to many vicissitudes. But this is clearly a stage in the political development of the West with enormous possibilities of good and evil, and it has been our good luck that the time has demanded precisely those forces of reconciliation and mutual support that have been lacking in the past and the lack of which has resulted in such monumental disasters.

The East Zone Revisited

The thaw in the East Bloc countries has now reached Middle Germany, the "German Democratic Republic." It remains, de facto, as the United States officially regards it, under Soviet occupation; although it exchanges diplomatic missions with Moscow, the East Bloc countries, Yugoslavia, and a number of the noncommitted nations and has its own parliament, president, and administrative apparatus, it is controlled by Moscow more strictly than any of the other satellites. No party leader in the East Zone would dare make the criticisms of Soviet policy that have, for example, been publicly expressed in Romania. The stirrings toward greater freedom, the revived clamor of nationalism in other Eastern countries have been but dimly echoed in Middle Germany. Until August 13, 1961, when the wall went up, it was a smoldering enclave of frustration and resentment; the hopeless rising of 1953, when the Germans attacked their *Volkspolizisten* and Russian tanks with clubs and stones, was not repeated but the walking plebiscite continued; the people who voted with their feet were moving to the West in such numbers that Middle Germany, had the wall not gone up, would have been a country only of old people too tired to move and a scattering of devoted party members. The migration, the constant loss of man and woman power, was the cause of the wall's being built, although the official reason was and remains the prevention of fascist, imperialist infiltration and aggression. But the zone had presented the Kremlin and the Communist hierarchy with two challenges they had never faced before: the first worker's uprising against a so-called workers' state and the unending exodus when 2,824,000 people, mostly those in their young productive years, moved out and the population, despite the excess of births over deaths, dropped from 18,388,000 to 17,012,000 between 1950 and 1964. It was a scathing rejection of communism in full view of the world.

Long before the end of World War II the East Zone was marked as a special area for the Soviet Union. It was to be her claim on the whole of Germany and the spearhead for the domination of Europe. Russian propagandists accompanying their army into Berlin at the end of World War II put up placards skillfully designed to appeal to the defeated, crushed Germans. They declared: "The Hitlers come and go but the German people, the German state remains." The propaganda still follows the same line. Former Nazis, having recanted, become good Communists. Party rallies, newspapers, magazines, officials, all unite to spread the word that the "German Democratic Republic" has once and for all broken with its infamous past of capitalist exploitation and conspiracy to become a truly democratic state of workers and peasants, and they piously and regularly pay tribute to the Soviet Union, which has made possible this leap into the socialist era. It is the East Zone, it is always said, as the socialist representative of the new era, in brotherly cooperation with the Soviet Union that represents the future German society. The theme of German-Russian solidarity is repeated in every possible context: in a museum in Leipzig is a large poster with a quotation from Gneisenau praising the Tsar in 1813 for having rescued Europe and the world from the tyrant Napoleon. One of Leipzig's broadest avenues is the Street of Liberation celebrating the day when the Russians occupied the city, which they have never left. Scarcely any public occasion or utterance fails to thank the Big Brother; in order to thank him properly Russian is the obligatory second language, taught from the fifth grade on and bolstered by exchanges of letters with Russian students, meeting with children of the Soviet occupation, and the constant reminder of how much the Germans have to learn from the Russians.

What the zone has achieved since the building of the wall is remarkable evidence of the industry of its people and their ability to overcome even the marvelous inefficiency of the centralized planning apparatus. The "German Democratic Republic" is now the ninth industrial power of the world despite the poverty of its resources—its only natural riches are brown coal and potash—despite the fact that it had no foreign aid to prime its pumps. Some of this flood of production has finally spilled over to the needy, hard-working people who made it possible. For a long time the Soviet Union bled the zone white; production rose steadily but little of it stayed in the zone and any exchange of goods was heavily weighted to provide cheap exports to pay for expensive Soviet imports. But in Middle Germany, as in the other satellite countries and in the Soviet Union, concessions eventually had to be made and consumer goods and food were in far better supply in 1966 than they were a few years before. The ruins from World War II, more evident in the East Zone than in any other country east or west, are slowly disappearing. Public buildings, new luxury hotels, and restaurants have been built, but these hotels and restaurants are not for the workers, they are for the party leaders, the visiting trade delegations, the managers, the people with big jobs, money, and connections. Housing for the masses remains a major bottleneck; people still wait years before they can get an adequate place to live; young married people still crowd in with their parents or into the single room one of them had before; what new construction there is, like that in Russia, develops cracks and fissures; the planned plumbing fixtures may run out after a start has been made to install them and the contractor has to begin all over again. It is the old story in the socialist countries where the plan, the norm, above everything has to be met and quality, craftsmanship, and common sense fall easy victims to their exigencies. The German technicians, the artisans, and well-trained workers were long in despair over the incessant, often impossible demands made on them—it was among the well-paid building workers in 1953 that the June uprising started—but they have come to accept what they must live by and with. A taxi driver who had been one of the masons who struck on that memorable June day thirteen years ago says he is better off now. He had given up the building trades, was one, he said, of the best-paid taxi drivers making his norms without difficulty; he had an apartment for himself and his family, he was doing all right.

His options had narrowed considerably since 1953 and 1961. The wall—the protective wall, as the Party calls it—is being breached daily but those who cross it risk their lives and many don't make it. The majority have come to accept their fate, and it is not as bleak as it was. But they continue to live in an atmosphere of double-talk, double-think. The wall is a protective wall to prevent capitalist infiltration, but those who are shot are not infiltrators trying to get in but East Germans trying to get out. Because manpower is lacking millions of women must work, and those who do, especially the wives and mothers, have a long day and week. There is the job at the factory, there are the household chores, the responsibility for the children, the waiting in line for food, and in addition the calls to join in demonstrations and rallies and to see to the proper socialist upbringing of the young. This opportunity to work eighteen hours a day is called equal rights for women. Children of working mothers are cared for in the *Krippenheime*, the nurseries and kindergartens, and all children must attend the *Oberschule*, which goes through grade ten. But schools, as the pedagogues keep reminding one another, are only part of the educational process, and the parents too are supposed to fire up the children in their zeal for the socialist state, see to it that they join the Young Pioneers at age six and the Free German Youth at age fourteen. The young people have a busy time; fifty hours of study and homework a week is reported as average in some areas for boys and girls in the upper grades of the *Oberschule* and then in addition are the extracurricular assignments of the youth organizations, the collecting of old clothes and bottles and metals as well as of wild plants that can be sold to add to the donations for the victims of American aggression in Vietnam. The boys and girls are told they are not only to love their democratic homeland, the Soviet Union, and all the peace-loving Communist world but to hate, and their teachers are explicit in these directives, to hate the wicked Americans and the West Germans who are determined to destroy the socialist countries and the nations seeking their freedom from capitalist exploitation. The American war in Vietnam is dutifully denounced in letters written by schoolchildren and by their teachers, and on almost any public occasion the phrases are always repeated, like the words lawyers throw into a document quoting long-dead authorities to fortify its legality. "The dirty American war," "the monopolists in Bonn," "the revanchists," "the militarists." They are a troop always at hand to be scattered into any speech or article to make it foolproof, to evidence its piety for the scrutiny of the censors and the party and state bureaucracy. Any phrase whether of the Marxist or capitalist world may be used that will strengthen the dose of propaganda. The German "miracle" of economic recovery that for many years was the subject of economic writing in the West was merely transformed to become the Russian miracle, and a propaganda film was made under that title. Words like "democracy," "individual initiative," "the full development of all the capacities of the human being," are freely borrowed from the centers where they have a real meaning and applied as labels to identify only activities of the Communist world.

Thus West Germany, which reluctantly armed long after the People's Army of the East Zone was a military force, is a bristling, war-mongering projection of the Nazi state of the militarists and monopoly capitalists who preceded Hitler, worked with him, and now plan to conquer the progressive, peace-loving Communist bloc with every weapon. The twentieth anniversary of the Nuremberg trials was an occasion for all the East Zone newspapers to remind their readers that Nazi criminals were still in power in Bonn and that, just as many representatives of the Western powers had predicted at the time, the conspiracy against peace did not end with the trial. But now the United States has become the major criminal at the bar with West Germany no more than its puppet. In this double-think it is a crime—*the* crime—to resist communism. The list of aggressors begins with those who do resist, and this occurs always at the instigation of the United States and its NATO stooges. Doves of peace appear throughout the zone, on restaurant walls, on postage stamps, on badges given children for learning their political catechism, on placards, on banners, on manifestos, and in the words of party orators. "The peace-loving, progressive forces of the socialist world" are forever locked in battle with the demons of monopoly, reaction, militarism. History is edited to the formula: the Russian attempt in 1948 to starve out the people of Berlin was owing to allied fascist anti-Soviet measures; the South Koreans attacked North Korea; South Vietnam attacked North Vietnam; and the deadpan commentators on the anniversary of the Nuremberg trials all reminded their readers of Germany's foul attack on Poland. That it was an attack in which the Soviet Union joined has disappeared from East Bloc history.

The people of the East Zone have learned to live with the slogans, the pseudo-history, the incessant demands for higher output, the secret police. They have learned because they had no choice. But since they are all prisoners together inside the wall and the regime cannot put seventeen million people in jail, they speak up more than they did before the erection of the wall. Their reaction to the system of norms was diverted to a joke: "Sleep faster, comrade." A group of students recently asked a party speaker why there were no exchange programs with the students of West Germany; why they could not get to West Germany to see conditions for themselves and why, if the workers of the West were so exploited, they lived so well. The answers were lame. The SED speaker was obviously put off balance by critical questions. He told his audience the Democratic Republic did not want to risk the mistreatment of their students by the brutal West German police—that is why the wall had been built—to protect them against armed incursions and forays. But the party speaker was on the defensive and the students knew it. Busy little members of the Young Pioneers may report that radio and television antennas are turned to receive the Western stations, but the people of the East Zone nevertheless continue to listen to the West. Cautiously, not with another fruitless rising in mind, but with unformulated hopes and the knowledge that otherwise they must live with lies and half-truths.

Nevertheless, the wall has divided German families in more than physical space. People can't live without pride, and the people of Middle Germany know how much they have achieved with how little outside help. They have grown deaf to much of the propaganda; party papers often complain of the small turnout for the demonstrations, of the resistance of students to the additional burdens imposed by the study in their "free time" of Marxism-Leninism, but the society has moved ahead. Its cultural life is thin but enriched by the importations of approved books and plays and ballets and films from other East Bloc countries, although the zone itself in 1965 produced a moving, expertly acted and produced film on the Nazi period—"The Adventures of Werner Holt." Painting, as almost everywhere under communism, is unimpressive, consisting too often of heroic revolutionary posters or propaganda pieces, but music remains in the great tradition, for it is one art not easy to politicize. Middle Germany remains a puppet state, but it is also the state of a hard-working, productive people, only a small percentage of whom have become convinced Communists despite the twenty-one years of unrelenting propaganda. But that they have moved away from former habits of thinking and the blandishments of the Western way of life seems clear too. They have made if not peace with the system, at least an armistice, for the way past the wall is well mined and the orders to shoot are followed out. And yet, as one of the former border guards at the wall said to me, a complete stranger, when I told him I was going to cross that afternoon, "Unhappily, I couldn't do that." It will be a long time before he is able to cross that wall in freedom; the East Zone remains the Soviet Union's bridgehead to the West.

1967

On the Durable
Conservatives

At the commencement exercises of a small Illinois college in June of
1966, I heard the main speaker of the occasion say that whether
the audience liked it or not they would all soon have to share their
neighborhoods with the deprived Negroes who would no longer accept
intolerable living conditions; the whites would have to move over—the
dwellers in the elegant and pseudo-elegant suburbs of Chicago and those
in the segregated city—for assimilation was written in the immutable, so
to speak, natural law of these times and they had better get used to the idea.
His remarks preceded the continual demonstrations that were to raise the
crime rate in Chicago by some 25 percent as the police were called upon
to leave their other duties to protect the "open housing" marchers from
the resistance of the community they apparently wanted to live in.

It was not at all an extraordinary statement to make to an academic
audience, in fact, in those days it was routine commencement oratory. The
well-heeled, successful businessman brandishing his liberal reputation
and baring his heart of gold, reciting such lines for a commencement
audience, is a standard part of the instruction of the young. In this scene
the prescriptions for social progress, which have made such faltering
cures in the course of the thirty years they have been offered, were
presented again with the new magic formula added, one that the liberal
academicians, the politicians, and speakers such as the above suddenly
discovered just a few years ago when they encountered still another
injustice they could see needed instant remedying.

June 1966, however, may have been the high point of such self-assured
exhortations. Up to then the waves of idealism, admonition, coercion,
and violence had irresistibly carried everything before them. The idea
that the traditions of a society, its mores, were what made it a society
had become derisory; injustice had to be obliterated with the sweeping
reforms that money could buy, and out-Marxing Soviet Russia or Red
China, to change the terms of the economic environment, was known
to be the key to social justice; a riot was automatically countered by an
appropriation of state and national funds to the disturbers of the peace,
for were we not all guilty when a shot was fired or a building burned down?
What else could be done after a riot in which in some mystical fashion

153

everyone had participated? Had not Goldwater and the conservatives been safely buried, had the liberals not triumphed everywhere, in the karate of politics and the universities, from the publishing houses to the television networks, and had not the glint-eyed men of business learned their lesson at long last and joined up with the forces of the Great Society? Had not even the president of the United States switched his longtime allegiance to Southern notions of race relations to match those of the Northern crusaders, and his economic principles from "Enrich thyself" to the heady plans for abolishing poverty for other people too?

But there are laws other than those written on the statutes and formulated in the courts. Prohibition gave evidence that no law can be stronger in the long run than those unwritten laws which collapsed enforcement of the Eighteenth Amendment from the day it became part of the Constitution. In the long run, you cannot force a remedy for however uplifting a purpose down the throat of a society that does not like the taste of the brew and that has a functioning electorate. Law emerges from the customs and habits of the community, and when it runs counter to them the lawmakers change and it is the non-law that crumbles. The elections in the autumn of 1966 threw out of office many of the men who had crusaded for views such as those presented by the commencement speaker, they broke into the pattern set by labor, religious, and political leaders and the courts, to revert to the kind of expression of individual judgment and conscience that had become hopelessly dated, or so it had seemed. The issue was not civil rights but the travesty the liberal cohorts had made of them.

There is a community in Chicago where Negroes and whites live together in peace and amity. But they live there, members of both races, because they choose to, not because they were told they had better get used to the idea. Such communities have grown up in various sections of the United States in the last years, communities in a real sense of the word, where people elect to live in a certain way and where they share one another's notions of the kind of society they want to have. But this is not the pattern the adherents of the Great Society have proposed—by way of tortuous court decisions, by way of political pressure, demonstrations, and riots the desegregated way of life was to be yours whether you wanted it or not. This is what the electorate in the autumn of 1966 said no to, although in Massachusetts a Negro senator was elected who may be said to represent voluntarism, as well as the people of his state.

The liberals were now building on sand, they had lost touch with their society while they thought they were dealing in the realities of politics, an art in which they had specialized for many years. But they were intoning empty phrases that no longer could exorcise the all too obvious evils they had in fact brought about. In New York City, despite the backing of Franklin D. Roosevelt, Jr., Mayor Lindsay, Senator Robert Kennedy, and Senator Javits, the electorate overwhelmingly defeated the proposal for a civilian review board for the police department; in California, despite the call to arms of all the liberal voices, the voters of the state chose a conservative. These events followed upon one of the most resounding defeats ever given American conservatives, that of the election of 1964 when it seemed that the liberal tide, the promises of the Great Society which had begun with the New Deal, had triumphed once and for all over the representatives of reaction and extremism. The alliance of the liberal intellectuals, of labor and of the minority groups had crushed their opposition; there were some twenty-seven million of the latter, to be sure, but they were at the end of the line, the remnants of faded notions that had no useful place in the dynamic surges of the New Frontier, the Great Society, and the space age. Was 1966 the start of a counter-revolution, or was it a temporary revolt to be explained in terms of the war in Vietnam, the white backlash, and the credibility gap?

It has been long observed that every society, once it gets past a tribal state, divides in time into conservative and liberal segments. In both Russia and China, communism has its liberal and conservative wings; so had National Socialism in Germany, so have the churches and the Negro movement and the labor movement and the groups within the movements. Age has something to do with this easily observable phenomenon, as does the historical experience of the society or group. But in any fraction representing a position or weltanschauung this split soon emerges, dividing those who see the pure doctrine in the light of the tradition and those who wish to adapt it to new conditions or to some blueprint they feel is more likely to lead to a world of their heart's desire. In the dynamics of change the pendulum of decision must move from one of these positions to the other. With the exception of some religious communities like that of the orthodox Jews in a small and isolated corner of the world, no past can remain fixed in the customs and pieties and ceremonials of the ancestors. An unstable balance will always be maintained between the traditions and the demands of a new order; even in the explosion of the great revolutions like those of France and Russia when the balance moved heavily to the side of change the old ways were never entirely obliterated even at the height of the terror.

No society, no party, can exist it seems without this division into these two factions. Age, temperament, experience, and the nature of the crises play a role in deciding which position the individual will take but the idea that the economic factor determines the weltanschauung requires a good deal of explaining when one considers the anti-Americanism of many countries where the United States has distributed its largesse, and the stampede of the capitalists—and above all their heirs—to the camp of those who for years have explained how dead capitalism is or should be. Of course, as in the case of Hitler, the leader's *explications de texte* may provide some imaginary nourishment for his bourgeois admirers. The Fuehrer told his business and industrial audiences that National Socialism admired them and would not think of turning the German economy dominated by private entrepreneurs over to the bureaucrats— who had their uses, although the running of a business was not one of them. German businessmen, once Hitler was in power, preferred to believe in such oratory rather than to continue in the state of doubt they had been in up to the time Hitler took over the country; for the most part they went along with the Fuehrer, some of them with enthusiasm, some without. So it was that businessmen who had always called themselves conservatives joined the brown revolution and the Resistance had very few among them in its ranks. The Resistance was made up of new revolutionaries who included old conservatives from among the Junkers and the army as well as Communists and disillusioned National Socialists.

Thus when the party formulae betrayed their inadequacy, the labels became confusing, as they became confusing some thirty years later in the United States. The "liberals" in the American Congress that met in January 1967 were now none other than the down-the-line machine Democrats who favored the seating of Adam Clayton Powell. For them his being chairman of an important committee, or his being seated, was not a question of morals or of whether he had broken the law, it was a question primarily of Mr. Powell's race and of the permissiveness necessary for party solidarity and winning elections. In this same Congress the liberals were still planning mechanically to force open housing on aroused communities and to continue to pursue domestic measures that had been conspicuous mainly for their failures; in foreign policy they planned to extend trading with the Soviet Union and the Communist bloc, which was providing North Vietnam with most of the war supplies that enabled them to shoot down American planes and to kill American soldiers. It was liberal to favor recognition or quasi-recognition of the

"People's Democratic Republic" of East Germany, a territory under Soviet occupation engaged in killing any of its citizens who attempted to scale its walls or cut through its barbed wire.

But the thirty-year-old formula was fading. The pendulum had moved as far on a Daliesque clock as it could go, and suddenly it was moving in the opposite direction. What had happened was not owing to the white backlash or to the war in Vietnam—these had merely triggered the revolt. Cliques and sects and parties that have their fixed answers to offer an electorate may last for indefinite periods if there is no clear test of their views, but they are no more long-lived than their eventual success in dealing with issues they favor or attack. The thirty-two parties of the Weimar Republic were mere debating societies in their day and all but three had disappeared in post–World War II Germany. What is lasting in the long run is not the issue but the convictions that deal with it; the political philosophy, not the knee-jerk reflex. The conservative position rightly taken is not an ad hoc stand; when conservatives have been resisting inflationary spending programs, the massing of federal power, the political decisions and legislation of the courts, and the invasions of the rights of local communities, when they have been preaching the need for consent, for voluntarism in race relations, for jobs in business and industry instead of handouts, when they have joined the battle against coercion on behalf of some fashionable nostrum they were expressing not notions that arise in connection with crises, or hotly debated measures, but the durable principles of a political philosophy that as guidelines outlast any specific issue. The cults and the sects like the Weimar parties come and go but the principles of change within a tradition remain. The liberal alliance with the labor unions (regardless of how corrupt or how useful they may be, or of the merits of the right-to-work laws for the welfare of labor and the country at large); with minorities (regardless of how parochial and shortsighted their aims and how detrimental to the common weal); with the political machines of the cities (regardless of how close to the gangsters and strong-arm men who are plying their trade under political protection); the institution of President's clubs, and the kickbacks from industry and labor for goodwill or more tangible favors were all part of a climate of corruption that had dominated the United States for many a long year. So apathetic in fact had the country become that Mr. Powell felt he had no particular reason to conceal his conduct; too many of his white colleagues, as he pointed out, were doing the same thing only in a more clandestine fashion, and his way of life only made him a hero in Harlem.

Paradoxically, it was a distorted civil rights issue that brought the revolution to a halt. Civil rights properly had little place in the current liberal dogmas that rely so heavily on coercion and a denial of individual rights when they oppose liberal notions of what is proper for society. Civil rights belonged essentially to the conservatives with their belief in responsibility and opportunity for every individual whether to get and hold on his own merits a job, or a place of dignity in the society. The bankruptcy of the liberal formulae had long been apparent even to the more perceptive people in the liberal ranks. Their economics had achieved little against the Depression of the 1930s, it was rearmament that had sparked the lagging economy; the inflation of the 1960s, the monumental confusions of the billion-dollar programs for complex problems that only deepened as ill-conceived measures demonstrated their futility, the rising tide of violence among the disenchanted people the programs were designed to help, the spread of crime and the malignant areas of the city jungles, the loss of consensus in American society had long been undermining the liberal position and turning the electorate in the direction of the very forces it had rejected only a few years before.

The swing of the pendulum was inevitable, what was new was that a good many people had noted that it was hung from a clock that no longer kept time. The political use, however, that can be made of the great change will depend on the conservatives' dealing not only with the issues that have been tossed in their laps but on their grasp of the abiding principles they say they have lived by and the finding of candidates who are capable of representing them.

"We Are All Guilty"

With our instant communications system the word gets around quickly, words, phrases, and punch lines that only a few years ago traveled leisurely by way of magazines, books, trains, and traveling salesmen now pour directly into the language from coast to coast in a matter of weeks or even days or hours and stay there if they have a tranquilizing or stimulating value. One of these phrases was and is "we are all guilty." The television networks helped to popularize this pious sentiment at the time of President Kennedy's assassination when their commentators explained what had happened with the help of interviews and interpretations, bringing up to the moment the solemn thought of Donne who had once beautifully expressed the sense of loss for the whole human race when one of its members dies. Hemingway, of course, had helped prepare the contemporary world to be aware again of the meaning of the tolling of the bell but it was the instant commentators who gave it universal currency. The tragedy could not be merely the result of the shooting of a president by a deranged killer. It was a time for sepulchral tones and portentous utterances. Hate had been stalking the land, a hate of our own engendering, and it might have been laid low, or at least that was the implication, by the same means that is suggested for ending the war in Vietnam: "make love not war." Had we all been gentler, had the social and no doubt political and economic climates been other than they were the president might still be alive. This is the "we are all guilty" syndrome; the analog of the one that was operative for a long time in American sentiments about post–World War II Germany, in the form of "they are all guilty."

Our society as represented by its public relationers constantly improves its image of itself with these clichés. Last March a sizable group of teachers in a Bronx junior high school resigned because of the repeated physical attacks made on them by some of their recalcitrant students. The teachers took an advertisement in the *New York Times* to explain why they had quit. Their advertisement said: "We are teachers. We became teachers because we want to teach. Much of the time we are unable to do so. . . . WHY? There are many reasons. Among the most important is the continued tolerance by the Board of Education of the problems of a small number of extremely disruptive children who openly threaten

159

teachers and defy authority. These disruptive children are the victims of poverty who, through no fault of their own, act out their frustrations through these assaults on teachers and other children. So much disorder exists in many classrooms that no learning can take place. . . . What is the Board of Education doing? In most cases, nothing. When serious assaults take place, the Board plays a game of musical chairs. A pupil who has committed an assault is transferred to a neighboring school in exchange for a similar case from the other school."

A most revealing advertisement. In it are signs of the "we are all guilty" piety but there is a new twist explicitly stated. That is that the guilty are not guilty. These children who have hauled off on their teachers and/or on other children often enough so that teaching could not go on are themselves victims, acting out their frustrations. The teachers have resigned and demand that the Board of Education do something more about inhibiting the assaults of the young delinquents, although it is not clear just what the board or any other minor authority could accomplish if the children are not responsible for their acts. The advertisement does not say so nor probably would the teachers, but they must know that the game of musical chairs goes far beyond that played by the board. Some of these children have been moved from old slum neighborhoods to housing developments that became merely new centers for crimes made possible by the provisions of elevators and the opportunities the separate entrances gave for attacking the inhabitants one by one. The advertisement called for public support of the teachers to urge the Board of Education to deal firmly with violators of school order. But if the violators are pinning back the teachers' ears through no fault of their own, it hardly seems fair to deal with the children instead of with the causes of their disorders, which must again lie in the social, political, and economic system that produces or tolerates the poverty at the root of, shall we say, their antisocial behavior. The Board of Education might put them in a special school such as the one that I understand exists in Manhattan where children who are merely serving out their time of compulsory education may be sent and where one teacher, a former football player, told me had had notable success in dealing with the more violent among his charges. He was forbidden by law to clout one of them even after they had attacked him but he had found a way. He had grabbed their arms and held them until they were out of voice and vigor and the children, accustomed to respecting that kind of show of strength, tried no further mayhem on him. Whether or not the children felt they were the victims of poverty before my friend took hold of them, they quickly learned to behave better in his presence.

His method, alas, could not be copied by all his colleagues but they too were impressed by it.

In the debate on the responsibility of the post–World War II Germans the question of collective guilt came up over and over again. Learned articles and books were written mainly to prove that it could not exist, and it was generally decided that the most that could be said of a people was that they shared a collective responsibility. This is true for those of us who deplored the use of the atomic bomb against Hiroshima and above all Nagasaki, when the war against Japan was already won and the Japanese government had been seeking peace terms through the Soviet Union for months. These were not your or my decisions; the order came from Messrs. Truman and Stimson. How could people who did not even know that research on the bomb was being done have any decision to make or share any guilt? Their responsibility eventually derives from their being citizens of a country whose government they participate in, and in the rough language of the street the bomb was dropped by the Americans. The language is indeed universal: when, during the Eichmann trial in Jerusalem, the papers printed the news of the attempted landing of anti-Castro forces in Cuba, a Czech Communist living at my pension waved a newspaper before me shouting: "What do you think you're doing invading Cuba? You can never win!" His last point at least as matters turned out was well taken. Thus there is no escaping the mark of a collectivity. Tribe, nation, color, race, sex are all generalized in the shorthand of everyday speech as well as in the writings of specialists. A woman or a Negro driver get automatic reactions the moment they chance to cross what a white man takes to be his right of way, and they too are catalogued by association out of the direct as well as sometimes distortedly interpreted experience of the male white driver.

Because this is a time dominated by genuine science, parascience, and pseudo-science, solid traditions as well as rooted prejudices are always open to inspection. "We are all guilty" is a statement about an allegedly illiberal, reactionary society where right-wing radicals especially are encouraged to sharpen their knives for crusades of hate. The left-wing radicals, one of whom actually assassinated President Kennedy, may be reluctantly admitted to the company of the guilty but they are not genuine members in the view of the "we are all guilty" people who indeed also argue, as the far leftists do, for the basic corruption of the capitalist society. The same thing is true of the "they are not guilty" people. The children who attack their teachers or mug one another, or anyone weaker than they are, are also considered the helpless victims of a corrupt society.

They commit these acts through no fault of their own and while the teachers who resigned would be glad to be rid of them without getting a set of duplicates from another school in return, what is obviously needed is another kind of society, one that would not reproduce them. A society without ghettos, without poverty, without exploitation and class warfare.

Imbedded in these articles of faith is the implacable conviction that the environment rather than the individual is the major cause of crime, that crime is a by-product of poverty and of slums. Actually, not much is known by criminologists about the causes of crime and there is much evidence that they are not closely connected with poverty. Michael Fooner, chairman of the Metropolitan Crime Prevention Project of the American Society of Criminology, in a recent article published in the *Nation* (March 4, 1967), pointed out that serious crimes have been increasing for decades in the United States while poverty has been declining. Crime went up 50 percent in the five-year period between 1962 and 1967 while poverty has been going down for thirty years. Crime has increased despite the higher standard of living, the drop in unemployment, the vast increase in earnings. I have already noted in these columns that a city like Taipei with a standard of living that is but a small fraction of that of a city like Chicago is a safe place to walk at night, even in the park. The easy assumption that impersonal forces, society, slums, and an inhumane economy produce crime, that they and not the individuals concerned are responsible, is well-nigh universally held but probably it is not true.

Other theories on the cause of crime are emerging in the face of the rapidly mounting crime rate that is clearly neither being slowed nor explained by the prevailing dogmas. Mr. Fooner refers to a book that was published many years ago—Hans von Hentig's *The Criminal and His Victim*. In this book the author calls attention to a kind of symbiosis that, as far as I know, was not remarked before Hentig wrote. Certain crimes are committed against certain kinds of victims. There are specific crimes committed against women, against children, against people who want to get rich quickly, against aliens, and so on. In this sense Hentig thought the victim participates in the crime, unwillingly, of course, in most cases, but in every case he participates in the nature of the act. The poverty theory does not, as Mr. Fooner points out, explain crime satisfactorily. About as many people, he says, citing S. M. Robinson's *Study of the Youthful Delinquent Behavior of Men Who Are Respectable Members of Society*, having successful and honorable careers as doctors, business and political leaders, clergy, and policemen have come up from broken homes, association with criminals and poverty, flawed family relationships, discrimination, and psychological abnormalities as have become criminals. And he quotes Robinson's conclusion: "The best cops and the best crooks come from the same place."

Something after all may be left to individual responsibility when the lethal dust settles over the grandiose formulations that have produced the articles of faith of the collectivists. Sin, wrong-doing, the act of a psychotic or of a criminal psychopath become objectified when the guilt is placed upon society, objectified and so diffused through the social space as to disappear. Just as the leaders of the Soviet Union thought the social space was to disappear, new society would no longer be necessary—why should women be prostitutes when they had no financial need to sell themselves or thieves steal when they could work without exploitation?—and therefore founded the forced labor camps where the victims of capitalism could be reeducated, so the faithful marchers for social justice in the United States would reform the wicked American society. Only thus, they hold, will the crime rate shrink and crime eventually disappear. But suppose the opposite is true, that the individual and not society is the criminal? Suppose, as Richard Weaver once said, that rising expectations without the possibility of fulfillment produce more crime than the knowledge that one's own possibilities are limited, that the individual in the free society must make his own way and must be given the opportunity to make it but it is he who bears the responsibility and not the society that gives him more options than any other known to man.

"Through no fault of their own," said the teachers in their advertisement. Did they really mean that? As the children attacked them or others young and old with fists or knives or guns, sometimes because their victims couldn't produce a cigarette on demand, did the teachers really think that the society must be revolutionized to cure such individual or gang behavior? Or did they, when they weren't writing advertisements, want the children, each one of them separately, held to account, disciplined, shown the error if possible of his or her ways, as did my hard-nosed friend in the tough New York school—to begin in some cases a longer-range therapy? What they want, they wrote in their advertisement, was the freedom to teach, one assumes, children who can and want to learn. That means making distinctions between the marauders and the genuine pupils on the basis of what they are and how they behave and not on some set finding of Marxist or other collectivist metaphysic. For it is precisely this capitalist society that has freed the great majority of the people of the

United States and of other Western countries from what was universal endemic poverty, and much of the world hangs on its largesse even when it denies the efficacy of its economic doctrines. And if we are all guilty it may be in this sense—that we permit the collectivist clichés to have authority long after they have been proven nonsense.

Plus Ça Change . . .

The changes occurring in the countries of the Soviet bloc in these last years are unmistakable. There is more open criticism, the secret police are operational but more secret, people talk to one another in restaurants, there are more cars, high-rise buildings go up—the surface differences between East and West narrow. A traveler in East Germany and in the Balkan countries is free to move about almost as much as he likes, providing the authorities know where he is spending the night, and if he stays in the chief tourist cities he can live at about the same prices and almost as well as in the West. Off the beaten track is something else again, there are not enough resources to build everywhere; roads, hotels, restaurants, housing are in dismal contrast to those in the main centers, although here too if a factory is in the neighborhood, the workers' apartment houses, multiplying in the same patterns from Berlin to Outer Mongolia, tower over the countryside. And in the remote villages of East Germany, but less so in the Balkans, are the same placards one sees in the big cities urging the people to build socialism faster, to help the Viet Cong in their struggle for freedom against the vile imperialists. The brilliant signs, often the only spot of color in the drab villages, are fewer in the Balkan countries but where they appear they carry the same messages on behalf of socialist fervor and triumph. This is the wide-angle picture of the East bloc; busy activity everywhere up and down the lands, soldiers in the streets and on maneuvers, Russian soldiers stiffly in evidence in East Germany, never mingling with the Germans; a huge dam building on the Danube by the Yugoslavs and the Romanians with Russian help, shipyards along the banks of the river, shiny new tourist buses running alongside the dilapidated trolleys and local buses for the use of the inhabitants who have to get to and from work.

The consumer spigot has been opened wide enough for a stream of mediocre goods to reach the people who make them. The censorship has been relaxed enough so that books and even films occasionally may appear that are critical of some aspect of life in a Communist country. The tourist attraction faucet is wide open. All these countries including Soviet Russia must have foreign exchange to finance their enterprises. It is not only the United States that is paying out huge sums for the Vietnam War; the war is also draining large sums from Russia and the East bloc, as are Cuba and Africa and especially the Near East, where millions of rubles' worth of hard-to-come-by resources either blew up in the desert sands or were captured by the Israelis.

The big gap in East German industrial production comes from the inability to get hold of many raw materials, spare parts of machines, and of improved machines that are produced in the West and that must be paid for by exports and tourism. Therefore, the virtual exclusion of visitors from the West that up to a few years ago kept businessmen and tourists out except for special missions, the Leipzig Fair, and heavily conducted tours is succeeded by a campaign that includes bourgeois travel posters to woo Westerners to visit and to see in all comfort the progress of socialist democracy firsthand. To be sure, there are incongruities in this grim wooing: campaigns are conducted among East German schoolchildren, for example, to explain why they must hate Americans and West Germans above all because they are fomenting World War III. The *Transparente* with similar messages of hate and the reactions to the Western visitors of the small proportion of the population who might take the party slogans seriously would not make for tourist attractions. Nor does news piped in from Moscow telling of British, American, and West German determination to start a new war set a festive tone for an international dance evening and get-together on a Russian Danube steamer. But these are incongruities the peoples of the Soviet bloc shrug off. They have seen the mighty statues of Stalin come and go and many of their own leaders rise and fall—they are used to this dialectic.

One of the extraordinary books on this theme to come out of the Communist world is by Ladislav Mnacko,[1] a Slovak journalist who spent some years in German concentration camps and escaped to become a partisan in World War II. Mnacko is a convinced and passionate Communist, and has been one since he was twelve years old. Or at least he was convinced and passionate up to a few years ago. His book not only deals with a case history of one of the party *Bonzen* of Czechoslovakia but also touches on the essential problem of power and its immanent misuse in a system that tolerates no loyal opposition; where you either are in or out depending on whose man you are and where, until recently, thousands of people paid with their lives when a chieftain fell from his high place. Mnacko knows this world from firsthand experience; his book is a roman à clef and the photographer who tells the story as he takes

---

1. Ladislav Mnacko, *The Taste of Power* (New York: Frederick A. Praeger, Publishers, 1967).

pictures at the catafalque of the fallen titan is not far removed from the journalist who writes the book. The non-hero of whom Mnacko writes was a mighty worker in the Communist vineyard; he took over when things were going badly and he drove at his task with all his furious energies, working night and day to clean out the enemies of the regime and to set production in order. His path was strewn with the political corpses and the human remains of people who got in his way, and he had no hesitation in destroying a man who had saved his life merely because he had himself behaved badly in the presence of his rescuer and the rescuer's well-disposed family. It is a violent world Mnacko describes, a primitive jungle of men whose jobs and lives are at stake whenever the hierarchy shifts. The commitment of these Communists is a total one to the idea, the mission; they become corrupt by the very nature of their commitment until ultimately nothing is left but the seizing and holding of power. It took Mnacko a long time to see this but he describes the career of his man with an unerring eye, and he has at long last been willing to understand what he sees. The book, it is said, has created a sensation in Czechoslovakia, and well it might. So far Mnacko has stayed out of the courts and out of prison despite his cautionary tale, and one can only hope that he will remain free.[2] What he has described is a phenomenon his fellow countrymen and the party big shots understand all too well; the question is not whether Mnacko's story is true but what its political effect will be. Socialist realism, as the imprisoned Andrei Sinyavsky wrote, is that which forwards the revolution and that which impedes it is treason in the republics of workers and peasants. Whether the party eventually decides it would be better to tolerate Mnacko's criticism than to have him join the ranks of the proscribed and often jailed writers depends neither on the literary merit nor on the accuracy of the author's work, which is weighed solely in a political balance.

The elbow room the East bloc countries have made for themselves is a precarious living space. Romania ostentatiously has stayed away from recent high conferences called by Moscow, conferences which are attended by the former apostate Yugoslavia, but the Soviet rocket bases aimed at the Ruhr, it is reported, are still in Romania unaffected by such gestures. The line is far more permissive than it was but the core remains hard. A Polish journalist who dared to differ with the official position on

2. Since this was written Mnacko has been deprived of his honorific title as "meritorious writer" of Communist Czechoslovakia, ousted from the party, and deprived of his citizenship. These measures were taken not as a direct result of his book but because Mnacko had openly opposed Moscow's Near Eastern policy. At this writing he is in Israel.

the responsibility of the Israelis for the war against the Arab states was first admonished and then recalled to Warsaw. The East bloc with the exception of Romania was unanimous in its denunciation of the Israeli "aggression" and in demanding that Israel be punished, and despite the brave show of independence it would scarcely be possible for Romania to adopt a pro-Israeli policy without incurring Soviet bloc sanctions. Apparently, the most Romanians can do is to disassociate themselves from the campaign to destroy Israel, to deal diplomatically with West Germany, to edge a certain discreet distance toward the West.

A tactical degree of freedom for the separate countries of the Communist International was foreseen from the time the Comintern was founded. In the early days of the Communist International, Lenin stressed in the fourth World Congress held in December 1922 the need for the reinterpretation of the Russian experience in terms of the separate nationalities of the countries making up the Comintern. He had criticized the resolution of the third World Congress as being too Russian, too unintelligible even when as well translated as it had been into the languages of the non-Russian world, to have the same meaning for those people as for the Russians. It was Stalin who attempted to impose a line-by-line adherence of every Communist everywhere to the Moscow position; since his death and demolition and the risings in East Germany, Poland, and Hungary and the success of the heretical countries in breaking away from the iron-fisted tutelage of Moscow, it is possible to stay away from conferences, even to differ on sensitive but nonvital interests, and still not be read out of Comecon and the Warsaw Alliance. The leash is longer, although it remains a leash.

Another evidence of the change has been seen in the continued outbreaks of the long-lived war between the party doctrinaires in the socialist countries and the new class of managers and technicians, a war that has spread to lower echelons. People who have work to do find the apparatchiks a constant burden. The complaints among workers, schoolchildren, and their families over the time given to political instruction that is often senselessly repeated is widespread in the East bloc, and it is reported over and over again that workers and students for the most part go through political motions only when they have to. They attend the meetings and the lectures but they do not listen. The head of a factory may be a party member but he is often described by his coworkers as basically uninterested in politics. Rarely is the head of an enterprise or even of a school regarded as a party fanatic. But this is not true of the newspapers and of the mass media dealing with the public.

However tongue in cheek the writer for the popular press may be, his reports on what the party has decided and the ecstasy with which the new measures have been received never vary from the official line. At most the papers may publish a letter complaining about the lack of enthusiasm in a given school or factory on a given occasion, and the reason for this is always ascribed to the poor performance of some local functionary. But the battle between the apparatchiks and the managers so well described many years ago by Viktor Kravchenko when he defected to the United States continues in the East bloc. Even the adoption in East Germany of the use of cybernetics in solving the incredible complexities of planning for everything was resisted for a long time by the party stalwarts because it would mean the strengthening of the hands of the technicians against the supreme authority of the party.

Skills in foreign affairs have declined. Soviet policy has made many blunders in its history, and the latest one may cost it and the East bloc even dearer than it has up to now. Soviet power politics, however brutal they may have been, have usually been framed in some kind of "humanitarian" or revolutionary context. But Russian intervention in the Near East has had little ideological cover and no humanitarian mask, its drive to dominate the Arab world would have had another "final solution" as a side effect and it was markedly unsuccessful as well. In the early days of the revolution the Communist party called on the oppressed of the earth, on the exploited workers and on the hungry peoples of the Far East to rise against their colonial masters and cast off their chains. Not only do millions of people in Europe and Asia now know what this call means in terms of their own bitter experience with communism, but ideologically too the call has lost much of its meaning. Who in Europe believes that the wall and mines along East Germany's border are there to keep out the imperialist aggressors? Who believes even in the Communist countries that the Hungarians revolted in 1956 against anything but Soviet chains? And in the case of Israel, who believes that the Soviet-triggered belligerence of the Arabs, who before the start of hostilities promised to kill off the entire population of Israel, was either a step toward the freeing of anyone from his imperialist masters or toward a sensible peace and the progress of mankind? The Soviet Union, whose contempt for the United Nations has been often made clear in word and deed and nonpayment of dues, wore a tattered pair of wings and carried a blunted avenging sword when she called on the conscience of the world to avenge an aggression she had precipitated. The great success of Soviet policy has been in the anti-American propaganda of the Vietnam War. It is a success not limited to Europe and Asia and the non-American continents, but one to which many Americans have contributed consciously and unconsciously, and it was made possible by American inability to distinguish between the impossible demands of an illusory collective security and the real world of functioning alliances.

Some seven years ago Mnacko said, speaking of the ultimate humanitarianism of Soviet policy, that when the chips were down and the great conflict between Israel and the Arab states would be fought out the United States would do nothing, but at the last moment Russia would intervene on behalf of the little state that represented a new order in the feudal Near East. Mnacko at that time still believed in the Moscovian heroes of his youth, but it must be clear to him now that it was a flawed vision he had, foretelling only what the United States would not do.

On Image Making

It is no longer easy to find stereotyped ethnic or racial villains on American screens. When a television series more or less accurately reproduces the life and times of Al Capone's Chicago some sensitive people of Italian descent protest about what this does to the Italian-American "image," or repute, as we might have said a few years back. But repute and image are not the same thing. A desirable image is a fixed forty-foot smile projected for a guileless public; it is part of a phantasmagoria of makeup, lighting, and the pitchman's arts. A good image is achieved by manipulation, by blurring undesirable features and touching up the pleasing ones. Repute on the other hand is often related to real activities, to what someone has done and to his character. For the image makers this direct relationship between the real person and what people think of him is of negligible importance. All you need to sell him with is a gimmick, a budget, and space. The ethnic stereotypes were easy images. Mexicans were invariably villains in the old westerns but this too has changed, perhaps in part owing to protests by the Mexican government. Jews have long been scarce as villains, and even the Japanese who for decades served as faithful prototypes of the unreliable Orient have emerged to walk side by side in the front ranks of glory with American Caucasians. The Negro, who on film as in the real society long had secondary roles, is being steadily upgraded on the screen as in the society. Russians, even citizens of the Soviet Union, are often hearty fellows speaking with comic accents who with a little more exposure to American customs and language could turn up in the Chamber of Commerce in Wichita. The Germans on the other hand can still be villains and/or stupid, nobody bothers about the German image, not even the Germans. And it may be said in passing that they have a remarkable gift even when they move into the field of public relations for presenting a broad target to their detractors, a phenomenon that is in remarkable contrast to the talents of the Austrians, who have succeeded in merging with the picturesque scenery of their winter and summer sports and their tradition of light opera. And yet the Austrians both in the days of the Third Reich and since World War II have actually presented a more serious problem to the conscience of Western man than even the Germans.

A recent book by Simon Wiesenthal, *The Murderers Among Us*, explains why he has his offices for the tracking down of the criminals of

171

the Nazi period in Vienna rather than in West Germany. Austria, says Wiesenthal, is far more than Germany a country with an undigested past, a country where after the *Anschluss* the numbers of the National Socialist Party were higher in proportion to the population than they were in Germany, a ratio that held for Austrian members of the SS and the administration of the concentration camps. Austrians, although only 8.5 percent of the population of the Third Reich, were responsible, Wiesenthal calculates, for the murder of half the Jews who were killed. And it may be added that the widespread view of the *Anschluss* as the "rape of Austria" is itself a myth. Never were foreign troops received with more rapture than the German soldiers in what they called "the flower war" to describe their triumphal, ecstatic reception by the bedazzled Austrians. Hitler had returned to the homeland he detested, but the homeland rejoiced in a wild tumult of adulation at his coming; it was the people, not the eighty-thousand-odd members of an underground Nazi apparatus, who swept through the streets of the mountain villages and the broad avenues of Vienna when the Fuehrer came. But the Allies, and after the defeat the Austrians, wanted it otherwise; Seyss-Inquart's lawyer, one of the few Austrians who had remained anti-Nazi, began the defense of his Austrian client at the Nuremberg trial with the words, "May God protect Austria." It was a logical ploy, unsuccessful in this instance of distancing Seyss-Inquart in the eyes of the judges from his German codefendants, but in the broader reaches of postwar opinion such rhetoric was to be much more successful. From the Austrian point of view, as observers have pointed out, World War II was a war they scarcely could lose. If National Socialism were victorious they could produce overwhelming evidence that they were fervent National Socialists, and if the Nazis were defeated they were the first victim of the imperialism of the Third Reich. A few months after the end of the war, at Nuremberg they were already a liberated country, although one with a number of unhappy representatives among the war criminals to be tried. It should be noted, too, that it was the Austrian government from 1945–1949, functioning under Allied occupation authorities, that made earnest attempts to bring their war criminals to trial. Thirteen thousand former National Socialists were convicted in those years and thirty executed.

But the story after the early postwar years of contrition and occupation is a different one. In an article in the West German publication *Der Monat*, in the September 1967 issue, Paul Lendvai writes a detailed account of the Austrian treatment of war criminals since 1949, and it is an illuminating account of how a nation can evade responsibility by way of adopting a protective moral coloration that is accepted both by itself and by much of the outside world. It has been the policy of the later Austrian governments to avert their gaze from the National Socialist past, to forget it, to reject it as an un-Austrian, nonhistorical event. How can it burden them, the citizens of a nation that was the first foreign victim of the National Socialist state? Lendvai tells story after story of legal and moral *Schlamperei* where murderers guilty of the deaths of thousands and hundreds of thousands of people have been set free by Austrian juries and the judgments confirmed by higher courts, many of whose members were themselves part of Hitler's judicial apparatus and among its most bloody practitioners. Herr Lendvai tells the story, for example, of Franz Novak, who was Eichmann's transport officer and as such, with full knowledge of the consequences, had sent some 1.7 million Jews to their deaths. Novak lived in Austria under an assumed name until 1957 when he resumed a civil career as business manager of a printing company and an officer of the *Kameradschaft IV*, an organization of former Waffen SS members. In 1964 he was brought to trial and sentenced to eight years of imprisonment, four of which he had already served while being held for trial. While Novak was in prison, an Austrian journalist tested public opinion on the case by passing the hat for Novak on a busy Viennese street. In twenty minutes the newspaperman had collected 150 shillings or about six dollars together with a pro-Nazi leaflet. He thought 45 percent of the passersby did not know who Novak was, 45 percent gave because they did know, and 10 percent were against him. The Austrian High Court, as a result of a public outcry in Austria and foreign countries at Novak's mild sentence, ordered a new trial on technical grounds and in October 1966 Novak was again found guilty but freed because he had acted under "irresistible compulsion," a defense that Novak had not himself attempted to make.

Two of the judges of the High Court that had annulled the sentence were former members of the National Socialist party. The president of the court, Dr. Hans Sabaditsch, had been suspended from his legal duties from 1946 to 1949 for his judicial services to Hitler's government. Another member of the Court, Dr. Konrad Zachar, had been a prosecutor in the Third Reich who had demanded death sentences for any anti-Nazi activities. One of his victims, a railroad worker, had given thirty marks to help the families of two fellow employees who had been arrested, and Zachar had demanded and gotten the death penalty for him. In 1946 Zachar had been pensioned by his thankless superiors but in 1949 he was again brought back into the service of Austrian justice in one of its highest places. A Catholic paper, *Die Furche*, commented: "With what

moral legitimacy can such a judge administer justice in the name of the
Republic whose foremost fighters he sent to the scaffold?"

Austrian juries free war criminals even when the evidence of their
guilt is overwhelming. Another case cited by Lendvai is that of Franz
Murer, known during the Hitler period as the "executioner of Vilna."
Murer had been turned over to the Russians by the English in 1949 and
sentenced to twenty-five years of imprisonment. The Russians released
him at the time Austria's independence was restored. Murer had quickly
made a new career for himself and he had been elected president of the
Farmers' Chamber (*Bauernkammer*) in Liezen. Brought before an Austrian
court in Graz in 1963, despite the testimony of fifty witnesses he was
found not guilty by a jury to the applause of the crowded courtroom. In
almost all such trials the sentences are either absurdly light or nonexistent.
The cases of Erich Rajakowitch and Robert Jan Verbelen are examples.
Rajakowitch, who was also a friend of Eichmann's, was in charge of
the Jewish Section in occupied Holland, and it was he who signed the
deportation orders that sent the Jews to the extermination camps. In 1965
an Austrian court sentenced Rajakowitch to thirty months in prison,
and since he had already spent two years in jail while he was being
interrogated, he was freed. He thereupon attended the trial of a former
SS leader, Robert Jean Verbelen, who had been condemned to death
in absentia by a Belgian court in 1947 for the murder of more than a
hundred Belgians who had served in the resistance. Verbelen had escaped
to Austria where, despite his known past, he became a citizen, writing
under an assumed name for neo-Nazi papers. Both he and Rajakowitch
are safe from trials in Belgium and Holland as long as they stay in Austria,
for Austria has no extradition treaties for offenses of the kind these two
have committed. As an Austrian citizen Verbelen was tried before an
Austrian court and acquitted. Because of a storm of protest in Belgium
and other countries a new trial was ordered, the preparation for which
could not have cost Verbelen much time since he was busily writing his
autobiography, *Mister Incognito*, which was published by an Austrian firm
as the trial was coming up.

Another group of sixty-five former Austrian officials in the extermination camps of Belzec, Treblinka, and Sobibor had been repeatedly named
by witnesses in various Austrian trials that had been held but only one of
them was arrested. While their opposite numbers in the Bundesrepublik
were brought to trial, in Austria 150 former members of the notorious
killing squads known as the *Einsatzgruppen*, 40 guards from Auschwitz
including an adjutant of the commandant, and more than 100 guards and

employees of other extermination camps together with a large assortment of additional war criminals were not only free men, but 100 of them were on the police force. These men continued in their ordinary pursuits in Austria even though many of them had refused to testify in the German trials for fear of the disclosures that might come from a court inquiry. This in spite of the fact that the German courts had guaranteed them immunity if they testified. Not one of these men was suspended from his police duty.

The Austrian equivalent of the German Center for the detection of Nazi crimes in Ludwigsburg, Section 18 as it is called, is a pale reflection of the activities of its German counterpart. Whereas the German center trebled its staff after the passage of the law extending the statute of limitations, its Austrian opposite number reduced its staff from ten to six after the statute of limitations for capital crimes was repealed. The investigation of the notorious *Aktion Reinhard,* which resulted in the destruction of two million Jews and which was planned and carried out mainly by Austrian Nazis, is conducted in the Austrian center by one man. Another single prosecutor is in charge of investigating the participation of Austrians in the murders at Auschwitz and Minsk. And both men have other duties to perform in addition to conducting these investigations. This compares in the Bundesrepublik with more than a dozen prosecutors at work in both these areas aided by so-called "flying commissions."

In the academic field there was the case of Professor Taras Borodajkewycz, who had joined the then illegal Austrian Nazi party in 1934. Borodajkewycz had been denounced in 1956 by democratic newspapermen for his anti-Semitic and anti-Austrian writings (he was a life-long pan-German) but the courts, says Herr Lendvai, condemned not him but his critics. It took nine years for the Socialists in Parliament to demand his retirement. The disciplinary committee of the faculty took more than a year to decide that Borodajkewycz should be permanently retired, something the minister of education had refused to do.

Herr Lendvai finds the chief causes for this sorry record in a combination of Austrian apathy, passivity, and self-satisfaction. The Austrians, he points out, lived for ten years under the bayonets of the Red Army, they had a long history of anti-Semitism before the Nazis came to power, and they remain uncomfortably close to the satellites of the Soviet bloc. Old Nazis became the new fighters against Bolshevism. The ordinary Austrian wanted peace, to put the past aside and to bask in the new prosperity that followed on the largesse of the Marshall Plan.

But at least as fascinating as the Austrian problem is American and Western opinion of the Germans and Austrians. The Germans for all their spotted past, abundantly shared by the Austrians, have tried earnestly to come to grips with it. They have made such restitution as can be made to the Jews and other victims of the Nazi terror, they have tried their war criminals when they could find them and turned their back on anti-Semitism. During the late Israeli-Arab war the Arabs complained bitterly of the uncompromising pro-Israeli stand of the Bundesrepublik where not only official policy but also public opinion was solidly behind the Jewish state. The Austrians on the other hand have difficulty remembering the period of National Socialism. They have made no restitutions, their war criminals are cheered in the courtrooms when they are freed, and when a foreign country wants to try them for murder Austria points to its statutes. The visitor will have a hard time finding any memorials to the victims of National Socialism, including the anti-Nazi Austrians, and July 20, the day the resistance made the attempt on Hitler's life, goes by unremarked. How could it be otherwise in a country that denies any responsibility for its recent past and lives in the myth that it was itself the first victim of the doctrines it embraced with such fervor?

Despite the contrasting records, the image of Germany remains gray at best and that of Austria either nondescript or a colorful picture-postcard version of neutral political virtue between East and West. Writers continue to speak of the rape of Austria, documentary films show Germany in a Marxist projection where the same classes and psychology continue to rule that produced Hitler and his Third Reich. Austria, whose son Adolf Hitler was only one in a long line of crackpot and seemingly imperishable anti-Semites, is the gay land of great mountains and high plateaus where, as in *The Sound of Music*, a happy people sings and romps in rural pastimes until it is undone by foreign foes.

Two answers to the problems of the difference in image making have been given, and both of them, I think, are inadequate. One derives from the propaganda image provided by the Communist bloc. In it West Germany is an unrepentant, biding-its-time imperialist power and a puppet of the monopoly capitalists of the United States, an image designed to play on Czech and Polish fears, to weaken NATO, and to keep West Germany as isolated as possible. The other comes from the readily understandable doubts on the part of the Jews and other victims of the Nazis of the genuineness of Germany's democracy and its wholehearted rejection of the National Socialist years. Both of these views no doubt are factors in the American image of Germany but not the most important ones. Images are not only created from outside, they are the cherished possession of the people who need them to make sense of an emotional segment of their world; like dreams they release tensions. A hated country must be strong, nationalist, and militarily dangerous or seem that it may become so and to be able to move in a direction opposite to where the observer wants it to go. It must also lack humanitarian ideals; Soviet Russia, even in Hungary and Cuba, seemed to many forward-looking people still a perch for Picasso's doves; pre–World War II Japan on the other hand was a warlike, inscrutable country that flooded the world with meretricious goods, which were not, it should be noted, in serious competition with American products. Japan after World War II, as one of the most redoubtable industrial competitors of many branches of American industry, fills us with admiration. It has no large army, or any intention of having one. Japan, like Austria, is no military threat to anyone, the Moscow Communist bloc with hope of some day taking power there mounts no wide-flung campaign against its Samurai or Zaibatsu, against the same classes who ran the country in its evil days of plotting aggression. Much the same thing is true of Germany's other former allies, the Finns and the Italians. The wave of pro-Finnish feeling that engulfed the United States when the Finns were attacked by Russia ebbed quickly when Finland joined the Reich in attacking the Soviet Union, but there is no anti-Finnish feeling in the United States and none directed against the Italians despite the American films about the Mafia and Al Capone. Italy has flourished in industry, in the arts, and in the affections of the Western world since the end of World War II and all Italian sins seemingly have been expiated in the death of the leader they shouted for for so many years. But again the Italians are not renowned as soldiers, they are a threat to no one even though they have one of the largest Communist parties in Europe and are colonizing the mainly Austrian part of the Italian Tyrol, to the huge distress of the Austrians, who bomb them in retaliation. The Germans suffer among their allies as well as their opponents from an after-image, from the tradition of their military prowess which no longer has any interest for them. And the Austrians who fought valiantly in the German Army, who manned the SS and its concentration camps in undue proportion to their numbers, and who deny any responsibility to redress the wrongs committed by so many of their citizens have projected nothing more than the *gemütlich* image the world preferred to have of them and which they gladly share. Their repute, however, which is still connected with a great European culture and a truly civilized non-Hitlerian past, may be in some danger.

1968

The Paraders

When the history of these years is written, or projected in some climatized, green-lighted, communal fastness it may well be titled the time of the parade, of the demonstrations, of marchers with signs. It is unlikely in all the days since Homo sapiens first stood erect that so many parades of this kind have taken place; they occur daily, seemingly every hour somewhere in the United States, Britain, Japan, and Western Europe, and on demand in the Communist countries. Very occasionally in the latter they have taken place without command, for example when Negro students in Moscow demonstrated against alleged discrimination and Chinese students marched against "Soviet imperialism," but such parades have a short life while the official demonstrations, like those of the Western marchers, may be repeated at any given moment and persist, to quote the words of an old song, "while life and voice shall last."

In the United States these parades are a growth industry increasingly supporting television programs, giving the onlooker an opportunity to get uptight between commercials and the participants a prime moment of propaganda truth for their protest or advocacy when for this brief space they fill the city with their signs and portents. Some of these marches must certainly express the deeply felt reactions of the participants to abuses or injustices; others arise from trivial causes and all of them are largely dependent, for their medicine to take hold, on one medium—television. The daily papers may report on the paraders and the reader may turn to these journals to find out more about what he has seen the night before on his television screen, but without the latter the concentrated actuality, the visible drama of protest would be gone; who day after day would read about a few dozen or a few hundred people marching with placards, or listen to an account of them over the radio? And what unknown, anonymous member of the crowd could suddenly become a leader, a spokesman, and be interviewed for millions of onlookers, as he struggles far more for words to make clear his discontents than for the opportunity to say them? On one such recent occasion a spokesman representing a group of parents of schoolchildren apparently demanding better schools in their district was asked what exactly his marchers wanted—smaller classes, more teachers, more books, better lighting—what? Yes, he said, they wanted all that, they wanted *everything* for the schools, and with this sweeping proposal he vanished from the screen.

181

The television parade goes hand in hand with the new leisure. Thousands of people, it appears, may take time out now to march who in the days before the affluent society had to work during hours that were inconvenient for parades and so were not easily available for protests, or love-ins, or throwing red paint and animal blood at members of the administration, except after hours. It is difficult, for example, to think of Dr. Spock when he was actively practicing pediatrics and writing helpful books for young mothers being available as a full-time marcher while his patients yelled with the pangs of colic or neglect. Or for the chaplain of Yale University, in days when the chaplain presumably had a full-time academic job taking care of the souls of undergraduates, demanding his own arrest for publicly urging the need for disobedience to the draft law while some of his charges took to drugs or drink, afterwards writing about their remarkable experiences without eliciting any kind of ecclesiastical commentary.

It is undoubtedly true that official acts of injustice, acts that counter rooted mores and notions of human rights and duties, may demand civil disobedience—the Boston Tea Party, the refusal of a large proportion of the American population to accept the Prohibition amendment, are cases in point, as is the right of conscientious objection of pacifists to any war. Among the paraders against the Vietnam War, for civil rights, and against unjust discrimination by reason of race there must be many such men and women of conscience and probity who feel that they must stand up and be counted when the summons comes either from without or from their own consciences. There was such an occasion for people of this kind when the television cameras were turned on police dogs unleashed against Negro protesters in the South a few years ago. Or when the accumulated resentments over what seemed to many an unjust as well as an undeclared presidential war were given an opportunity for expression through action as well as through pronouncements. That these marchers, like the pacifist Quakers, may have been linking their arms with the militants of the Communist bloc, who were serving quite a different cause from that of peace or civil rights, is a price one assumes that they are prepared to pay.

But scores of these parades have no moral purpose whatever. They are performances given before an audience. Recently in Chicago some elderly people mounted a march to picket *Readers' Digest* because it had run an article they thought was unduly critical of Social Security. No more indignant letters to the editor, but the prompt taking to the streets before the ever-ready television cameras. Parading has become a tedious pastime, like the tree-sitting and marathon dancing of the Depression years. People parade because their landlords have failed to make house repairs, in some instances they parade against the paraders and, like the slow circulation of the *Paseo* in Spanish towns in the evening where the girls walk in one direction and the young men in the other, these two streams move in opposite directions watching one another out of the corners of their eyes. There is nothing that eventually cannot be paraded for or against. No sooner were two successful heart transplants made than an American senator proposed that a commission be set up to determine priorities; he asked whether it was enough to be rich or in close proximity to a hospital to be in a position to be operated on or whether measures should be taken to establish more reasonable criteria. In South Africa, where the first successful operations took place, one of the heart donors was a mulatto, and the surgeon announced he would like to perform his next operation on behalf of a colored person or a black because they are more given than whites to a disease that specifically attacks the heart. Had a Negro's heart been given to a white man in Mississippi, it is inconceivable that it would not have been the occasion for parades across the United States. Here, in South Africa, a country where apartheid is strictly enforced in the most casual social situations, was a doctor putting the heart of a colored man into the body of a white one. What would not the black and white marchers have made of that to give muscle to their disquiets? And not only was the patient given the colored man's heart a white man, but he was a Jew, the exploiters, according to many Black Power spokesmen, of the Negro ghettoes everywhere—the parades in the United States would undoubtedly have been given more television time than the operations.

The marchers of the past were inner-directed, and their goal was reform. The free silver advocates of the 1890s, Coxey's army that marched on Washington, were bearers of convictions that impelled them to action for their souls' or pocketbooks' sake and that was true, too, of the "Bonus Marchers" of the thirties. Coxey led only a hundred men to Washington but it was a long march, without benefit of cameras, and if it ended ignominiously when the "army" was arrested for trespassing on public property, it remained a historical occasion. General MacArthur led a contingent of soldiers to victory over the trespassing Bonus Marchers with no more than newspaper and newsreel coverage. The great march on Washington of the Civil Righters, on the other hand, was performed before the eyes of millions of American viewers, the marchers were greeted by scores of cheering congressmen, the legislation they sought was enacted, and it was a Metro-Goldwyn-Mayer love feast of the good guys, black and white, who linked arms and sang "We will overcome," as indeed they had, the legal caste barriers of centuries.

But the time of the parades was with us, the marches not for reform but for pie in the sky, for equality in everything, super-equality. America, however, was not ready for that; it was one thing to be liberal in a burst of camaraderie but something entirely different to flesh out the egalitarian hopes of the marches. Civil rights legislation was felt by the Negro and the white liberals to be just a beginning, and the linking of arms came to an end, clubbed down by the violence in the streets and the growing demands of Black Power. Black Power arising from the frustration of unrealizable hopes wanted no more of white leadership or the participation of whites in the Negro leadership; its leaders would hear nothing of gradualism, and the appointment of a Negro to the Supreme Court or to the Cabinet and the election of a Negro senator filled them not with pride but with bile.

Black Power demanded a change of life for the Negroes in the ghetto, on the farms, and in integrated areas, and demanded it right away. It spearheaded the protest of whites and blacks against a society they found loathsome, to be endured by many only with the help of drugs. So the parades, whether headed by a white priest in Milwaukee or by a white spokesman for the substitute, mainly Negro teachers, who have not been able to pass their examinations to qualify as regular teachers of Chicago have tended more and more to be Negro marches. White marches of dissent without Negroes tend to be tepid, colorless, non-soul-brother affairs. It is the Negro presence that gives them tone. The white paraders have wholeheartedly accepted this state of affairs; the Peace movement, the dissidents on Vietnam and on the square American society, baby, cannot stage a proper rally without the Negroes who are tired of them. The New Politics meeting in Chicago may have been a shambles, but the Negroes dominated it. The election of a Negro mayor in Cleveland or in Gary, accomplished in both cases by the almost unanimous vote of the Negro districts, the Black Power spokesmen regard more as a token than a triumph. It is the Negro who is the essential ingredient of the latter-day American revolution.

It must be clear, however, to many Negroes as well as to whites that the Negro is now often parading against himself. The call for Negro athletes to boycott the Olympics is a call to segregation that a few years ago would have been just cause for both the Negro and white communities to rise in protest. Athletics have provided the Negro with unparalleled, enormous public acceptance and adulation, the tumultuous approval of the grandstands has indeed at times spilled over into a cult. And it has indicated that despite all the disclaimers there are stubborn racial differences and the Negro on the average seems to be a better athlete than the white man. Negroes who are 12 percent of the population make up some 53 percent of players in the National Basketball Association, 27.7 percent of the players in the National Football League, more than one-third of the baseball players in the American and National Leagues, and they have long dominated the American track teams that went to the Olympics. Even the U.S. Army fitness tests in which the Negroes do not do well on the mental side show they are in better physical shape on the whole than is the white man. The mental tests tell another story, of course. There three out of five Negroes fail the army tests as against one white man in seven. These tests, it should be noted, are not intelligence tests, they are aptitude tests to enable the army to tell in advance whether a man can carry out a soldier's assignments; the results vary for both Negro and white from state to state and regionally. In Mississippi, for example, 82.4 percent of the Negroes fail the tests as against only 29.9 percent in the state of Washington. The white failures ranged from 5.9 percent in the state of Washington to 31.9 percent in Kentucky. Although it might be argued that the more up and coming Negroes have migrated from the South to such states as Washington, it would be difficult to make the same argument for the differences in the white scoring between Washington and Kentucky. The differences seem to lie mainly in the cultural environment, although there is a distinct racial differential as well.

Other figures bear this out. For example, recent tests made on behalf of the federally financed Center for Urban Education in New York and by the Stanford Research Institute in California indicate that the high hopes many people have had for the effects of integration on Negro children's school performances are not being borne out. In both states the latest tests reverse those made in 1966 on behalf of the United States Office of Education and show no significant change in the reading ability of Negro children bused to integrated schools as compared with those who have remained in segregated schools. And the formula always at hand that what schools need is more funds to enable them to undertake special, remedial programs has also come up against some hard facts. According to a 1967 New York City report, made by the Center for Urban Education, even schools costing $7.7 million by reason of their special programs and high ratios of teachers to pupils are making heavy weather. The 1967 report issued on the results of "A Special Enrichment Program of Integrated Education in Transitional Areas" shows that while reading achievement did go up from grades three to six, the students in these junior high schools were relatively more retarded than they had been at the start of the program.

The substitute Chicago teachers, mentioned earlier, paraded in the winter of 1968 against the injustice of their not having received accreditation as full-time regular teachers. They had failed to pass a written or oral test, or both, and what they wanted, since they did not seem able to pass the examinations, was for experience rather than the passing of an examination to be the decisive factor in awarding them full teaching status. It may be true that an oral test is inaccurate in assessing abilities and should be replaced with something more objective, but the same anti-examination trend is apparently in the offing in the New York school system where unduly few Negro high school students have had sufficiently high grades to enable them to be admitted to one of the city's colleges. As a result a movement is on foot to change the requirements so that more Negroes, as such, may be admitted. So far there have been no parades either of the high school students or of a faculty committee that would change the rules, but they will doubtless come as they have come in other parts of the country when the word "prejudice" may be substituted for the failure of someone to get something to which they or their spokesmen feel in their bones they are entitled. A parallel in athletics would be to permit a white basketball player, in an interracial game, to stand on a ladder in front of the basket.

Parades are an essential part of the permissive society. When rioters are arrested they are soon set free with little or no punishment, because every right-thinking, liberal American knows that the conditions in which they live are not of their own making but the fault of someone else. When garbage is not collected in Harlem it is owing to the prejudice of the white power structure controlling the Department of Sanitation and not to the people who throw garbage into the streets instead of cans.

The time of the parades has developed the wider de facto segregation of the races. On the one hand the Negroes, frustrated in their hopes of being able to achieve everything they had been promised, deprived of that full equality they had demanded and been told they were entitled to, are turning more and more away from integration as an end and toward solutions of their own, some of which involve violence. It has been reported from observers in Harlem, for example, that nine out of ten of the young Negroes in high schools are advocates of Black Power and want nothing to do with integration. That this attitude is not confined to students is apparent in the shift in the Negro leadership and of their demands; it is the radicals who are the heroes and who capture the imagination of the rank and file. How could it be otherwise? Astonishing figures turned up at the end of the year 1967 showing that in all the time between the Supreme Court's decision in 1954 ordering integration, segregation has actually increased. According to a *New York Times* report of January 12, 1968, there are now 2.5 million children in all-Negro schools as against 2.2 million before the Supreme Court decision. Attempts to bus children either to or from Negro schools are met with a storm of white protest and whether these protests are made out of prejudice, or as a reaction to the rise of Negro crime and to riots, they are undoubtedly not to be assuaged by the white community's being told they must learn to live with the Negro. Increasingly, they are refusing to live with the Negro and the Negro to live with the whites.

Cities are getting tougher. After the days of the police dogs being turned on demonstrators, the dogs are now being used with strong public approval against criminals. In Miami, where the Negro crime rate was such that law-abiding Negroes stayed indoors at night, with a police crackdown violent crimes have been reduced 60 percent in a few weeks, the Associated Press reported in January. The criminals may have merely moved to easier hunting grounds but the rate of violent crime is nevertheless down sharply for one city. The pressure for civilian police review boards to curb alleged police brutality has all but ceased since the resounding defeat of the proposal in New York City. As was duly noted by the commentators on the president's State of the Union Message, the only part of the speech that evoked cheers from Congress was the declaration that the rise in crime must be stopped. When the president talked of civil rights there was silence.

With the Negroes in American colleges demanding freedom from white tutelage, keeping to themselves, looking to themselves to win their place in a white environment despite the attempts of the authorities and of undergraduates to break through the barriers and to return to the good old arm-linking days, we have obviously come to a new phase of the race problem and one that will not be as accessible to the television cameras. These dissident Negroes, like their dead heroes, Malcolm X and Dr. Fanon, reject the white society lock, stock, and barrel although they make use of its opportunities, and by their violent rejection of it they become an avant garde not only of Negroes but of the radical white wing that has no revolutionary drama without them. They are in fact the front line of the left-wing environmentalists who believe we can change anything we will to change, aptitudes, intelligence, athletic ability—all we have to do is to expend enough energy and money and transform our economic and political system, and the job will be done.

These are old illusions, optimistic, wishful, giving rise to impossible hopes, but because they are illusions they are damaging. It is in the differences between races, between people, as well as in their basic similarities that culture and the good society are formed. As the Pan-Negro patriot Edward Wilmot Blyden, who before the American Civil War emigrated to Liberia where he became professor of Classics and president of Liberia College, said: "The duty of every man, of every race is to contend for its individuality—to keep and develop it . . . Therefore honor and love your Race. Be yourselves . . . If you are not yourself, if you surrender your personality, you have nothing left to give the world. You will see, then, that to give up our personality . . . would really be to give up the divine idea . . . and this is the worst of suicides."

These were the words of a remarkable, self-educated man born in the Danish West Indies who had been denied admission to American theological schools because he was a Negro. He learned Latin and Greek and taught himself Hebrew. He lived in a harsh world for the Negro in the mid–nineteenth century. In the United States of the late 1960s, however, he would have been awarded any number of scholarships in almost any university of his choosing, but in the time that had become one of vast opportunity for Negroes of promise he might well have used more energy in parades than in study.

Presidential Wars

The Fund for the Republic and its offspring, the Center for the Study of Democratic Institutions, have been noted far more for their overblown prospectuses than for any subsequent performances beyond the scope of commencement oratory. It is possible, say their detractors, that no institutions in the vast, uneven landscape of American higher learning have spent more money to less effect than these two. There was for example the case of the reference books dealing with communism that made their grand appearance in 1955 under the auspices of the Fund for the Republic, only to be found somewhat lacking in references to books such as David Dallin's—highly esteemed by eminent scholars, but also well known for their critical attitude toward Soviet Russia and the Communist party. And then, only last year, at the end of May, came the loudly heralded *Pacem in Terris*, Peace on Earth Convocation in Geneva, which had the purpose, as announced in January 1967, of bringing together leaders from all over the world including possibly Ho Chi Minh from North Vietnam, and certainly members of the Viet Cong, representatives of Red China, the Soviet Union and the East bloc, South Vietnam, Western Europe, and the United States. The convocation was duly held but there were many vacant seats. Ho Chi Minh couldn't make it, Soviet Russia refused to participate although it had been announced in January that a Russian was helping with the plans for the convocation; the Swiss Foreign Minister, Willy Spuehler, canceled his appearance when he discovered that U Thant, who was busy in New York with the Middle East crisis, would not attend. The *New York Times* reported rumors that Herr Spuehler didn't approve of the financial support of the convocation by Investment Overseas Service, a firm that had been attacked for its methods of selling mutual funds. No one came from either North or South Vietnam. South Vietnam's representative, Tran Van Do, had his speech canceled by officials of the convocation because the North Vietnamese and the Viet Cong had sent no representatives. Even Ambassador Goldberg found he couldn't attend, the American Ambassador to the UN in Geneva couldn't make it either and sent a deputy in his place. Senator Fulbright, however, was present and declared the conference to have a useful purpose. U Thant sent a televised greeting from New York, and a message from the Pope, who had spoken in 1965 of *Pacem in Terris*, was read by Cardinal Journet.

189

No dialogue, as the center likes to call it, borrowing from Martin Buber who did not use the word as a euphemism for long-winded discussions between liberals of varying degrees of intensity, took place in this instance, nor does it in any meaningful fashion in many of the tableaux put on at the center. Nevertheless, the center in its campaign against American involvement in Vietnam has unexpectedly turned out a most useful pamphlet handsomely printed in two colors of ink and written by a political scientist from the University of Utah, Francis D. Wormuth; its title: *The Vietnam War: The President versus the Constitution.*

Professor Wormuth, who believes the Vietnam War to be illegal because under the Constitution only Congress has the right to declare war, has written a learned résumé of the ebb and flow of the battles of decision making that have preceded this latest war decreed by a president. Demonstrating the clear intention of the Founding Fathers to place the power to declare war in the hands of Congress and not in the hands of the president or of the Senate, which were other possibilities debated before the adoption of the Constitution, Professor Wormuth traces the development of the argument that has led to the widest possible claims by the State Department on behalf of the presidential power to make de facto war. According to the State Department, sending armies to foreign countries on order of the president without a congressional declaration of war is sanctioned by some 125 precedents that began almost with the founding of the Republic. It is against these sweeping pretensions that Mr. Wormuth lays his barrage to show that from the early days of nationhood, beginning with the undeclared war with France that lasted from 1798 to 1801, it was Congress, not the president, that properly made the decisions to issue letters of marque and similar authority to commit acts of limited but nevertheless shooting war, although war was never actually declared. This was a state of hostilities described at the time as "imperfect war" to be distinguished from the all-out or perfect war in which, for example, France and England had long been engaged. But in the course of American history the clear wording and intent of the drafters of the Constitution have become increasingly blurred with regard to presidential and congressional prerogatives.

A key case cited by Mr. Wormuth, used by the State Department on behalf of presidential power, is the shelling of Greytown in Nicaragua in 1854 by an American warship. The British had claimed a protectorate over the Mosquito Coast, as it was derisively called, and under the alleged jurisdiction of the Mosquito King and the British Consul a company was formed to conduct travelers, at a price, from one side of the Isthmus to the other. An American group set up a rival company under Nicaraguan jurisdiction on the shore opposite from Greytown and inevitably incidents occurred as a result of the conflicting claims of the two companies. The American minister to Central America suffered a slight cut from a bottle thrown by a member of a Greytown mob and as a result, after damages and an apology had been denied, the secretary of the navy ordered the shelling of Greytown by the USS *Cyane*. Following a day-long bombardment the American ship landed its crew, who proceeded to burn down the buildings that remained standing, to the huge distress of the British company and the subsequent delight of State Department lawyers. Despite the fact that the bombardment was widely condemned at the time in the United States, the captain's act was not repudiated, and the State Department has pointed to Greytown as a precedent for the right of the president to send the armed forces of the United States into combat without a declaration of war. State Department lawyers have held Greytown to be a blank check for the president to order hostile acts in an emergency and as a reprisal. Professor Wormuth points out that President Pierce in recounting what had happened to Congress exaggerated the facts, alleging, for example, that Americans had consistently been damaged and humiliated by the British company. This was not true, only the one incident had occurred and that had been enough to touch off what many contemporaries thought was a reaction of undue proportions to minor damage done an American official. However, as President Pierce pointed out, Greytown was less a political community than a "piratical resort of outlaws" and it was thus that the use of armed force might best have been justified.

American presidents, however, have taken other action against sovereign states or authority in the Far East, in Mexico and elsewhere in Latin America, and in Hawaii. Some have asked for congressional authority, some have acted without it, but since President Buchanan, Professor Wormuth informs us, no presidential request for authorization to use force has been refused. In the case of Vietnam, we have a full-scale war that has made clearer the dangers to which this equivocal course has led and the threat to the American balance of powers of the State Department's extravagant claims. Many of the previous cases, Mr. Wormuth points out, that the State Department cites have had to do with very minor affairs. It is one thing to order a longboat ashore to protect American lives and quite another to send some five hundred thousand troops together with a great fleet and air support to a foreign country on a presidential order. Nor are treaty obligations a sufficient justification for sending such armed forces into battle. If signing a treaty could under any circumstances automatically put the United States at war, then a subsequent declaration of war by Congress would be a meaningless flourish. As for the Tonkin Bay resolution, it cannot be a legal blank check for the president to initiate war and to order out the army, navy, and air force in any numbers at his discretion. Congress simply does not have the power under the Constitution to confer its prerogatives on the president; it cannot legally delegate its constitutional authority to the president. The power to declare war rests with the Congress, it cannot be voted away by approving a course of action the president has undertaken or by conferring on him the right to take any further steps he may deem necessary to prosecute an undeclared war. Thus Mr. Wormuth's persuasive argument buttressed with many historical examples of presidential pretensions and renunciations and of congressional assertions and denials of its authority under the Constitution.

What Mr. Wormuth does not mention, perhaps because the acts merely led to hostilities but were not direct orders to send large numbers of troops and planes and ships into action, are the policies and activities of two other American presidents, Messrs. Wilson and Roosevelt. Like the chiefs of the Fund for the Republic, they saw their roles in cosmic perspectives. For Wilson the war of 1914 was a conflict between good and evil, and not one of the interminable wars between shifting European power structures that had been erupting on the Continent for centuries. As a result he took theoretical positions and made practical demands that could only result in war, and Congress ultimately could only ratify the inevitable effects of his belligerence. Woodrow Wilson from the start of the war pursued a one-sided neutrality: Allied ships, although armed, he regarded as peaceful merchantmen, German submarines that could be and were sunk by one shot from such peaceful merchantmen had to follow the rules of cruiser warfare and visit and search a ship, placing its passengers and crew in a place of safety, before sinking it. No submarine can operate in this fashion, and in World War II no American or British submarine attempted to. In Mr. Wilson's view American citizens had the right to travel anywhere, even in war zones, not at their own risk but under the protection of the U.S. government, and any harm that might come to them under these circumstances was the result of an illegal attack. Under the Wilsonian doctrine a British ship like the *Lusitania*, carrying as the most valuable single part of her cargo ammunition to be used against the German army, had to be granted immunity from being torpedoed by the German navy because Americans were on board.

Only three Americans lost their lives on American ships sunk by German submarines before the breaking of diplomatic relations in 1917; these men died as a result of the torpedoing of the *Gulflight*, which the submarine commander correctly believed to be under Allied convoy. The German government, despite the circumstances, offered to pay reparations for the incident. When the Germans, in a final effort to counter the British blockade, a blockade which they and many neutrals regarded as illegal under international law, announced their purpose to sink on sight any ship within the war zone they had proclaimed around the British Isles, Mr. Wilson had his war. Diplomatic relations between Germany and the United States were broken, American ships were armed by order of the president, not of Congress, and American ships were sunk. Congress could only respond to the predictable results of Mr. Wilson's lopsided neutrality by a declaration of war that as much as any act in recent history has helped to bring on the catastrophes of the peace treaties following World War I and the subsequent period of international violence.

President Roosevelt went further. He not only denounced and took measures against countries with which the United States was not at war, he committed acts of war without congressional authority and then attempted to get Congress to take further measures of hostility to back up what he had done. In the present American view a nation's coastal waters end at the three-mile limit, and not the twelve miles claimed by the North Korean government in its accusations that the *Pueblo* violated its territorial waters. But before the United States entered World War II, President Roosevelt proclaimed a three-hundred-mile neutral zone within which no German submarine would be permitted, and even this generous expanse of territory was widened to twenty-three hundred miles, described as an American security zone by Admiral King. In addition, American war vessels convoyed Allied shipping before the United States entered the war, and American destroyers reported to the British the position of German submarines they had tracked and in at least three cases participated in an attack on submarines with depth charges. When the submarines replied by firing torpedoes, Mr. Roosevelt charged Germany with having initiated hostilities against the United States. "The shooting has started," he said, "and history has recorded who has fired the first shot . . . America has been attacked." It was because the American navy and Congress were of another opinion that the shooting war in the Atlantic remained a limited war. This and the fact that Hitler had his hands full with his conquests and plans of conquest in Western Europe prevented full-scale hostilities. American acts of war there were a plenty, but Hitler forbade his submarine commanders to penetrate the three-hundred-mile security zone that Roosevelt had proclaimed and to retaliate against any American provocations.

The situation in the Pacific was in a sense easier to manipulate, and Mr. Roosevelt worked with a will. Filled with the Wilsonian notions of the need for the United States to play its full part in the measures of global collective security, he announced his purpose in 1937 to quarantine the aggressors, and from then on Mr. Roosevelt struggled steadily against the strong noninterventionist sentiments of Congress and American public opinion to have the United States join in the anti-German-Japanese front. That Hitler and the war party in Japan were potential dangers to the United States may be conceded, but Mr. Roosevelt did not confine his animus to Nazis and Japanese extremists. The members of the German Resistance to Hitler and the Japanese moderates who were battling the war party were given the back of Mr. Roosevelt's hand with the same vigor with which he smote their enemies.

The ultimatum of November 26, 1941, that Secretary of State Cordell Hull presented to the Japanese emissaries came six days after Japan had made a conciliatory offer for a modus vivendi and a day after Mr. Roosevelt, Secretary of War Stimson, Secretary of the Navy Knox, General Marshall, and Admiral Stark had discussed how to "maneuver" the Japanese into firing the first shot. Mr. Hull on November 26 told the Japanese in effect to retreat to their islands. Get out of China and Indochina, support no government in China other than the government of Chiang Kai-shek, Hull demanded; go back to your jumping-off places in the homeland and desist from any attempt to deal except according to American prescriptions with the Chinese revolution or to make use of the disarray of the Allied Powers to the disadvantage of their holdings in the Pacific. Together with economic sanctions Mr. Hull's memorandum was an invitation, from the Japanese point of view, to become a second-class power. It shattered the influence of the moderates and placed the war party in Japan in a position where it could give the final go-ahead signal to the task force that had been sent to bomb Pearl Harbor but that could have been recalled up to a certain critical time if the United States showed itself willing to negotiate. Roosevelt, Stimson, Hull, and the other members of the American war party knew what kind of reply they would be likely to get, for the Japanese cables were being deciphered by American naval intelligence and they also knew, after the Hull ultimatum had been received by Japan, that an attack was imminent, although they may not have known at what precise point it would occur.

The attack was made on December 7, and Congress had no choice but to declare war on Japan even had it known all the facts of American intransigence that came to light at a later period. Hitler solved the remainder of Mr. Roosevelt's problem by declaring war on the United States. But the hue and cry over the Rooseveltian methods has not died down. The books of historians like the late Charles A. Beard, the memoirs of generals and admirals, and now the Vietnam War have kept alive the question of the consequences of Mr. Roosevelt's policies and pretensions.

There is no question of the dynamism of world communism that intends in the long run to overthrow the existing non-Communist orders. Had the United States not resisted in Greece, Berlin, and Korea, had its armed forces backed by nuclear bombs not been available in Western Europe and the Far East, local Communist cadres with the aid of the Soviet Union and/or Red China would undoubtedly have overrun many independent areas of the world that wanted no part of communism. When the American commitment aided an independent people, ready and willing to fight for themselves, the main opposition to these interventions has come either from fellow travelers or from pacifists or the new isolationists. But the very success of these operations, the relative ease with which they have been secured, made possible the major intervention in Vietnam, which could only be successful, in view of the uninspired military and political performance of the South Vietnamese, by a full-scale American war and the risk of extending it beyond Vietnamese borders.

The United States did not, like Russia and Red China, confine itself to training, organizing, and supporting its Vietnamese allies; it took over the war. What President Johnson has done in waging a major undeclared war against the Viet Cong and North Vietnam is in the direct line of the Wilson-Roosevelt policies supported by "liberals" such as Senator Fulbright as long as the enemy was one of whom they too disapproved. The present war is being waged with the same vapors of collective security, an alliance of the "peace-loving nations" in the background that provided Messrs. Wilson and Roosevelt with their sense of messianic national mission. Secretary of State Rusk still pays homage to them when he speaks of the need for "organizing peace" in Southeast Asia, words that are in the context of the Four Policemen mirage that glittered so enticingly for Mr. Roosevelt when he was dreaming of a postwar world to be run by the good guys before at least two of them, Chiang Kai-shek and Stalin, came to be regarded with deep suspicion by Mr. Roosevelt's successor.

Perhaps it will be through this most unpopular war in the jungles of Vietnam that a distinction will once more come to be made between the president's duty to defend the United States against attack and Congress's duty to declare war. The question before Congress and the American people is whether it should be possible for any president to send a half million men together with the American navy and air force into action thousands of miles from the American coasts by way of capricious increases in military advisers or extensions of so-called police actions. This question is in turn linked to the claims of Messrs. Wilson and Roosevelt that they were defending the United States when they took their own roads to enter a foreign war which they had decided the country must join. It is not enough to pass laws like the Neutrality Act of 1935. Congress must actively participate in any decisions for armed intervention and keep a wary eye on every presidential move, however exalted its stated purpose, that will in effect take from Congress its constitutional duty to declare war. This may be one of the chief things we can learn from Vietnam; the other is that American power, moral and material, is not unlimited. It must be husbanded for areas that are critical to the United States and with a people and government ready and willing to defend themselves.

The American Condition

A n American presidential election summons up the ghosts of the past, the demons of the present, and the integrated heavenly hosts of the future. It is a time of circuses, of celebrating famous men and idiots, a time of self-praise and of hand-wringing. We have, from pole to pole, smug societies, self-critical and self-congratulatory societies, and societies where a master race or a master dialectic confer an uneasy superiority on their people, but the United States in its awesome power and affluence prefers to call itself sick and violent, and proclaims its guilt for every ill everywhere—for alleged crimes that occurred four hundred years ago, for war and pestilence and hunger, for the whole wretched state of mankind. There is hubris in this self-flagellation; it is an indulgence, a luxurious exhibitionism, a show of strength through masochism to confess one's guilt on every possible occasion, above all if the guilt is imaginary.

Americans compare their society with no other actual society but with a promised land. They want a place to live and where others may live without war, without poverty, and without hunger. They look forward—or at least their great liberal president did and millions cried amen—to a whole wide world of the four freedoms: freedom from want, from fear, freedom of religion, and of information. Everyone who comes within the penumbra of this cosmic undertaking is subject to its rhetoric, whether he be a Vietnamese being bombed out of his hutch for his own good or a Mexican migrating to the United States. Mexicans may come for the higher wages they will earn in upper California, but as soon as they have crossed the Rio Grande and made their way to the wine country, their condition immediately becomes equated to an American standard which is called inhumanely low, demanding massive public indignation and legal action although it beckoned the migrants from whence they came.

By all the measuring rods of altruism the United States has not done badly. It provides more help than any other nation for the indigent both within its borders and in underdeveloped countries; it has saved the independence of Western Europe and of some of the Far East; it has rescued the city of West Berlin and large populations of the earth from starvation; and it has made possible a higher standard of living for its own people as well as many foreign peoples than has ever been known in all

197

the history of a troubled planet. Let us now look for a moment at some of the chief charges against America's moral health.

The race problem and poverty. In no other country of the world have such large numbers of ethnic and racial groups—historically at one another's throats—accommodated themselves to the enemy and flourished as they have in the United States. Racism, ethnocentrism is worldwide. Soviet Russia is accused of it by Negroes, by Chinese, by Jews, by Ukrainians; the British, conservatives and labor alike polls tell us, want no more colored immigration and would like to be rid of what they now have; the African states proclaim their devotion to *Negritude,* and a good many of them deport people of other races. The Congo and Nigeria slay their thousands because they are white or belong to another tribe; the Indonesians murder their Communists; the Pakistanis the Indians, the Turks the Armenians, the Greeks the Turks, the Germans the Jews, and the Communists their millions of wreckers and saboteurs who were later solemnly rehabilitated. The Israelis and the Arabs fight on. The war of the country against the city, of the nonwhite peoples of the world against the whites is proclaimed from Peking, which, however, has not hesitated to kill Chinese by the millions. The words are reechoed in Cuba and in Harlem and many other parts of the United States.

Violence can be done on any conceivable pretext; Jonathan Swift described one war between the big and little Endians, referring to a quarrel about the end of an egg to be opened first. Race throughout the world remains a visible point of acceptance and rejection as it was before the Greeks and Chinese called the outsiders barbarians. Although racial differences have over and over again been explained away on religious, humanitarian, and cultural grounds by theologians, anthropologists, and psychologists, no society or subsociety has really believed them. The Negro has complained, and justly so, of being discriminated against in the United States, but he can make the same statement about any country where he lives as a minority. In fact, nowhere else in the world does he live as well, nor can he advance himself more easily than in America if he has any luck and skill or intellectual capacity and either conforms in a minimal way to the norms of public order or denounces them. It is perhaps a small matter compared with what we should like the human being to aspire to, but our impoverished people, black and white, have more television sets, automobiles, and washing machines than the middle classes of many European and Asian countries. If there is hunger and malnutrition—and there is—it exists mainly as a result of dubious choices on the part of those who prefer the television sets, liquor, and washing machines. The Columbia Broadcasting System reported that the poor often do not spend their money on better or more food for their families. Hunger also stems from the bureaucratic ineptitude of the responsible government offices, which do not adequately distribute the excess commodities that are available and in large supply. In any event, deprivation does not exist because the American people have shown themselves unwilling to be taxed to provide proper nourishment for the hungry or decent housing or medical care for the underprivileged of any color. It was the local doctors provided by the local counties who made the reports on which the Columbia Broadcasting System and other critics of the present state of health of the poor have based their findings.

Billions of dollars have been spent on slum clearance, on free food, and on medical, welfare, and special educational programs. If they have failed in their high objectives, what part of their failure can be attributed to the openhanded American society and what to the administration of the policies, the planning, and the recipients? In the last issue of *Modern Age*, an article dealt with the situation of that most renowned of welfare states—Sweden. It told a cheerless story where the economy and the spiritual life both stagnate; where 120,000 out of 800,000 Stockholmers are looking for apartments that have not been built; where, because of the high taxes, doctors and dentists often work only half or three-quarters of a year, and patients wait months to get into a hospital. In Britain, a country that in 1900 led the world in economic well-being, and, like Sweden, a welfare state, the situation is equally catastrophic, and for the same reason, say suddenly awakened British economists. One of these economists declared, in a recent lead review of the *Times Literary Supplement*, that the public sector has swollen to such a cancerous growth that it has consumed the energies of the society, leaving Britain's development far behind that of its European neighbors where the private sector can operate. On the record of its consequences, it is the welfare state that produces the economic sick society, and it is because the contagion has spread to the United States that we are in danger.

Crime. Homicides in the United States are eight times those in England and Wales, four times those of Japan, New Zealand, and Canada. These figures are somber, and so is the fact that arrests of Negroes for homicides in some American cities are ten times those of the whites. Since the rate of crimes of violence, including homicides, is rising rapidly, we require rapid explanations of this epidemic. It is popularly ascribed to poverty, to slums, to television, to the war in Vietnam, and to racial discrimination, but, as we saw in an earlier issue of Modern Age,[1] it seems unlikely that these are actually the causes. Poverty in the United States has been declining steadily for decades while crime has been rising; Negroes for the most part kill not whites but other Negroes; and many crimes such as mugging are committed by repeated offenders who suspend their activities only for short periods in jail. While it is undoubtedly true that harsh punishment, such as the death penalty in the eighteenth century for stealing a purse, does not stop thievery, it is equally true that violent crime is neither curbed nor prevented by judges merely slapping the wrists of perpetrators, or by political and religious leaders, social scientists, and commentators telling criminals that they, and not the people they slug, are the victims.

Crime is to a degree a specialized product of every society: the Malay runs amok; the Mafia organizes its operations of terror among its victims in Sicily and the United States; the Japanese, when political assassination was in vogue before World War II, did in chiefs of governments or departments on allegedly patriotic grounds; the anarchists of Eastern and Southern Europe, in search of a great nonsociety, tossed their bombs at a wide range of heads of state. There are styles of crime as there are styles of working and living. Our political assassinations have been the deeds of isolated psychopaths, criminals, or fanatics whose presence is probably inevitable in a population of two hundred million people where strong emotions on issues of race, nationality, war and peace, communism versus alleged reaction can either be readily imported or bred from native stock. The politicos dutifully intone the liberal litany of the time and tell us we must get to the roots of these malheurs, by which they mean we must not turn to the police, to coercion, or to swift judicial punishment, or deal harshly with arsonists and thieves who are merely unhappy progeny of this sad, sick society. But every society must defend itself against criminals, either collectively through law, the courts, and the police or by more informal individual efforts such as Europe and Asia and the American West knew in the centuries before a central authority supplied the protection. How can these peacekeeping, law enforcing powers function in a climate where muggers and killers are daily brought the happy tidings that it is they who are the victims of circumstances? When a vice president of the United States declares he too would riot if he lived in the slums, and we discover that most of those who rioted in

1. "Editorial," Modern Age, vol. 2, no. 3.

Detroit had jobs and were earning well over a hundred dollars a week, we have some measure of who is sick.

War. Millions of people, Europeans and Asians, are living in their national styles with all the advantages and disadvantages of their traditional societies beefed up with American aid because of the armed forces of the United States. The American umbrella held off Stalin and although it blew inside-out in China, without it much of the free world would have been drowned. There is no sickness in helping nations keep their independence, but there is a limit to American manpower and resources, and these must be husbanded for the vital areas and above all for those willing and capable of fighting and sacrificing for their own independence. President Johnson once said he thought the people with whom he had talked on a trip to Europe and Asia would have liked, if they could, to live in Johnson City. He was wrong. Even the wretched half-naked cadres of despair and revolution, not to mention sizable numbers of Mr. Johnson's own countrymen, might reject such meager values of the good life. Florence was poor by American standards, so were Athens, London, Paris, Rome, Madrid and Weimar, it may be that American cities are poorer than they were by the measures that are used over a long period of time. But there is nothing morally corrupt, nothing sick in being willing to make sacrifices of one's own substance to permit the countries of Southeast Asia to choose their governments without the aid of strong-arm cadres recruited in Moscow and Peking. The enormous vitality and goodwill of the American people make it all too easy for a president to apply primer formulations of moral uplift to areas and peoples where they are worthless and where they will be counter-selective. For only those can be aided who will willingly put their own lives and property on the line for their freedom. This happened in Greece, in Latin America, and in Korea, and it will happen again: so-called wars of national liberation are a relatively cheap means of advancing the revolution that both Moscow and Peking do all they can to make inevitable. But it is not a sick society that has stood in the path of a totalitarian communism and that has given freely of its resources, its brains and manpower, with no notion of any material profit to be gained. Naive perhaps, given to foolish oversimplifications and ever ready moral purposes, but it has held off the barbarians both beyond the wall and on this side of it.

And where are these utopias where there is no sickness? The German Democratic Republic, East Germany, is the second-largest industrial power in the East bloc, following only the Soviet Union. It has the highest standard of living among the communist countries outside of Russia and from it more than two and a half million people fled before the wall and the barbed wire were put up in the summer of 1961. Since 1961, 240,000 more have left, half of them illegally, at the risk of their lives, across the wall and the mine fields and despite the armed guards who have orders to gun them down. In the Communist bloc, the liberalization policy so widely praised as a sign of better days is a minuscule approximation of the Western economic system, substituting some measure of consumer choice for the heavy stamp of the Plan, permitting some breath of criticism of the basic orthodoxies, and withal continuing to send those to Siberia who dissent too widely or too publicly.

Is it in the welfare states of Europe that utopia is to be found? That is something Mr. Wilson's government is having increasing difficulty in explaining to his electorate as it votes against his statist policies in British cities where labor has held office for decades. It is something the Social Democrats are having similar trouble in explaining to the harried Swedes, who complain of the increase in crime and delinquency among the young and wonder why Sweden, spared of the bombing that devastated Germany, has such an acute housing shortage compared with the West Germans.

Man, even American man, is born to trouble as the sparks fly upward. Maybe he's had it too good. Maybe all the opulence, the automobiles, and the drip-dry culture has led him to think that the real four-star paradise is a commodity and all he has to do to get it is to make more money for himself, pay out a larger portion of it to those who need it, and help the rest of the world to settle down. Maybe he thinks with this he'll have it made, and if he does it will be at that point that the sickness will be upon him.

The New Conservatives

In the early years of the twentieth century William Graham Sumner wrote an essay that has become far better known by its title than by its content. It was called "The Forgotten Man," and it referred to the part of the nation that uncomplainingly went about its business, paying taxes and bills, doing its job, demanding no handouts or government subsidies either directly or in the form of high tariffs—the people in short who never got into the newspapers or the halls of Congress with their petitions and lobbyists, but who carry the charities, the workload, the lame, the halt, and all those in need as well as free-loaders and those who live by good deeds and a fast buck. Franklin D. Roosevelt liked the title of the Sumner essay and used it in a speech referring not to the patient citizens Sumner was writing about but to the third of a nation which then in the deep Depression he declared to be ill housed, ill clad, and ill fed. In the election of 1968 the phrase was revived again, this time by Mr. Nixon, who said it applied to the hard-working people of the suburbs, those who joined no television demonstrations, took part in no riots, who presumably mowed their lawns and washed their cars and themselves. Nixon was closer to the original text than Mr. Roosevelt had been, and he was in fact praising a segment of the population that is vastly larger than a suburban habitat would support and that represents in its power and influence a revolutionary change in American life.

The 1968 presidential election was made manifest in the combined Nixon-Wallace vote and in shifting emphases in the Democratic party as well as a new pattern not only of voting but also of social-economic stratification and habits of thought. What had been for years a seemingly unbreakable alliance of ethnic, racial, and religious minorities, plus labor unions, plus the liberal intellectuals of the mass media and the universities, has been broken into by long damned-up torrents of public sentiment that have swept aside many of the leaders and policies dominant since 1932. It is an ad hoc coalition that has replaced this old alliance, a coalition of millions of blue-collar workers and Southern agrarians, of people from small towns, clerks, storekeepers, Middle and Far West farmers, employees, enterprisers and pensioners, a vast, partly new middle class that is rapidly becoming for the first time in history the class of a majority of those who have taken pride in being gainfully employed. It is a class that cuts across historical cleavages and symbols of status and color, and in its proportion to the population and in its potential influence it may be far more powerful than the massed activists of the Kremlin and Mao Tse-tung. For these are the legions of the wage earners, the working people, the makers; they are the squares, the anti-hippies, the anti-pot and acid heads, and millions of them have had it up to here with the give-away programs and the burnt offerings of the liberal voodoo. Not all of them have broken with their traditional political allegiances but the yeast of change is in them all.

Although many of them are critical of the Negro, they include Negroes and a respect for Negroes who have joined their ranks. And make no mistake about it, Negroes have joined their ranks in increasing numbers as the opportunity has been open to them. A recent newsreel of a housing development on the outskirts of Cleveland recorded interviews with a number of the Negroes who live in a well-kept suburban middle-class section they had created. Their indignation at Mayor Stokes' plan to move slum Negroes out from the city to a government-subsidized housing development that would be next to their tidy home sites would have matched any backlashes in Cicero, Illinois, or London, England. The interviews were most revealing; one neatly dressed Negro woman said flatly: "We don't want any of those project people in this neighborhood, we've come away from the project by the sweat of our brows, we know what it means to have the handout people at your doorstep." Or words to that effect. These Negroes may still follow the voting habits established during the Depression but their sentiments are different now and they too are the unmistakable signs of the new wave, of an artisan middle class that has spread out over the stratifications of the nineteenth century and over the educational gaps that were often more apparent than real, for the children who use the going vocabulary of easy learning with its words like dialogue, communication, power structure, charismatic, alienation, cultural deprivation, and such are not so much better educated than their parents as they are the parroters of a vocabulary diffused by a swinging technology.

All this is not to be explained in purely economic terms. Many, most in fact, of the rioters in Detroit and Watts were employed, some of them at high wages. The disaffected youth have come from all strata of society; the battle in Chicago was fought far more by the sons and daughters of the conventional middle-class people in the suburbs than by the inhabitants of the ghettoes. It is the rich who have been conspicuous among the leaders in the fight for busing, for integration, for open housing, for increased benefits to the fecund mothers of dependent children. It is also the rich, and the comfortably affluent liberals, who, having paraded in the civil rights demonstrations and agitated for all the benefactions of the Great Society from busing to Black Power, continued to live untouched by them in their personal and domestic life. A few years ago one of my liberal friends, a historian who was doing research in Germany and slowly making his way back home to the city of Washington, told me he was dreading his return. His children were of school age and most of the liberals he knew—this was in 1962 or 1963—were taking their children out of the Washington public schools, including those who a few years before had been most enthusiastic for integration. And this remark of my historian friend has long since been borne out by the statistics, which show that only two or three of the children of members of the House of Representatives or of the Senate now attend Washington public schools, which became black far more quickly than the general population of the city as parents voted one way in public and another in private.

An even more striking example of this is to be seen in the behavior of the very rich liberals, especially of those in public life. The Kennedys and Rockfellers have no immediate prospect of being forced by open housing laws to accept Negroes as neighbors or by the policies of school integration to bus their children to a school in the slums. Their passion for the integrated society can be expressed on their own terms and in graceful ways with chosen representatives of any of the races that meet their fancy. Otherwise, they are threatened by no invasion of project housing or of people furnished with rent subsidies; their children are not forced into schools where they are regularly chased home at the end of the day by gangs demanding money, as has happened day after day in integrated schools in Chicago.

But things are different with the blue-collar workers and with the moderately well-off middle classes. Much of what they have in the world's goods and in pride is centered in the house they live in, in their neighborhood. They have fewer options, be they black or white, than the people with the acres of rolling lawns and a wide choice of private boarding or local day schools. It was the way of life of this middle group that was being threatened at every hand by the coercive society of the liberals who told them through the courts and federal and local governments they had better get to like the new era or else. And it may be noted too that the rich and the very affluent were not in the least affected in their standard of living by the costly enterprises of the Great

Society. The rich liberals suffered the deprivation of not one trip abroad or one ball less; they were no Lord Buddhas retiring from the fleshpots of the world; no St. Francises or Simone Weils sharing the life of the poor and distressed. However high their pulses beat for the Lumpenproletariat and all the dispossessed, they made not the slightest move to dispossess themselves. It was the middle class they called on to bear the burden of their welfare state, and it was millions of the members of the middle class who said they had had enough.

This enormous middle class is a truly modern phenomenon; more modern than the hippies who in other disguises have long been with us, more modern than the pot and acid heads, for the drug takers too have a long and disorderly history. But for a great class of wage earners to live well, even opulently, with short work weeks, the opportunity for a higher education open to them, aided if they have any talent for the higher learning or technology by private corporations that will pay their way; with art, literature, music, theater on their dials or down the street if they want them; this is something the planet has never seen before. Luxuries that a few years ago were available only to a handful now are taken for granted by the masses who have earned the right to have them. And it was these hard-earned material goods that were being defended together with the even more important feeling of having made it, of status, of being a full-fledged citizen who also had the right to say no, to dissent from union leaders, from politicos who had given them little enough choice among all the legislative panaceas and court decisions that had cascaded over their heads. They wanted no more of the facile promises that bigger doses of spending and more welfarism would at long last make it safe to walk on the streets, to use a park or travel on public transportation after dark. They were not on the receiving end of the public cornucopia; it was mainly they who were pouring in the taxes on behalf of a war for which they had no enthusiasm and for the welfare programs they knew were supporting too many people as able to work as they were. Their revolt was based on a revulsion against the collapsed liberalism that has been dominant over so many decades far more than it was a crusade for a new politics, a new society, or the call of new leadership toward a transcendent order.

The conservative alliance is a loose conglomerate of many factions, sentiments, and beliefs. Like many other mass movements it is mainly an alliance against something, a repudiation of measures that have not worked and could not work, a denial of the proposition once overwhelmingly agreed upon that it is the state that should provide, the state that must create the great and good society, and the conviction that if enough money is shoveled out on the public sector we may have it. The fallacies in these arguments have been long exposed in a few places; in a few, very few universities, in scattered publications, by a relatively few economists, and still fewer social scientists and writers. The overwhelming majority of these pundits were on the other side but they too have been disenchanted, many of them, and from their advance guard curiously enough have come recently the most vehement denunciations of the facile liberal formulations of the last years. Some of these disillusioned liberals have joined this precarious conservative coalition, but only a few because it is always the intellectuals who are most reluctant to give up their prejudices or to admit that they exist. An interesting example of this myopia was to be seen when President Johnson to the vast distress of Arthur Schlesinger, Jr., appointed Senator Hruska and Eric Hoffer to the commission investigating violence in the United States. Schlesinger said indignantly on learning of these appointments that both these men should disqualify themselves, for Hruska was opposed to gun control and Hoffer had said that the slaying of Robert Kennedy was not symbolic of the sickness and violence of America so much as it was typical of Jordan from whence the alleged gunman had come only a few years ago. Such opinions in Schlesinger's view disqualified these two men, but their real disqualification came from disagreeing with Mr. Schlesinger's prejudices or, if you like, opinions on what to do about guns and on the nature of such political assassinations as that of Senator Kennedy. There has been little evidence that Mr. Schlesinger has been willing to disqualify himself from any commission whatsoever because of his own partis pris.

This middle class of the new conservatives may not be cast in a heroic mold. It has engaged in no Long Marches nor does it aspire to, nor in fact did those who followed and fought with Mao over the six thousand miles of the march want to do that either. It could be that the heroic demands of the modern world are of another order, although these people too may be called on to fight and die as they have been before in the recurring wars in Europe and the Far East. But another kind of virtue may be needed to live and do one's job in this world of the Great Technology—it may demand above all the ability to participate in the automated society as its master with something more, much more than the satisfaction of spiraling material wants as the goal to be sought. The United States continues to be the leading power among those who keep Communist imperialism from further conquests, the crisis of the cities and of other conclaves of poverty has still to be met, the plight of the *Lumpenproletariat* to be dealt with, and aid afforded to those who cannot provide adequately for themselves without depriving these recipients of the incentives and means for climbing out of their dependency. The United States must refashion a domestic policy based on individual responsibility and a foreign policy based not on collective security, which does not and cannot exist in the present real world of international conflict and divisions, but on regional alliances of nations that have similar interests and the same desire to defend themselves. This middle-class conservatism is basically a reaffirmation that a society is made not by government but by its people and its institutions, and that the individual not the government is responsible for his actions, that it is to his own efforts he must turn and that law and order must invoke the sanction of force when the other sanctions fail and the burnings begin. But whether this loose coalition will provide more than a stopgap against the forces set in motion in this century under the banners of the Left will depend on the fortitude and integrity with which it proceeds. It is one kind of victory to take over from a spacious liberalism; it will need more than the notion that what is good for General Motors is good for the United States to go from here.

1969

The Prisoner
of Spandau

O f the original seven major war criminals sentenced in Nuremberg in 1946 to various terms ranging from ten years to life, only one remains in the Berlin prison of Spandau. The others of the twenty-two accused were either hanged, as were Ribbentrop, Keitel, Streicher, and seven others; or like Goering committed suicide; or like Bormann were not to be found; or like Papen, Fritzsche, and Schacht were set free by the International Military Tribunal. The last of the Nuremberg prisoners and the last man to be the cause of military collaboration by the four powers whose common deployment has long been limited to Spandau, is Rudolf Hess, the Fuehrer's deputy, the man who on May 10, 1941, a little more than a month before the German attack on the Soviet Union, flew to Scotland on a self-appointed mission of peace to prevent the two Nordic powers, Britain and Germany, from shedding more of their precious blood. Hess told his British captors he saw more unspeakable horrors ahead unless peace were made, he saw long lines of women grieving over the bodies of their uselessly slain in a conflict that was "suicidal for the white race." Convinced that only a dramatic gesture would bring an end to this civil war of the Germanic brothers, he had flown to Britain without Hitler's knowledge but with the conviction that peace would be made if the British would only listen to him.

The British, a few of them at least, did listen. The Duke of Hamilton; the Lord Chancellor Sir John Simon; Lord Beaverbrook, another member of the Churchill cabinet; and Ivone Kirkpatrick from the Foreign Office were sent to the house where Hess was confined, and they questioned him closely. Although Hess had planned to go to Britain for only a short stay, a few days he thought, he had landed with a large store of homeopathic pills and an elixir from Tibet. Doctors including psychiatrists examined him, as did members of the intelligence service, and his endlessly repeated monologues were useful mainly to the psychiatrists, who pronounced Hess schizophrenic with a hysterical overlay. At least twice in Britain Hess attempted suicide, his first lunge over a banister the doctors thought had really begun as an attempt to murder his physician but Hess had changed his mind and tried to kill himself. Later he would stab himself in the chest and attempt to poison himself.

Such behavior as well as his flight were merely additional evidences of the mental disorders from which the Fuehrer's deputy suffered. Hess had a long history of bizarre behavior. One visitor saw him in bed in Munich with a large magnet suspended overhead to deflect evil influences and a dozen more under the bed in case the malign powers came from that direction. Hess had been one of the privileged few who could lunch with the Fuehrer any time they wished, but Hitler had discovered Hess was carrying his own raw vegetables in a briefcase to the Fuehrer's cook and told him angrily that the Chancellor's kitchen was able to provide him with proper nourishment when he came to lunch and forbade him in the future to bring his own food.[1] During his confinement in Britain, Hess was always suspicious of the meals served him and he would often swiftly exchange his plate with that of the prison commandant at whose side he ate. At times he writhed on his cell floor suffering from real or imaginary stomach cramps, and these seizures together with constant complaints that he was being drugged and poisoned and kept from sleeping by his ubiquitous enemies, his frequent lapses of memory and his haranguing answers to any precise questions, made him generally useless to the political interrogators who were trying to find out why he had flown to Britain and what he knew of German plans. Hess's British doctors believed his personality still to have some clear areas which the schizophrenic process had not yet invaded and these, they thought, enabled him to function under certain circumstances with seemingly normal reactions. Thus he could talk lucidly at times to the men who interviewed him. Lord Beaverbrook reported to Churchill that Hess seemed sane to him. In the same way he had been able to carry out his party and governmental functions; although he was widely thought of as erratic and peculiar, his behavior was not considered unduly eccentric in an environment of mystical theories of blood and Nordic destiny and of fanatical loves and hates. Alfred Rosenberg shared Hess's belief that the former Chancellor of Germany, Heinrich Bruening, was a secret agent plotting to bring communism to rule the Reich and thus to get rid of Protestant Prussia and deliver the country to the Catholics. Respected scholars like the Haushofers shared Hess's views on the blood brotherhood of the Germanic races and the necessity for organizing peace between them; the Fuehrer himself was a vegetarian as Hess was; astrologists and soothsayers were in high fashion—when Mussolini was taken prisoner by the Badoglio government in 1943 so-called psychics were employed by the

---

1. This scene is described in Albert Speer's memoirs, *Inside the Third Reich*.

SS to divine his whereabouts; the genuineness of the forged Protocols of the Elders of Zion was taken for granted by the Nazi leadership. In a time of revolution, murder, arson, and sudden disappearances into concentration camps, Hess with his particular brand of paranoia attracted no undue attention until he flew to Britain on his mission of peace.

It is the ambiguities in the search for peace that have been his downfall. For Rudolf Hess is the only man in all history to be sent to prison—in Hess's case the sentence is for life—for having plotted to wage aggressive war and then to have waged it. The decision to make war has hitherto been regarded as an act of state, an impersonal act made on behalf of a government and its people, and it was only the Nuremberg Tribunal that stated this new and retroactive law that sent Hess to Spandau for as long as he lives. The Russian judge had demurred at this leniency. Soviet authorities were more skeptical of Hess than of many of the others among the twenty-two defendants, for they saw in his flight to Britain, six weeks before the German offensive, a confirmation of their most dire forebodings—a combined attack on the Soviet Union by Hitler and the capitalist powers. At Potsdam, Stalin questioned Attlee closely about Hess's treatment and asked suspiciously when he would be brought to Germany to trial. When the Western judges voted to sentence Hess to life imprisonment the Russian judge Nikitchenko wrote a dissent saying Hess should have been sentenced to death. As the Fuehrer's deputy he had had a hand in the main Nazi atrocities, and Nikitchenko stated flatly that Hess's flight to Britain had been for the purpose of getting the English out of the war temporarily while the Germans attacked the Soviet Union. Actually, however, when the British questioned him during the six weeks before the German advance, Hess denied any German intention of attacking Russia. His interrogators were naturally interested in finding out what they could of the truth of the many rumors that a German assault on the Soviet Union was imminent, but the subject was not one that had much interest for Hess. He kept repeating how much Hitler wanted to come to an understanding with Britain, and, in fact, while Hess remained in the Reich he had opposed the attack on Russia on the ground that a two-front war had been disastrous in World War I, in which he had served. He agreed with Haushofer that a victorious Russia would mean the end of the British empire and the triumph of communism on the continent of Europe. In any event, what Hess yearned for was the collaboration of Britain and the Reich. Germany would get its colonies back, control the continent of Europe, and would help preserve the British empire. The Soviet Union was secondary in his thinking, the problems she presented might be worked out by treaty or by war—the main thing was to convince England that the Reich sought friendship and peace with her and the fratricidal war with her must stop. It was only three months after the German attack on Russia that Hess proposed to Beaverbrook that England join the Reich in the war against Russia.

The Court at Nuremberg decided that Hess was sane enough to be tried after another panel of doctors, chosen from among the four powers, had examined him for a few hours. The psychiatrists said that he was not insane in the strict sense, although they noted that his amnesia would prevent him from understanding completely what was going on around him and would interfere with his defense. Hess in fact made no defense, he addressed the Court only twice, at the beginning and the end of the trial, telling it first that he had been feigning amnesia and that he could remember when he wanted to; and, at the end of the trial, telling it of the plots against him and the strange phenomena he had to endure: "I said before that a certain incident in England caused me to think of the reports of the earlier trials. The reason was that the people around me during my imprisonment acted towards me in a peculiar and incomprehensible way, in a way which led me to conclude that these people somehow were acting in an abnormal state of mind. Some of them—these persons and people around me—were changed from time to time. Some of the new ones who came to me in place of those who had been changed had strange eyes. They were glassy and like eyes in a dream . . ." His behavior had been odd enough for the Court toward the end of the trial to order a further mental examination, this one was conducted not by a psychiatrist but by an Austrian-born psychologist, G. M. Gilbert, who cordially detested all the defendants and pronounced Hess still able to stand trial without having to appear before another panel of psychiatrists.

Behind the scenes the evidences for Hess's insanity had nevertheless multiplied. He had been brought before a group of people he had known well to refresh his memory; Haushofer, Goering, Papen, Messerschmidt, and he could recognize none of them. Goering, strutting on this occasion as he did at every opportunity, reminded Hess of his having stayed at Goering's princely residences in Berlin and Karinhall but all Hess could say was that he remembered his name but knew nothing else about him. Hess's first lawyer, who because of an accident had to relinquish the case, told the court that Hess was incapable of helping in his own defense, and in fact Hess never took any part or seemed to have the slightest interest in the trial. Sometimes he would bring a book to read in court, sometimes he seemed to follow the testimony, but for the most part he sat day after day alone with his own private meditations, lost in his dark broodings over the hostile world in which he found himself and unconcerned with the outcome of the proceedings that had brought him to Nuremberg.

Many people including Goering thought Hitler had secretly sent Hess to Britain so that if the mission failed he could disavow it, and if it succeeded England would at last be out of the war. But this seems an unlikely hypothesis. It was unnecessary for the Fuehrer's deputy to fly to Britain to make contact with British representatives. Switzerland, Spain, and Sweden were all used during the war for negotiations between nationals of the warring powers, and Hitler had no need to place such high propaganda cards in the hands of the British to make his "peace offers" known. Hitler's propaganda chiefs could not possibly make any capital from the flight, but Churchill could not use it to full advantage either. Hitler was beside himself when he heard the news. Here was his deputy taking off on a private peace mission, a demonstration to all the world of political crack-pottedness in the Third Reich, and this at a time when the preparations for the war with the Soviet Union were going into high gear. "I hope he dives into the ocean," Paul Schmidt, Hitler's chief interpreter, heard Hitler say, and the Reich propaganda apparatus after a period of silence could only report that Hess's health had suffered of late because of overwork and that he had had dealings with astrologers and fortune-tellers as a result of his impaired state of mind. Hess's adjutant, who had brought the news of his flight to the Fuehrer, was arrested, streets and public buildings named for Hess were renamed. Churchill thought it best to treat the flight as a medico-political problem; to play it up as evidence of German weakness could be a double-edged sword for there was a peace party in England and a sizable group might like to know what kind of proposals Hess had brought with him to Britain on behalf of a war they too disapproved of. Goering, upbraiding Messerschmidt for letting Hess have an airplane, told Messerschmidt he might have known that Hess was crazy. To which Messerschmidt gave a reply that was soon quoted widely in many a delighted gathering of those who were less than enthusiastic about National Socialism and its leaders. Messerschmidt said: "How could I be expected to suppose that one so high in the hierarchy of the Third Reich could be crazy. If that was the case you should have secured his resignation."

Hess was indicted on all four counts of the Nuremberg charges—on the two counts of plotting to wage and waging aggressive warfare and also for committing crimes against humanity and war crimes. On the latter two he was found not guilty but concerning his crimes against peace the Court was stern. Hess's signature appeared on the law of March 16, 1935, establishing compulsory military service, the court said, and he had known how determined Hitler was to realize his ambitions and how little likely the Fuehrer was to refrain from resorting to force. Also the court declared that Hess had been an informed and willing participant in the aggressions against Austria, Czechoslovakia, and Poland. All this was the dogma of the New Revelation written under pressure of the gaseous notions of a world order to be administered by peace-loving nations; an imaginary order that had already broken down long before the end of the trial.

As for the court's findings, how could it be criminal for any member of a government (Hess was a minister in Hitler's Cabinet) to sign a bill establishing compulsory military service when every country in Europe had conscription? How could Hess have been aware of Hitler's belligerent intentions when Hitler himself shifted as opportunity offered from pro-Polish to anti-Polish, from years of denouncing the Soviet Union as the arch-enemy to making a pact and even a short-lived military alliance with her? As for the aggression against Austria, the German soldiers were joined by Austrian units in their "flower march" and were received with wild enthusiasm by the rejoicing millions of this most pro-Nazi segment of the Germanic peoples. As for Czechoslovakia, she had been partitioned with the aid of Britain, France, and Italy in as legal a fashion as any nonviolent change of borders in Europe has ever been effected. And as for Poland, almost every serious writer on the subject of Germany's post-Versailles boundaries had said the next war would be likely to originate there in the land of the Corridor and of a Polish state that has existed in modern Europe only when either Russia or Germany or Austria-Hungary were unable to partition her or to bring her in one piece into the Slav or Germanic orbit. In any event, Hess had had nothing to do with Hitler's orders to invade.

No, Hess was a victim not only of his own impaired mental processes but also of the illusions of his judges. The war against Hitler had to be fought and won but neither the war nor the victory could result in a world order under the combined banners of the Soviet Union and the Western powers. Communism has its own definitions of aggression, and who can doubt that a court composed, for example, of North Koreans, Cubans, North Vietnamese, Red Chinese, and judges from the Soviet Union would find former President Johnson guilty of aggression? "Aggressors" like Israel can be and indeed are named in advance by the Kremlin, and along with Israel, West Germany, the United States, Britain, France, Finland, or any other country that opposes communist expansion. Aggression, like sin, may be more readily identified than defined, and despite the labors of recent generations of international lawyers its definition still eludes any formulation. It is what the enemy does, it is what those who disturb the status quo do, it is any move made by any power we dislike or fear and above all it is the notion that we can never be safe until the world is molded in our own image. Hess, the man who flew to England to stop the war, committed no crimes whatever against peace, and it is unlikely that anyone in a position to act on behalf of a sovereign power commits such a crime as a personal indulgence, persuasive as it may seem to equate members of governments with common law breakers. Heads of state and their advisers act for better or worse, mainly it seems for worse, on behalf of their own people. To prepare an invasion of a neighboring country like Cuba, which has intercontinental missiles aimed at the United States supplied by a hostile foreign power, can be regarded either as self-defense or as an act of aggression, and any decision as to which it is will depend more on one's ideology than "pure" legality. So with the decision of the Israelis to attack in the Six-Day War of 1967 after the Arabs had closed the Gulf of Aqaba and had promised to kill all of them. So with Korea, with Vietnam, and with the invasions to come. We are a long way from the dreams of the One Worlders who gave us Nuremberg, although we, like Hess, are their victims.

Hess is seventy-six years old and he lives alone now, alone with forty guards and two cooks and any spiritual advisers or physicians he may consent to talk to. He has never seen his family since he flew from Germany in 1941, he refuses to permit them to visit him, although he has written a good deal to his wife and seems well disposed toward them. A son is attempting to organize a worldwide protest against his further imprisonment and were it not for the Russians this would undoubtedly have a good chance of success. Admiral Raeder, too, was sentenced to life imprisonment, as was Walter Funk, and both were released from Spandau with the consent of the Soviet Union on grounds of ill health, but this is unlikely to happen in the case of Hess. Hess is an old man wrapped in his own thoughts who perhaps has no objection to being where he is. He refuses to work in the prison garden at Spandau, although most of the other prisoners thought gardening a healthy diversion in their confinement. But Hess is a man of a different kind. He seems to have had some remission from his schizophrenia, although he retains many of his ties, he is still the minister, still the man who could order others to do his gardening, still the victim of mysterious enemies and of a court that had no jurisdiction over him. So Hess probably doesn't care where he is as he sits in the most expensive prison in the world alone with his haunted musings. The Allies who put him in prison have long since abandoned any notion of bringing post-Nuremberg aggressors to trial, they have no means of doing so and presumably it suffices to use the term as an epithet and a routine characterization of the enemy. Only this extraordinary precedent of the case of Rudolf Hess, who flew off to stop the war and so landed in prison for the rest of his life, remains, for a time at least, a living reminder of the mental aberrations of those presumably sane people in high places who were building a world order of law and peace no wider than the Nuremberg courtroom.

The United States and Europe

The promise of sensible, rational, mutually advantageous developments in the area of American-European relations is superficially more glittering now than it has been since the early days of the NATO alliance. In economic policies, the United States and the countries of the Common Market, with the exception of France, aim at fostering wider trading areas, reducing tariffs and any other artificial restraints to the exchange of products wherever trading can have a free run. In political matters, since the invasion of Czechoslovakia on August 21, Western European critics of the United States are far less inclined to wish to see the American presence in Europe diminished to a shade that can be exorcised or summoned at will. The rising tide of anti-Americanism, which was given great impetus by the Vietnam War, has at least been held in check by the force of the more than two hundred thousand East bloc troops that moved swiftly into Czechoslovakia. Europe has always been sensitive to troop movements; even a few regiments sent up to a frontier have been immediately registered in the seismographs of European capitals, and this massive movement of Warsaw bloc forces had no need of the seismographs in chancelleries, every man and woman in the street registered the change out of their own experience. Thus the illusion of the last decade, that Europe was safe for a long time to come, that it could, like Japan, indulge itself in the ever-mounting luxuries of peacetime with the comforting notion that both non-European powers, the United States and the Soviet Union, had successfully nullified one another's atomic arsenals, leaving Europe not only in a state of détente but in a state of a peaceful euphoria—this illusion was rudely shaken.

It is all too easy to think in terms of a stable, ordered, long-range peaceful community achieved by rhetoric when the going is relatively easy. It is then that traditional patterns of thinking like de Gaulle's can be tried out in their new blueprints; a Europe happily free of non-European powers, of both Russia and the United States, under the hegemony of France, economically and militarily flourishing as a third great power, not to be told off again by outsiders—as France and England were at the time of the Suez crisis; in short, a Europe combining the politics of Richelieu and the high living of the 1960s. And such a program, although demonstrably

219

short-sighted, is not without its reasonable grounds. Western Europe has had good reason, at times, to be doubtful that they might not fall victim to an American-Russian agreement made at their expense. The spirits of Camp David, of Glassboro, and so many other encounters of short-lived hope could, if pressed too far, leave West Germany, for example, permanently divided and with such armed forces as she has under the command of an organization that has lost its vitality, for without the unswerving support of the United States, NATO is a paper shield. Developments such as the long, inconclusive war in Vietnam and even the Pueblo affair have made it seem likely to many friends of the United States that American power, for the time at least, has been stretched about as far as it will go, or as far as prudent American political leadership would have it go. Russian goals of containing Red China in the Far East, above all of preventing any kind of Japanese-Chinese bloc, of aiding wars of liberation like the one in Vietnam, are being attained by means that do not require the participation of Soviet fighting troops in the front lines as has been true for years of American soldiers in Korea and in Vietnam. And in Europe when the time came for the invasion of Czechoslovakia, it was accomplished by a direct order from Moscow and accepted without debate by the other members of the Warsaw Pact who participated. The United States must pursue its policies under vastly different conditions; it cannot by itself order NATO into action, it cannot send its tanks and the tanks of its allies into the cities and villages of a state that only last night was part of its bloc and then tell its NATO partners that their sovereignty is of no importance compared with the overriding importance of defending capitalism. But the Soviet Union can do all these things, and this is precisely the claim that it made to justify its actions when it announced the overriding necessity of defending the socialist world when any one of the members of the East bloc is endangered by nonconformists within or revanchists without.

Nationalism in all the countries of East Europe, but especially in Romania, Czechoslovakia, Albania, and Yugoslavia, as well as separatist or particularist movements within those countries all take the form of moves toward decentralization, toward polycentrism, toward a revival of an ethnic or national history, away from Moscow. That the Soviet Union will permit Romania more autonomy than is accorded Czechoslovakia is due almost entirely to the geographic situation of the Czechs. It is one thing for the Romanians to remain aloof when the East bloc war cries resound against Israel, it is quite another when the Czechs bordering on West Germany show signs of turning toward the West in any important matters whether cultural, or economic, or political. If the Russian nightmare in the Far East is an alliance of the Chinese and the Japanese, in the West it is a strong Germany, backed by its NATO allies and the United States in any kind of *Drang nach Osten*. Soviet policy in the West continues along the same lines as it has since the formation of NATO—to weaken that organization as far as possible, if it can't be gotten rid of entirely; to edge the United States out of Europe; and to isolate West Germany. Any attempt toward a conciliatory West German Eastern policy—such as was urged for years by the Bundesrepublik's Social Democrats and to some extent carried out under the foreign ministry of Willy Brandt—is met with prompt hostility by the Soviet Union and the East German government.

In the West, too, the signs of increasing nationalism, of getting away from under Washington, have been evident. France under de Gaulle pursued her recently chosen courses, anti-British, anti-American, anti-NATO, that de Gaulle imagined would bring her great-power stature; West Germany, for the first time, refused to act in a spirit of humble reconciliation with de Gaulle, who has just come close to recognizing the permanence of the Oder-Neisse boundary, and refused to revalue the mark to help the French government to live beyond its means. The West European trend toward more independent foreign policies—of trading with and recognizing Red China, for example—of dealing more closely with the East bloc, of mounting resentment and criticism of the United States, has led some European observers to believe that the time may come when some sort of Rapacki plan of a neutral zone encompassing both Eastern and Western Europe might become a reality. It could be, they say, assented to by the United States as an extension of the détente, and by the Soviet Union, which in exchange would achieve its goal of getting the United States out of Europe and at the same time reducing the latent menace of a West Germany that it regards as the edge of the American glacis on the frontier of its domain. But these are the speculations mainly of people who lack confidence in the United States and who have mixed feelings for the Soviet Union.

At this point in history, the national interests of both the countries of the East and West blocs and of those between—like Yugoslavia—point toward preserving the status quo. Unlike the situation in the 1930s and 1914, few countries in Europe have any bleeding frontiers. With the exception of the Oder-Neisse territories of Germany and the tribulations of the Austrian population of the Italian Tyrol, the people of Europe are at least reluctantly content with their boundaries and even with the balance of power between East and West as they now exist. Germany and Berlin are divided and the Bundesrepublik's allies give lip service to the necessity for reunification, but the division in Germany, too, is accepted as a fact and among many governments both East and West it is considered desirable.

Europe is in no danger from the status quo on the continent. Berlin is intermittently rocked by the propaganda wars, but it, too, is part of the détente marking the fields of force where the two worlds meet and rest on their arms. The grave danger to the American-European alliance lies primarily in other parts of the world, in the Middle East for example, where France has moved over to the neighborhood of the Soviet-Arab camp and where any day could see the resumption of fighting that, if it lasted longer than the Israeli-Arab Six-Day War of 1967, might well spread to far wider areas. Even Castro's Cuba, Santo Domingo, and other countries of Latin America are more likely settings for brushfire wars that—like Vietnam—may involve both worlds than are the countries of Europe.

It is primarily the United States that for better or worse will continue to guide the defense policies of the European nations. They form of themselves too amorphous a coalition to have anything approaching the strength to create the independent and countervailing forces that General de Gaulle had in mind. When the Russians march into Czechoslovakia, the countries of Western Europe look not to themselves but to the United States for reassurance against a further Soviet advance; this is as true for the French for all their atomic weapons as it is for the Germans without them. It is at this point that the belief in the durability of the status quo and in the satiety of the Soviet Union is shaken and the threat of Soviet power reasserts itself.

The crucial questions then for these countries are: How reliable is the United States? To what extent are American vital interests parallel or identical with their own, so that they may depend on the collective defense that NATO calls for where an attack on one of the partners will bring all of them into action? Such questions are answered in different ways in different capitals at different times, for those old societies have long racial and ethnic memories that become more vivid as the immediate dangers subside. But Europe has no alternative to this military alliance. Short-lived ideas of a world order of peace-loving states, of the four policemen who once long ago at the time of Teheran were supposed to patrol the world on behalf of these peace-loving states have gone the way of an international force of Keystone cops. The United Nations are looked on now by both East and West as a convenient propaganda forum, a meeting place where nudges may be given and received and aggressors denounced, but the UN is no longer a forum of man's hopes for peace or the base of an international army intent on putting down evil-doers. American policy hammered out in the hard realities of the post–World War II world has become far more realistic than it was in the days of the Kellogg-Briand Pact, disarmament treaties, and the long and repetitive articles in learned journals about the World Community and the necessity for treating aggression as a criminal act.

But always lurking between the lines of public pronouncements are the old ghosts, the old fantasies that since 1917 have enticed both liberals and conservatives—especially in the United States—with the idea that the Communists are just another political party and that once the Communist countries attain a decent standard of living, once they are convinced that the United States really means well by them and will not organize an encirclement of them, we can all live together happily, if not in one, then in two worlds. The ever-ready praise of the Soviet Union when it has given American presidents and other high officials, as well as the *New York Times*, the slightest occasion for it is matched only by their short-lived disappointment when the Soviet vetoes some measure they take to be on behalf of the peace they seek, or openly takes hostile positions in Cuba, Korea, or Vietnam, or moves its troops and tanks into Berlin, Poland, Hungary, or Czechoslovakia. But the hopeful theory of convergence, the need for showing our good faith and allaying the seemingly bottomless, as well as ill-founded, suspicions of the rulers of Russia and other members of the East bloc, are deep articles of faith that will reappear as soon as the dust of each crisis settles. We have some evidence, for example, that former President Johnson even after the invasion of Czechoslovakia was anxious to initiate talks with Messrs. Brezhnev and Kosygin despite the consternation this quasi-recognition of the legality of an act of sheer force would have spread throughout the nations of the West and many countries of East Europe as well.

Such unilateral acts of confidence and goodwill have been conspicuous and far-reaching in their consequences over a period of decades and, allied with a vague internationalism, they have succeeded in producing the state of permanent world crisis in which we live. But the actual, direct American experiences with world politics have rubbed away many of the unrealistic notions of a world order; it is these experiences which have led the countries of Western Europe, and the United States as well, to rely far more on regional pacts like NATO than on their own divided strength or on the UN, which, without the surrender of sovereignty that no nation in the world would give it, could not operate in the image in which it was conceived. The essence of international life, as it is of all biological forms, is to retain the imprint of the past and yet to change; and in international affairs the possibility of change must exist without every minor realignment of forces triggering a major war on the pretext that an assault has been made on a nonexistent world order. What is fortunate in the present European situation is that illusory notions of the kind that sired the League and the UN have been burned away by the experience of the last generation and of this one. No country in Europe relies on the UN for its security, but they do rely on their respective pacts and on the two great powers that guarantee their efficacy. So the United States and Europe have the opportunity to deal forthrightly with realities, and these realities fortunately include the moral values they share, the similar cultures, and the identical goals of preserving them against not only communism but also the anarchism that seems to be an inseparable part of the affluent societies that promise and produce so much and leave so much unfulfilled.

It is melancholy, for example, to reflect on the diminishing of the British estate in these last years. In the early twentieth century Britain was the foremost power in the world, flourishing economically, sure of its mission and with not only its flag planted throughout the globe but its civilization as well. Joyce Cary gives a touching picture of the unconscious effects of the British mission when he has one of his sympathetic black characters, who has never been outside his native district in his life, talk of "going home to England." No country performs admirably on all fronts and at all times, but the British had done well in the annals of civilization despite many and repeated lapses, and it remains to be seen whether the new countries it has left as a legacy of its imperial standards will do nearly as well. But Britain is a shadow of its former power; after two victorious wars and a technological revolution it helped to set in motion it is reduced in its economy and perhaps even in its self-regard below the two nations it has helped to defeat, Japan and Germany. The Soviet Union is not responsible for this change in the fortunes and position of Britain, which is due instead to a whole series of developments that occurred as much within the British empire as outside it.

The renunciation of grandeur may have its beneficent as well as its negative aspects. In Italy, for example, the idea of an imperium that led Italians by the thousands to cheer and march for Mussolini is entirely dead. There are no more heady dreams of an Italian Ethiopia and an

Italian-dominated Balkans, no more shouts for Nice or Corsica being returned to Italy. The Italians are reasonably content with their industrial, aesthetic, and cultural revival, and although millions of them vote against the establishment and seemingly against the Western orientation of their foreign policy, their Communist party, too, finds it necessary to denounce the Soviet invasion of Czechoslovakia, and in no part of the electorate are there any signs of a return of the dream of mighty armed forces and a major role in Europe and Africa. Italy, like Britain, accepts a reduced status in the age of the superpowers; she has no interest in German reunification, the only borderland that disturbs her is her own South Tyrol where the Austrians of Italian nationality wage an intermittent partisan war against the Italianization of their province. Thus in Italy, too, any threats to her security come from inside the country, from the large section of the electorate that rejects or would like to water down the Western alliance and enter either a zone of neutralist powers or the Eastern alliance. The scars of the defeat and whatever laurels may have been plucked from the victory that resulted when the nation abruptly changed sides in World War II are worn lightly. The Italian people were led into both of the world wars against what would undoubtedly have been an overwhelming majority of the country had a plebiscite been held in either case.

The United States is a nation at the peak of its power in the economic, technological, and military complex, sporadically intent on certain goals and then wavering and self-doubting with regard to these and others. The Vietnam War is the symbol of these conflicting tendencies. No question can exist in the minds of anyone save the most doctrinaire but that such a war could have been won speedily and economically had the military power of this country been fully brought to bear on behalf of a speedy victory. But it was a presidential war, a war that involved the commitment of more than a half million men thousands of miles from the United States not by a declaration of war by Congress but by a series of presidential orders. It is therefore an undeclared war, a limited war prosecuted piecemeal, and because the risks of bringing in either Russia or China or both were unacceptable to the administration that was responsible for the commitment of the mass of the troops, it was a war fought inconclusively and at a cost that seemed to an increasing number of Americans incommensurate with any victory that might eventually be achieved. The allies that once in the age of innocence were supposed automatically to join in the posse comitatus against the aggressor were sparse, and it must have become plain to even the most stubborn advocate of collective action on behalf of moral principles that nations simply do not risk the lives and treasure of their people on behalf of any such dicta but only on behalf of what they take to be their own vital interests, their security.

It is here that our present situation with regard to Europe is manifestly different—it is in the individual and common interest of the United States and of every state in Western Europe to provide for the defense of the alliance; a continent controlled by the Soviet Union would force the United States to breathe economically with one lung, not to mention the impairment of our strategic position and the inevitable consequences of our isolation in every other part of the world. For Western Europe, the alliance is a matter of life and death as far as the independence of national cultures and political traditions are concerned. There is no substitute for this alliance in the foreseeable future. Thus, what NATO offers us all, Western Europe and the United States as well, is the only kind of collective security that has any validity in the contemporary world, for it is forged out of common needs and purposes and with no echo of the cries for a spurious global police force of which we have found by experience we are the only active member. Our goals should have again become clear, as they were in the early days of the Republic; they are not goals of world peace, which is so often trotted out as the pious hope of this well-meaning land. Since the end of World War II there have been no less than fifty-four armed conflicts, revolutions, police actions, wars of one kind or another. They continue the ancient pattern of resolving conflicts by conflict despite the dire threat of the atomic bomb and the lofty findings of the Nuremberg Trials that found aggression to be a criminal offense. It is a depressing fact that we have as yet found no substitute for the force of arms as the ultima ratio when irreconcilable quarrels between nations reach their critical mass. The United States cannot prevent them, but what it can do is to lend its assistance to those peoples who are ready to sacrifice and defend themselves against the encroachments of a Communist attack. And this does not mean the fighting presence of American soldiers in every part of the globe; for the direct intervention of our armed forces must be reserved for the areas deemed vital to the protection of this country and after the most searching scrutiny of the priorities of these vital interests.

The United States has the means to carry out a successful policy of containment and of maintaining Western superiority without bankrupting itself or draining its resources of manpower, raw materials, and industrial production. But the problem is obviously not one of manpower and physical resources alone. We, like the countries of Western Europe, face an internal crisis of great dimensions. Part of it may be seen in the revolt in the universities, where it merges with the race conflict; in the violence of our cities, where the lack of security has brought about in some areas a demand for the private organization of elementary protections. Hand in hand with these well-known phenomena are others that also betray a deep change in contemporary attitudes toward the homeland, the defense of the nation. The repute of the internal forces of law and order is not high among the youth of the nation, or among its intelligentsia, and the dim view extends to the armed forces. When universities like Yale and Harvard stop giving academic credit for ROTC courses and withdraw faculty ranking from the officers teaching them, we witness a considerable change in the attitude of the predecessors of the same young men who joined the Lafayette escadrille a half century ago during World War I. The attitude may arise, as it has in so many countries, out of the disillusionment of the young men who returned from fighting on behalf of world democracy or of the peace-loving nations or of some other abstract goal, but what of the changed climate among the faculty, the alumni, and students who for years fostered or at least accepted such courses and who now in 1969 find it necessary to turn their backs on them?

What is lacking in the West are the psychological, the spiritual, the moral convictions that are part of being a great power, not the material factors. We react to what the Russians do, we do not originate the policies that in the past have stirred men's spirits. A Prussian general once said his answer to "Liberty, Equality, Fraternity," was "Cavalry, Infantry, Artillery," but it was not a durable answer; the West has still not found a satisfying answer to the problems arising out of the technological society and its abundance. When the youth of our time are alienated, this is not the result of a conspiracy, although the conspiracy makes all the use it can of their revolt and strives to turn it into the desired channels. But the United States has a far better case than the one we tell the world or that we tell ourselves about. It is we who keep the doors open for all the dissident writers and thinkers, geniuses and crackpots, who are sent not to Siberia, but to the lecture circuit; it is we who pour out our substance on behalf of such principles as independence and self-determination, and then lament the fact that the results are in no proportion to our expectations or the expectations of those for whom we were making the sacrifices. It is necessary to conserve even such enormous material energies as we can generate, and it is necessary to hold and harden our lines. American interests may be clearly defined; it is for those interests that we need fortitude and determination, and it is possible that if we are able to forge a foreign policy that conforms to the genuine needs of this country—which are also the needs of that other part of the great world of traditional culture in East and West—the disillusioned ones who lost track of themselves after the fruitless search for worldwide four freedoms may return to the ranks of civilization.

Castles in Spain and Other Countries

N o man or country can have everything. If, as in the United States and West Germany, the technological society builds computerized spaceships, overnight roads, stratospheric planes, and chemical industries for and against the plague, new industrial and social diseases created by the processes themselves immediately begin an attack on the altered structure of the society. Spain, on the other hand, which has had a slowly developing technology, has its old immunities, it bears its dictatorship stoically as it has other centuries of hard living, joins the modern world only in unavoidable places and moves not outwards toward the void of the cosmos, but inwardly toward the smaller goals of keeping body and soul together and perhaps repossessing Gibraltar. Quixote still lives in Spain, the man from la Mancha is as alive to the Spaniards as his creator, and inns where he might have stayed can be pointed out as readily as the house where Cervantes once lived in a narrow street in Madrid. The Moorish past too lives on, a powerful aesthetic impulse that has never failed to stimulate the Spaniards however much they may have hated the infidel. The inhabitants of Cordoba were bitterly opposed to the transformation of the gracefully vaulted mosque built by Abd-al-Rahman I in the eighth century into a holy Christian church, even in the days when the passions of a religious war were still smoldering and the man who managed to convert it narrowly escaped paying with his life for his bad taste and excess of piety.

Spain has long had a powerful magnetism for a wide variety of foreigners for its grace, its *corridas*, its harsh, bright landscape, its Catholicism more rigid than any other excepting perhaps that of parts of Ireland, its habits of introspection and eloquence, its simple dignity. So inefficient that their armed forces at the turn of the century simply fell apart when they encountered a fairly modern armada of American warships and troops, Spaniards fought and died gallantly in their Civil War and on the Russian front just as they had fought and died, and that time won, against Napoleon. What they have lacked has been the marvelous machinery of the contemporary world. They have lived in a tradition, part feudal, part clerical, part mystical, and like the Chinese, they knew despite

229

all the evidence to the contrary that they were the central kingdom, the preservers of the true faith that has little need of so-called modern enterprise.

Spain in the twentieth century was the only country in Europe where anarchism was and still may be potentially a powerful political movement. When the Communists during the Civil War moved in to take over the Loyalist forces it was the anarchists who were their most formidable opponents. The revolution was presented to Americans—the liberal tide was already running strong in the United States—as one of the crucial battles between Good and Evil, but we know now that it was much more confused and heterogeneous than that. The Communist leaders, sure of their historical mission, slew Loyalists and Francoists impartially. The dictatorships of Italy, the Third Reich, and of the Soviet Union joined the struggle that could have no outcome which would resemble the inflamed hopes of the American liberal media. Spanish friends tell me that the dictatorship is riding with a lighter rein in these last years and, as is the case in all dictatorships right or left, there is, despite the censorship, the controls over speech and action, talk of some modified kind of democracy. But, as one Spaniard observed sadly, the moment a modifier is placed before democracy, whether people's democracy, organic democracy, socialist democracy, or any other, it means no democracy exists.

As in the Middle East, it is the past that dominates the people and the landscape. The fury of building is spotty, it runs along the coast, in the cities, on the roads that may run smoothly for some miles before the driver encounters a man with a red flag or sometimes a fistful of poppies to warn that for another space he will be back on the dirt highway with the interminable construction done more by hand than by machines. Burros at a building site stand patiently on their stilt legs that do not buckle even when workers slowly load them to their ears with debris that one scoop of a bulldozer could carry off. But the rickety system has its human compensations, even its virtues, for when a motorist drives behind a truck on the narrow roads, a truck always belching a cloud of black smoke from a laboring engine, the truck driver signals to let him know whether he can pass safely. When the stranger asks for directions in no matter what part of the country, the response made with eager helpfulness is likely to be beyond his desserts; and a policeman gestures with a flourish like that of the matador's cape to set him in the direction he wishes to go.

Spanish newspapers may be read in a few minutes. They tell what impressive things the *Caudillo* did the day before, they report at great length on endless local festivities, they print, usually in one paragraph, brief accounts of happenings in foreign countries and a two-column headline on the first page may tell the reader: " 'Man is made in the image of God,' says Pope Paul," a pronouncement that could be true but that was not spot news. Any thaw in the dictatorship must be observed by reading between the lines of the newspapers and by such dispensations at the permission to publish the works of Garcia Lorca, who up to a few years ago was still proscribed for his association with what plaques marking the site of battles during the Civil War describe as "Marxist hordes." But a Spaniard need not apply for a university post unless he is politically beyond reproach; the Spanish universities like others in the free world wish their professoriat to hold sound political and economic opinions, the main difference being that in Spain they must be Franco's and in the United States until a very short time ago they had to be those of admirers of the Great Society.

Poverty still haunts Spain as it has for centuries. The workers who every day by the hundreds took the ferry from Algeciras to Gibraltar were paid at a scale similar to that in other Western countries to which Spanish labor has flocked in these past years. They go, men and women both, to France, Switzerland, and West Germany, where in July, despite all the guest workers migrating from southern Europe, 850,000 jobs were open, almost all of them providing a standard of living far beyond the reach of those who stay in Spain.

Unlike the peoples of the Communist bloc, the Spaniards are allowed to travel, to take a better-paying job in another country, although no longer in Gibraltar, and to compare what they have at home with the freer political and economic systems of the North. The long-haired, unwashed Hippie contingents are scarce in Spain. The few who are there are mainly visitors, and their way of life seems to have no attraction for the Spaniards. Spaniards have had their own Gypsies for long centuries, and it is no novelty for them to live in a pair of worn pants and a shirt. But Spain is clean; not as hygienic perhaps as the health codes of some other countries would require but there is no filth, there are no slums such as one may see in New York or Chicago; laundry may be spread out on the scanty grass in front of a whitewashed house, but it is clean and so is the house and so are the people, even the humble, even the very poor of whom there are many.

As you move north into France, Switzerland, West Germany, you move into a different time scheme. The past of these countries lives on as it does in museums to be visited from time to time and then forgotten for the trials of the day. Their troubles are part of their development, of new tensions and dilemmas, rooted not so much in their history as in their present condition. The French, tired after a decade of an old man's dream of recovering a grandeur and a hegemony they have long lost, settle down again to a mainly conservative way of life at the edge of which rumble the forces of another revolution. Millions of Frenchmen vote Communist, and thousands have been ready to take to the streets despite their relative well-being and the era of peaceful détente that has come to Europe by way of the ideas and forces they deride. It was the calcified Establishment ruled by an old man that the disenchanted rose against, the Establishment with its unfulfilled promises; and in any serious economic depression the left wing will again want to blow it up and may succeed. De Gaulle came to symbolize no more than an empty tradition, and millions of Frenchmen knew that the postwar Europe they lived in demanded different, more generous solutions than his.

The Swiss for their part continue to keep their inns, they retain their mountainous smugness and self-satisfaction. They are prosperous as ever and what is useful in their past is what is in demand by the tourist trade. They live well, all of them, even in the cantons that demand separate autonomy, and they have one of the highest suicide rates in the world.

And then come the West Germans, who have bounced back from a short-lived economic slump to even higher levels of industrial production and building and travel. Their *Autobahn* set a world style of rapid transit, and for years proportionally more people have been killed on them and the other streets of West Germany than on the roads of any other country that keeps reliable statistics. The Bundesrepublik suffers from all the modern ailments; a creeping inflation, universities that open and close as the students attend classes or demonstrate, scandals of a kind never experienced before in the Fatherland. These scandals have recently erupted on front pages when it became known that high-ranking officers of the army and navy have been involved with the secret agents of Soviet Russia. A defection that began with the conversion to the Soviet cause of Field Marshal von Paulus and his generals and officers has reappeared in the free and unstable climate of the Bundesrepublik with its tarnished past and uncertain future. A new generation of writers, cynical, original, amusing ironists, has replaced the coterie of translators who seemed to be the only living examples of a former high literary *Kultur* for many years after the war. Germany for better and worse has lost much of her tradition; this is evident not only in the repeated scandals affecting the armed forces but also in the rejection of the military life, in the heterogeneous building styles, the low level of film and theater, in the readiness with which American and other foreign styles are adopted, in the recently acquired good habit of Germans—doctors, for example—to go to other countries for part of their training. Fifty years ago the traffic went all in the other direction, but the Germans lost ground under Hitler that has never been recovered. Germany's universities, which were the light of the scholarly world up to World War I, suffer, as does the army, from a past of glory that ended in bankruptcy. Academic morals did not keep pace with the research; in the Hitler period it was pedantry and opportunism that won the allegiance of the professoriat, and these two academic vices are still there as they are here.

It is still to the United States that these countries look for their ultimate protection and for a future closer to their hearts' desire. To the United States, with its riots, its disorders, its race problem, its universally unpopular war, and its journeys to the moon. It is American technology and politics that fascinate and repel the countries of Europe, both East and West. The press of the East continues its denunciations of American imperialism and American lust for war, but the people, like the people of Spain, react apathetically to the one-tone picture of the world outside their enclaves. Unlike the Spaniards, the peoples of the East bloc are taught to be gruff and suspicious of foreigners whose sole aim is to sabotage their building of the socialist future. The Communist texts are forging a continually amended tradition of socialist virtue and capitalist perfidy that must be revised with every new edition of speeches made in the Stalinist, Khrushchev, and succeeding periods. (When Walter Ulbricht called Stalin a genius in the late 1940s this is omitted or completely altered when the speech is reprinted in 1960.) But millions of the inhabitants of the bloc, Czechs, Hungarians, Poles, East Germans, and Russians, too, know better than what they are taught. It is the human capacity to think and to struggle despite all the odds against their own suffocating dogmas and for something better than the substance of the day that many of these people have in common with many of the people of Spain and the United States, although it is hard to see how this capacity can do more than endure.

Index

235